The Sound of Silence

The Sound of Silence

Ryan Gosling, Expressionism and the Silent Hero in 21st-Century Film

NANCY EPTON

BLOOMSBURY ACADEMIC
NEW YORK • LONDON • OXFORD • NEW DELHI • SYDNEY

BLOOMSBURY ACADEMIC
Bloomsbury Publishing Inc
1385 Broadway, New York, NY 10018, USA
50 Bedford Square, London, WC1B 3DP, UK
29 Earlsfort Terrace, Dublin 2, Ireland

BLOOMSBURY, BLOOMSBURY ACADEMIC and the Diana logo are trademarks of
Bloomsbury Publishing Plc

First published in the United States of America 2024

Copyright © Nancy Epton, 2024

For legal purposes the Acknowledgements on p. x constitute an extension
of this copyright page.

Cover design: Eleanor Rose
Cover image: Ryan Gosling in *Blade Runner 2049*, 2017, dir. Denis Villeneuve © ArenaPAL

All rights reserved. No part of this publication may be reproduced or transmitted
in any form or by any means, electronic or mechanical, including photocopying,
recording, or any information storage or retrieval system, without
prior permission in writing from the publishers.

Bloomsbury Publishing Inc does not have any control over, or responsibility for, any
third-party websites referred to or in this book. All internet addresses given in this
book were correct at the time of going to press. The author and publisher regret any
inconvenience caused if addresses have changed or sites have ceased to exist,
but can accept no responsibility for any such changes.

Library of Congress Cataloging-in-Publication Data
Names: Epton, Nancy, author.
Title: The sound of silence : Ryan Gosling, expressionism and the silent
hero in 21st-century film / Nancy Epton.
Description: New York : Bloomsbury Academic, 2024. |
Includes bibliographical references and index. |
Summary: "An exploration of non-verbal communication,
shown primarily through the acting of Ryan
Gosling, to provide an expressive space in which audience viewing - an inherently passive
experience - is made far more active by removing the expository signifier of
dialogue"– Provided by publisher.
Identifiers: LCCN 2023029385 (print) | LCCN 2023029386 (ebook) |
ISBN 9798765108055 (hardback) | ISBN 9798765108048 (paperback) |
ISBN 9798765108079 (pdf) | ISBN 9798765108086 (epub) |
ISBN 9798765108062 Subjects: LCSH: Silence in motion pictures. |
Expressionism in motion pictures. | Heroes in motion pictures. |
Gosling, Ryan, 1980—Criticism and interpretation.
Classification: LCC PN1995.9.S545 E78 2024 (print) | LCC PN1995.9.S545 (ebook) |
DDC 791.43/6115–dc23/eng/20230926
LC record available at https://lccn.loc.gov/2023029385
LC ebook record available at https://lccn.loc.gov/2023029386

ISBN: HB: 979-8-7651-0805-5
ePDF: 979-8-7651-0807-9
eBook: 979-8-7651-0808-6

Typeset by Newgen KnowledgeWorks Pvt. Ltd., Chennai, India

To find out more about our authors and books visit www.bloomsbury.com
and sign up for our newsletters.

King Philip II of Macedon's message to the Spartans following his successful invasion of Greece:

> *'You are advised to submit without further delay, for if I bring my army into your land, I will destroy your farms, slay your people, and raze your city.'*

The Spartans' response:

> *'If.'*

Contents

Preface viii
Acknowledgements x

Introduction 1
    A Real Hero? 1
    Taciturn Femininities: A Female Silent Hero 3
    Expressionism and Expressionism 6
    Silence and Movement 15
    Feeling Theories: The Silent Hero as Affective Vessel 19
    The Sound of Music 21

1 Mythologies of the Silent Hero 25
    Film Noir 38
    The Western 46

2 Silent Heroes in 21st-Century Film 55
    21st-Century Expressionist Film 61

3 Ryan Gosling and the Star System 109
    Critical Responses 111
    'Literally Me': Ryan Gosling and Silent Hero Masculinities 122
    Acting Techniques 129
    Gesture 134

4 Sound and Music 149
    The Heroic Leitmotif 150
    Emotive Sound 156

Conclusion: 'To Be Born Is to Have a Soul, I Guess' 165

Filmography 171
Bibliography 173
Index 181

Preface

This work is concerned with 21st-century films that create meaning and narrative through a focus on a silent hero and through the utilization of non-verbal techniques to create heightened individual emotional response. It positions these films within a tradition of expressionist filmmaking that is characterized by a more subjective, non-representational articulation of the human experience and that stands in stark contrast to a more naturalistic depiction of physical reality.

It is important to distinguish between the general and specific definitions of expressionism that feed into the mythology of the silent hero. I pursue this distinction with particular reference to Rudolf Kurtz's early but highly influential *Expressionism and Film* (1926), and will also detail the key themes and techniques from the German Expressionist art movement that fed into these early films and on into the 21st-century films that I will discuss. I will analyse early notable German films such as *The Cabinet of Dr. Caligari*[1] and *Metropolis*[2] and move on to look at the way these films went on to influence later 20th-century genres such as film noir and the Western. To explain how expressionism has influenced film in the 21st century, I will link these ideas to techniques and styles exploited in contemporary films such as *Drive*,[3] *Arrival*[4] and *Blade Runner 2049*.[5] I will focus on key modern directors such as Nicolas Winding Refn and Denis Villeneuve, whose approaches I will discuss, and I will look at the way their films are marketed to appeal commercially to audiences.

The term 'silence' will be explained in the context of my research, defining the word as applied to film as any form of non-verbal expression, or where speech is only used episodically. This will include an examination of the use of laconic dialogue but will also involve a study of the use of sound and music as well as the use of movement (facial expression, gesture and physical action) to inform the narrative in film. Defining silence as a productive way of creating

---

[1] Robert Wiene, dir. (1920, Decla-Bioscop), BFI Player.
[2] Fritz Lang, dir. (1927, Parufamet), BFI Player.
[3] Nicolas Winding Refn, dir. (2011, FilmDistrict), DVD.
[4] Denis Villeneuve, dir. (2016, Paramount Pictures), DVD.
[5] Denis Villeneuve, dir. (2017, Warner Bros. Pictures), DVD.

PREFACE

meaning and inviting personal audience reaction, I will draw on key works such as Susan Sontag's 'Aesthetics of Silence' and Tanya Shilina-Conte's 'Silence as Elective Mutism in Minor Cinema'.

A lot of contemporary cinema places great emphasis on high-decibel action, both in terms of movement and dialogue, the editing process and use of camera focus. Many blockbusters now contain more than 3,000 individual cuts, for example, and commercially successful franchises like *Transformers* and *Fast & Furious* are filled with 'noise', bombarding viewers with both visual and audio stimulation. I will show that, by saying less, 21st century-expressionist films can be understood to say far more.

Acknowledgements

I would like to thank the people who have supported me throughout my research. Special thanks to my supervisor Lucia Nagib for helping to direct the building blocks of this work, and to my teacher Jess Parker for providing me with constant inspiration during my independent research on German Expressionism. Thanks to friends and particularly family who have provided me with moral support, especially my mother and father, who have been constant advocates of my studies and interests.

Introduction

A Real Hero?

At the start of *Drive* the audience are presented with the sounds of wind and moving cars, followed by the techno beats of The Chromatics' 'Tick of the Clock'. Shortly after this, Ryan Gosling's Driver is heard giving a terse, authoritative list of instructions over the phone before we see him. Aside from a few brief, neon-tinted opening credits, the film begins in literal darkness, demanding complete auditory attention. Even when some limited vision is granted, the camera focuses initially on a detailed road map of Los Angeles – the source of the voice remains unknown. As the camera slowly pans up to the speaker, the audience only witness the back of his figure facing a window.

While his reflection can be seen, it remains dark and vague against the pitch-black night, and it is almost impossible to see his mouth moving as he methodically dictates his rules to an unknown contact. Presently, the camera slides away to a television showing the half-time scores of a basketball match. The camera finally comes to rest on a suitcase lying on a bed; the individual collects this item and walks left out of shot as the camera pans out on a dark, threatening Los Angeles outside his window (Figure 1).

This opening sequence of *Drive*, the journey of a nameless mechanic and getaway driver adapted from James Sallis's novel of the same name, illustrates various traits of contemporary silent hero films through its use of sound, image and laconic dialogue: the deceptive location of sound eliciting audience confusion, the lack of any expository backstory, the distinctive visual aesthetic and sense of intrigue and moral ambiguity. A silent hero must be constructed from what is not clearly heard, seen or spoken. Mystery is paramount. In his analysis of *Drive*, film theorist Justin Vicari asserts that the heroic figure must

FIGURE 1 *The audience's first image of Driver's upper figure. Even the body shown in the reflection is obscured, only providing a fractured, ghostly image of half his face, with the scorpion adorning his jacket in clearer view. Mystery and intimidation, key features of the silent hero, are already firmly established.*

be 'one who exists outside these bonds [of humanity], almost inhumanely but with solemn and undying love for the human (as he or she perceives it)'.[1] The silent hero must enter a society to purge it from evil, but they are unable to survive and live within its confines. In his groundbreaking *Audio-Vision: Sound on Screen*, Michel Chion describes the essential vococentrism that is at the core of sound cinema, where 'in any given sound environment you hear voices, those voices capture your attention before any other sound (wind blowing, music, traffic, a roomful of conversation)'.[2] In the example of *Drive*, however, what catches our attention first *are* precisely the noises of traffic, wind blowing and music. When a voice is subsequently heard, with the screen still black, Driver's statement that 'there's a hundred-thousand streets in this city' provides the audience with no clues as to time, place or Driver's identity.

Only after this first snippet of spoken dialogue are the audience finally taken out of the darkness and provided with the image of a map. Without an expository narrative voice, the audience must work hard to fill in the gaps, using subjective, emotional responses to decipher meaning from sounds and images. Whilst the screen is dark, the bracing sounds of wind immediately locate the viewer in an outdoor environment, as do the surrounding noises of traffic. When the techno beats play and the first few spoken words are heard, one might assume that the opening images will likewise situate the audience

---

[1] Vicari, *Nicolas Winding Refn and the Violence of Art*, 181.
[2] Chion, *Audio-Vision*, 6.

INTRODUCTION 3

in an outdoor space, and that these techno sounds will originate from a diegetic source. However, the opening panning shot disorientates the audience both with its interior setting and the extradiegetic form of the music. An extra level of confusion and intrigue for the audience is added as they try to orientate themselves through listening to the calm, commanding statements of a man they have barely seen. Chion notes the overwhelming effect of cinematic sound that, unlike the image, 'can become an insidious means of affective and semantic manipulation' which influences the audience psychologically and can completely change the audience's interpretation of the pictures before their eyes.[3] By eschewing traditional ocularcentric approaches, Chion establishes a point of hearing where sound becomes an essential means of configuring and manipulating the audience's emotional response.

This work discusses the portrayal of silent heroes in 21st-century film. The central films I will be analysing are *Drive*, *Only God Forgives*[4] and *Blade Runner 2049*. These works do not bombard us with the empty, cacophonic action and expository dialogue that pervade many modern franchises. In them, imagery and non-verbal sound frequently replace the spoken word, creating a productive space between artist and audience which can, as Susan Sontag argues in her seminal work *The Aesthetics of Silence*, 'constitute the grounds for ascetic affirmation'.[5] Sontag's use of 'asceticism' does not refer to the term in its religious sense, but rather as a practical means, in film, of denying the most common instrument of comprehension (speech) to an audience and replacing it with more challenging alternatives (sound and image). The audience is often forced to negotiate meaning from what is *not* said. In *Audio-Vision*'s preface, sound designer Walter Murch similarly talks of Chion's 'sound *en creux,* "in the gap"', which provides a 'fruitful tension between what is on the screen and what is kindled in the mind of the audience'.[6] Directors like Nicolas Winding Refn and Denis Villeneuve force the audience to utilize conceptual, imaginative faculties and thus form a more incisive response.

Taciturn Femininities: A Female Silent Hero

Opening credits appear on a black, noiseless screen in small white font, pushed to the left. Studios involved are listed. The director is noted, as is the film's main star, but no one else. The star's name then disappears, leaving the audience

---

[3] Ibid., 34.
[4] Nicolas Winding Refn, dir. (2013, Scanbox Entertainment), DVD.
[5] Sontag, 'The Aesthetics of Silence', 5.
[6] Murch, 'Preface', in Chion, *Audio-Vision*, xvii.

with the same black, noiseless screen. Then, suddenly, a flurry of rapid violins is heard while the screen remains black, gradually increasing in volume. The strings become more violent, more jarring, to the point of overwhelming. Only then do the audience receive their first image. It is not an image that fills the whole screen, or even half of the screen. It is a dot, bright and miniscule in the centre of the black screen. The strings remain insistent as this lone dot suddenly becomes a bright light. Two barely distinct white circles appear around the light and increase in size as a larger circle appears outside the brightness. The shapes continue to expand as the strings continue to demand attention, evoking further disorientation alongside images the audience cannot yet understand. The following image shows the light adjacent to a spherical object with a hole in its centre, both entities now occupying the sectioned-off space in the image where the opening text formally stood. As these objects start to merge with a black circle on the right, the unsettling violins are joined by a new sound, a voice. This voice speaks, but the audience cannot make out any decipherable human language. Sibilant, hissing sounds are heard alongside guttural hums, then plosive 'd's and 'p's, as the circles converge and the screen returns to darkness. The camera slowly pans in on a single dark circle as the voice's pronunciation of the repetitive sounds becomes faster. Suddenly, the audience witness their first all-encompassing image, an extreme close-up of an eyeball. Initially, the pupil appears as a menacing, inhuman, black disc surrounded by pale white that slowly evolves alongside the voice's evolving human language, with the image zooming out and only finally becoming a recognizable human eye, still in extreme close-up (Figure 2).

The opening scenes of *Under the Skin*,[7] the journey of a humanoid alien (Scarlett Johansson) loosely based on Michael Faber's 2000 novel of the same name, initially employ similar techniques of disorientation to *Drive* in terms of both image and sound. Both examples utilize the black screen as a blank canvas to play with audience orientation, but *Under the Skin* manages to cultivate yet more narrative confusion and ambiguity with the abstract nature of the imagery that emerges from the darkness – right from the start of the film, the very nature of what it means to be human is questioned. The audience are not in a recognizable apartment. The audience are not sure where they are at all.

Director Jonathan Glazer noted how he wanted the sequence to evoke recognizable images in the sci-fi canon such as 'the alignment of planets, or the docking of a spaceship', and then subvert it, 'turn it, and suddenly, that isn't a planet, that isn't a spaceship, that's an eyeball'.[8] Filmmakers draw the

---

[7] Jonathan Glazer, dir. (2013, BFI), DVD.
[8] R. Kurt Osenlund, 'Interview: Jonathan Glazer Talks Under the Skin' (2014). *Slant*. https://www.slantmagazine.com/film/interview-jonathan-glazer/.

FIGURE 2 *The Woman's cold, alien eye before it morphs into a more recognizable human structure. Johansson's sounds in the opening scenes are also the recordings of her voice exercises as she learnt how to do an English accent while she drove around in Scotland. Both the actress and her character are learning to play their roles through language.*

FIGURE 3 *In* Blade Runner 2049, *K walks slowly through a dystopian Las Vegas that has been ruined by nuclear radiation. The thick orange mist serves as both a practical effect to emphasize the doom-laden landscape, as well as a visual form of pathetic fallacy that reflects K's confusion.*

audience into a false sense of visual security before turning this familiarity into bewilderment (Figures 3 and 4).

While my work primarily centres on films that depict male silent heroes, drawing on a particularly male iteration of the silent hero in earlier film genres, it is nonetheless intriguing to observe how these stereotypically masculine

FIGURE 4 *The claustrophobic, saturated halls of* Only God Forgives *play a central role throughout the film, representing Julian's constant tension and dread at the thought of confronting his mother.*

traits are coded in cinematic narratives which focus on female silent figures. The key films I will be analysing as an interesting point of comparison are *Incendies*,[9] *Under the Skin*, *Arrival* and *The Neon Demon*.[10] Like expressionist films before them with their pronounced stylized aesthetic and sparse use of dialogue, imagery and sound become central components in constructing and complimenting the elliptical narratives.

Expressionism and Expressionism

I argue that, with their focus on alienated, disillusioned loners and their frequent use of stylized, often violent action, many of these 21st-century films can trace their lineage right back to the Expressionist movement of the early 20th century. In Chapter 1 I will be drawing on key historic texts such as Rudolf Kurtz's *Expressionism and Film* (1929) and Lotte Eisner's *The Haunted Screen: Expressionism in the German Cinema and the Influence of Max Reinhardt* (1974) as well as contemporary texts to show that these films are rooted in beliefs of subjective, emotional audience experience, and often feature symbolic figures with a tumultuous psyche which can

---

[9] Denis Villeneuve, dir. (2010, Entertainment One), DVD.
[10] Nicolas Winding Refn, dir. (2016, Amazon Studios), DVD.

be difficult to fully articulate through dialogue alone. In art, the Tate Gallery defines Expressionism as a movement where the image of reality is distorted in order to make it expressive of 'the artist's inner feelings or ideas' and that in terms of art it is 'characterised by simplified shapes, bright colours and gestural marks or brushstrokes'.[11] Writing about film as early as 1926, Kurtz defined Expressionism as an urge to 'get away from the time-bound, away from the moment, away from "impression" and toward creation'.[12] This is an urge shared by the 21st-century directors I am focusing on, Nicolas Winding Refn and Denis Villeneuve, with their frequent lack of expository dialogue and depiction of stylized settings where external environments are distorted to reflect inner psychological turmoil.

Refn was keen to set himself apart from the 'more classical tradition' of the filmmaking of his director father Anders Refn, which he describes as like 'a story, it's a narrative; by contrast, Refn sees his filmmaking as 'an act of expression'.[13] He neatly articulates one of the main tenets of expressionism: that no strictly linear, expository tale is required to craft elements of expressionist cinema, which are, like the urge described by Kurtz, formed from a less time-bound, spontaneous act of creation.

It is important to stress here the difference between Expressionism, with its capital 'E', and expressionism. The former is understood as a specific artistic movement, originating in Germany at the beginning of the 20th century, which has inspired many thematic and stylistic elements in the contemporary films I will discuss – their use of claustrophobic, stylized sets and dramatic lighting effects, for example, that frequently articulate characters' emotions and the use of still, controlled, often exaggerated gestures to complement their themes of chaos, angst and disillusionment. However, in terms of these films' employment of a silent hero, I am more interested in a *general* definition of expressionism, as signified with a lower case 'e'. I am interested in a general artistic style that moves away from objective, literal depictions of physical reality (in film, a concern with more 'realistic' acting techniques and depictions of naturalistic settings) towards a more subjective depiction of emotions and responses. Specifically, I will focus on the categories set out by J. L. Styan in his key 1981 text on expressionism in drama, *Modern Drama in Theory and Practice 3: Expressionism and Epic Theatre*. These include atmosphere

---

[11] 'Art Term: German Expressionism'. https://www.tate.org.uk/art/art-terms/g/german-expressionism.
[12] Kurtz, *Expressionism and Film*, 11.
[13] Xan Brooks, ' "My Father and I Disagree on the Purpose of Cinema" : Anders and Nicolas Winding Refn on film-making' (2021). *The Guardian*. https://www.theguardian.com/film/2021/feb/11/my-father-and-i-disagree-on-the-purpose-of-cinema-anders-and-nicolas-winding-refn-on-film-making.

(often vividly dreamlike and nightmarish), settings (avoiding naturalistic detail), plot and structure (often disjointed, episodic), characters (often nameless, mythical), dialogue (laconic) and acting style (a move away from traditional, realist techniques).[14] In film, I will show how this expressionism can take the form of a bold and stylized use of dramatic lighting effects, distorted camera shots, lack of expository dialogue and imaginative use of both diegetic and extradiegetic sound effects. Villeneuve, when considering the original *Blade Runner*, for example, noted that he wanted his sequel to retain a strong similarity in terms of sound design, with 'the spirit of that atmosphere, expressionist'.[15] The long takes on still facial expressions in *Drive* (a technique that is often utilized in German Expressionist films) prompted unenthusiastic responses from financiers when it was pitched, with Refn noting how 'we're so used to sound, meaning dialogue, moving story along. Cinema becomes less cinematic and more about logistics of verbal explanations'.[16]

An example of Refn's expressionist 'spirit' can be found in the scene where Driver first enters the flat of Irene (Carey Mulligan), bringing back her groceries once he has driven her home from the garage. After providing Benicio (Kaden Leos) with one of his signature speech-blocking toothpicks, Driver tactfully places his own toothpick behind his ear in preparation for verbal communication. He accepts the offer of a water from Irene with a simple 'ok' as the camera rests on him in the kitchen. Not a 'thank you' or a 'yes please', but a single, ambivalent word of acceptance. He answers Irene's questions about his living situation with polite but vague answers and listens to her talk about her husband. When Irene asks about his profession, Driver states simply that he drives, at which point the calming synths of Cliff Martinez's appropriately titled 'I Drive' start to play and fill the laconic space as the camera focuses on Driver's figure resting against the wall. The audience receives a close-up of his still facial expression as he begins to describe his day job at the garage in more detail. It cuts back to Irene's silent, serene expression before Driver politely but taciturnly states that he needs to leave. Verbal exchanges in this example are measured, thoughtful and carefully spoken.

Equally, Refn's dislike of 'verbal explanations' can be seen in the interaction between Driver and Irene just after 'A Real Hero' has concluded. Driver is staring out of Irene's window as she walks up to him, holding his scorpion jacket; his violent behaviour currently repressed, he turns around, but doesn't

---

[14] Styan, *Modern Drama in Theory and Practice* 3, 4.
[15] Michael Ordana, 'How Do You Follow Pp a Sci Fi Classic without Cloning It? If It's "Blade Runner", You Rewrite Its DNA' (2018). *LA Times*. https://www.latimes.com/entertainment/envelope/la-en-mn-denis-villeneuve-20170104-story.html.
[16] Film at Lincoln Center, 'Nicolas Winding Refn on the Power of Silence' (2013). *YouTube*. https://www.youtube.com/watch?v=6sLr5_1eo7U&t=7s.

speak, and several seconds go by where the two stare at each other without exchanging words before Irene placidly comments on how nice the day was. The camera – and thereby, the audience – focuses intently on the two. Driver smiles, but makes no immediate response, staring at the ground before laconically stating that he had a nice day too. Another punctuated pause takes place as the two continue staring at each other. Irene apologizes for him having to drive her home, and Driver quietly responds that it's ok. Another long pause as they both stare. Driver politely retrieves the jacket, cue more staring. Driver then offers to take Irene out again at the weekend. This time, Irene doesn't respond, and they both share shy smiles as Driver abruptly stands up and leaves. Both remain incredibly still throughout the sequence, with only subtle changes visible in their smiling facial expressions. Each verbal pause provides affective space for the audience to contemplate their burgeoning relationship. It is not a case of, as Refn's financers seemed to suggest, the two characters doing nothing, but rather evoking feelings of affection through deliberate, unsettling moments of silence. This silence presents a challenging and novel way to interpret meaning without the oversaturated presence of the voice and it is this decisive, driving factor that becomes what Kurtz calls 'the emotional logic' of the film.[17]

It is interesting to note that the Icelandic academic Sif Rikhardsdottir in her work *Emotion in Old Norse Literature: Translations, Voices, Contexts*, describes the epic *Poetic Edda* as 'an *emotive script* that favours somatic indicators over verbal expression'.[18] Refn clearly positions himself in this Old Norse tradition of stylized emphasis on physical environment, mood and economy of language. Far removed from popular Hollywood depictions of Norse mythology, with their noisy action set-pieces and glorious battle regalia, Refn's Odin in *Valhalla Rising*[19] is an inscrutable monolith who does not utter a single word. The audience are forced to create meaning from the elemental natural world surrounding the figure and the few words provided by other characters. One Eye's enigmatic and intimidating nature is highlighted at various points in the film when his head is presented as a statue carved into the landscape alongside natural forms such as mountains and clouds (Figure 5).

The image mirrors angst-ridden Expressionist art such as Karl Schmidt-Rottluff's visceral 1918 woodcut *Did Not Christ Appear to You* ('Ist euch Kristus nicht erschienen'), where harsh cuts depict the Redeemer staring blankly at the viewer with unfocused and uneven square pupils. Even the light that emanates from his figure is depicted with a stark stylized aesthetic, with his

---

[17] Kurtz, *Expressionism and Film*, 56.
[18] Rikhardsdottir, *Emotion in Old Norse Literature*, 1. Emphasis in original.
[19] Nicolas Winding Refn, dir. (2009, Scanbox Entertainment), DVD.

FIGURE 5 *The saturated blood-red that envelops One Eye's statuesque profile highlights his inherently violent, dangerous character. Like the weather that sits alongside him, he is a force of nature that cannot be reasoned with.*

hair blocked into an exaggerated, jagged chunk of black and the year of the First World War's end etched onto the figure's forehead. Jacob Phillips, Head of Theology at St Mary's University, London, notes that 'an axe had been laid to Europe's roots' when Schmidt-Rottluff created the work, and likened the violent act of creating the woodcut – comparing the gouging chisel to an axe – to the brutal nature of war itself.[20] Refn's formalist approach to film focuses on the technical – set design, composition, sound and light – rather than dialogue and expository narrative, creating images and ideas that are often unexplained. His silence thus presents a direct artistic rebellion against the noisier interpretations of Norse mythology and depictions of Odin in recent texts and films.

Refn's is a form of expressionism that draws heavily on a distinctly Northern European tradition of Romanticism, which sought to raise the status of the imagination and intuition, and expression of strong emotion, to new heights. According to Isiah Berlin in *The Roots of Romanticism*, Romanticism embodied

> a new and restless spirit, seeking violently to burst through old and cramping forms, a nervous preoccupation with perpetually changing inner states of consciousness, a longing for the unbounded and the indefinable,

---

[20] 'Did Not Christ Appear to You? Commentary by Jacob Phillips'. *VCS*. https://thevcs.org/psalters-darkest-hour/did-not-christ-appear-you.

for perpetual movement and change, an effort to return to the forgotten sources of life, a passionate effort at self-assertion both individual and collective, a search after means of expressing an unappeasable yearning for unattainable goals.[21]

This Romantic strand translates into many of the 21st-century expressionist films I discuss, particularly in relation to the idea of the artist as tortured soul, with disillusioned, taciturn heroes often embracing violence in their journeys of self-exploration and transformation or as a means to protect those they love. The 'perpetually changing inner states' Berlin mentions are part and parcel of these characters' emotional make-up as they strive to find identity and meaning in unsympathetic, alien worlds, and this Romantic emphasis on imagination and heightened emotion, striving to be something more than they currently are, necessarily positions the silent hero against or outside of the bounds of human society.

The two artists who are generally considered to be the founding fathers of German Expressionist art, Vincent van Gogh and Edvard Munch, both drew heavily on this earlier Romantic tradition and famously articulated in paint the themes of angst, disillusionment and doom which preoccupied their troubled psyches. Both moved away from the Impressionist fascination with imitating nature, the attempt to capture effects of light and atmosphere, towards a far more introverted, personal (often tormented) depiction of emotion and inner truth. *The Oxford Dictionary of Art & Artists* refers to Van Gogh's 'spontaneous, irrational side'[22] – both key elements of Expressionism that have followed on from the Romantic glorying of the artist's subjective imagination. During his later work in 1866, Van Gogh himself noted that 'Instead of trying to reproduce exactly what I have before my eyes, I use colour more arbitrarily so as to express myself more forcibly'.[23] An example of this distinct artistic change in his use of colour and the way he applied it in thick, textured marks can be found in his 1888 work *Night Café*. He explained: 'I have tried to express with red and green the terrible passions of human nature.'[24] A similarly heightened orange colour palette and doom-laden atmosphere is evoked in *Blade Runner 2049* when Deckard and K enter a desolate Las Vegas bar, as Deckard notes that there are 'millions of bottles of whiskey' left while he pours a bottle for K and himself, and even deigns to spill some on the floor for his dog (Figure 6).

---

[21] Berlin, *The Roots of Romanticism*, 92.
[22] Chilvers, *The Oxford Dictionary of Art & Artists*, 257.
[23] Vincent van Gogh: The Letters, 'To Theo van Gogh. Arles, Saturday, 18 August 1888'. https://www.vangoghletters.org/vg/letters/let663/letter.html#translation.
[24] Chilvers, *The Oxford Dictionary of Art & Artists*, 258.

FIGURE 6 *The lingering decadence and debris of the abandoned Las Vegas bar reflects Van Gogh's famous composition due to the area's vivid unnatural colour, with a similar air of social tension present as a haggard Deckard initially refuses to engage with K's questions.*

In *The Story of Art*, historian E. H. Gombrich observes that van Gogh used his distinctive brushstrokes not only as a technique to break up colour into separate marks 'but also to convey his own excitement'.[25] In other words, the expression of emotion was paramount. Van Gogh was not concerned with merely imitating nature, what he himself called '*trompe-l'oei'l* [stereoscopic] realism',[26] but rather wanted to use colour and form to reveal what he *felt* about his subject matter.

Similarly with Munch, we can see a clear link between creativity and extreme psychological states (bordering on mental illness). Munch expertly summarizes the ideals of Expressionism when he declared: 'Just as Leonardo da Vinci studied human anatomy and dissected corpses, so I try to dissect souls.'[27] His wish was to portray internal, emotional, subjective truths as opposed to the physical, external reality in front of him. As well as drawing upon earlier Northern European philosophical and artistic traditions, particularly from Germany, this desire to express inner tormented reality was likely influenced by his own personal experiences. He remarked how 'illness, insanity, and death were the black angels that kept watch over my cradle'.[28] The idea of personifying internal turmoil as spiritual apparitions also plays an intriguing role in many of the silent hero iterations I discuss – with

---

[25] Gombrich, *The Story of Art*, 413.
[26] Vincent van Gogh: The Letters, 'To Theo van Gogh. Arles, Monday, 3 September 1888'. https://www.vangoghletters.org/vg/letters/let673/letter.html.
[27] Stang, *Edvard Munch*, 1979.
[28] 'Edvard Munch: Norwegian Artist'. https://www.britannica.com/biography/Edvard-Munch.

INTRODUCTION

stillness, mysterious pasts and an almost robotic indefatigability contributing to the sense of a ghostly, rather than a fully human, presence. Film critic Mark Kermode highlights how 'these characters [21st-century silent heroes] are supernatural. There is a suggestion in some of them that they are actually ghosts ... they're real, but they're not human'.[29] Not only do these figures sit outside the boundaries of human society, but they almost exist on a different, sub-human plane altogether.

As with Van Gogh, suffering was an essential element of Munch's creative prowess, with Munch himself acknowledging: 'I would not cast off my illness, for there is much in my art that I owe to it.'[30] His description of his motivation for creating his seminal work *The Scream* is very reminiscent of key aspects of Expressionism in relation to both the emotional content of the work and the use of distortion and vivid, unnaturalistic colour:

> I was walking along the road with two friends. The Sun was setting – / The Sky turned a bloody red/And I felt a whiff of Melancholy – I stood/Still, deathly tired – over the blue-back/Fjord and City hung Blood and Tongues of Fire/My Friends walked on – I remained behind/ – shivering with Anxiety – I felt the great Scream in Nature[31]

In *The Art of Scandinavia*, Andrew Graham-Dixon calls this distinctly Northern European anxiety a 'Nordic Angst', bringing with it a 'sense of becoming un-moored in a hostile universe'.[32] This alienation is a constant theme throughout the 21st-century films I study, again in particular relation to one of my central films, *Blade Runner 2049*, where, in one scene, a bandaged K, questioning the nature of reality, stares over a bridge in an expressionist close-up of angst and despair (Figure 7). The inner worlds of chaos and subjective imagination depicted in Expressionist art take on an intense cinematic form in these 21st-century narratives of fractured worlds and tortured psyches.

The end of the First World War saw the emergence of an even darker strand of Expressionism. Under Hitler, and particularly under Joseph Goebbels's Reich Ministry of Public Enlightenment and Propaganda, Germany saw an attempt to control all forms of mass communication, including film. Entartete

---

[29] Epton, Interview with Mark Kermode, 10 February 2021.
[30] Books & Boots, 'Edvard Munch: Love and Angst @ the British Museum'. https://astrofella.wordpress.com/2019/07/22/edvard-munch-love-and-angst-british-museum/#:~:text=I%20would%20not%20cast%20off,art%20of%20one%27s%20innermost%20heart.
[31] Abdullah Ryan, 'The Scream Is One of the World's Most Famous Paintings. But What Does It mean?', *bdnews24*. https://bdnews24.com/arts/obydgcu7g2.
[32] TV series, BBC4. 2016.

FIGURE 7 *K stares into the void after listening to the taunting words of the black-eyed Joi, questioning if the one he loved was truly real. Freysa's comment about 'dying for the right cause' is repeated in extradiegetic form and provides no more emotional respite, with K ultimately deciding to defy her orders by saving both the child and Deckard.*

Kunst (Degenerate Art) was the term the Nazis in Germany assigned to most modern art forms between the wars. It was also the specific name of an Exhibition of artworks in Munich in 1937. This attitude to perceived degeneracy in modern art, of which Expressionism was an important part, had developed from a theory about degeneracy in modern culture in general. In 1892 Max Nordau (who was, ironically, Jewish) had written 'Entartung' (Degeneracy) in which he had criticized the various art movements which had fed into Expressionism: Aestheticism (for its lack of a moral code), Symbolism (for its mysticism) and Impressionism (for the indistinctness of its painterly technique). Interestingly, these all remain key elements of the silent hero archetype in the 21st-century films I will discuss: the distinct sense of mystery and moral ambiguity lending them almost mythical status, combined with a stylized aesthetic. Nordau's criticisms harked back to an idealized past in the search for a 'pure' German spirit, tapping into earlier Gothic and Romantic artistic strands within German history. However, with the Nazis these became muddled with ideas about racial purity and idealized classical beauty and order – themes which were highlighted in another exhibition of 1937, this time titled 'Great German Art'. The two contrasting exhibitions drew attention to the significant underlying fight over control of society and definitions of 'truth' and 'reality'.

A similar attempt to control and shape a sense of German identity occurred within the Nazi film industry, which released a swathe of propaganda films. Murch notes chillingly how 'Hitler's ascension to power marched in lockstep with the successful development of the talking film', linking the emphasis on language and the spoken word with Hitler's nationalist agenda.[33] He contrasts this with the more universal appeal of earlier silent films, which he describes as 'Edenically oblivious of the divisive powers of the Word'.[34] He particularly highlights the major success of the early Danish Nordisk Films industry, which was able to achieve far greater universal appeal precisely because it did not rely on time-bound, expository narrative.[35] Silent film provided an opportunity for filmmakers to engage with their audiences on a subjective level, allowing space for individual, imaginative interpretation of image and the live music that accompanied film screenings. Ironically, through Hitler's banning and shaming of Expressionist artists and filmmakers (many of whose works were destroyed or kept in private collections by the Nazis themselves) he simply highlighted their work by collecting them together in one space, bringing them to a far wider public attention, both within Germany and further afield.

As a result of this treatment, many artists and filmmakers working in Germany subsequently emigrated to America and other parts of Europe to continue their work, thereby spreading the various principles of Expressionism beyond Germany. Despite great personal suffering (many lost their jobs, had their exhibitions closed and paintings removed from public collections), their work gained significant attention and popularity abroad. The failed suppression of Expressionism allowed it to flourish and expand on an international scale, and traditions of Expressionist art continued to thrive after the movement's immediate popularity in post-war Germany. Clear examples of Expressionist influence can be seen in the work of various artists and musicians who fled Nazi-occupied Germany, and this becomes increasingly obvious in the popular and influential sphere of film with the influx of émigré filmmakers into America like Austrian-born director Billy Wilder. Chapter 1 of this book will look at the ways in which these traditions were upheld within the film industry in Hollywood by tracing expressionist links in genres like film noir and the Western, which were major influences both aesthetically and thematically on the 21st-century silent hero films I will discuss.

Silence and Movement

It is important to emphasize that, in my original research concerning ideas of the 21st-century silent hero in film and their links to expressionism, the silent hero is rarely completely silent and is not always easily defined as

---

[33] Murch, 'Preface', *Audio-Vision*, x.
[34] Ibid., ix.
[35] Ibid.

entirely heroic in black and white terms – they are often morally ambiguous. In Chapter 2 I will therefore continue to draw on sources such as Sontag's 'Aesthetics of Silence' and Chion's *Audio-Vision* to explain my precise use of the term 'silence', as often involving a lack of expository dialogue, and I will acknowledge the comparative importance of all other sound – in all its diegetic and extradiegetic forms – in creating a heightened emotional and subjective experience for the audience. In 'Silence as Elective Mutism in Minor Cinema', this is something Shilina-Conte describes as a useful 'tool of film philosophy', which permits us to 'supersede traditional film analysis and examine silence not as an interpretative condition but as a critical-clinical mode of experimentation'.[36] In these expressionist films, sounds are not always used to merely replicate reality but rather can be 'liberated from their original causal connection' and used imaginatively to manipulate an emotional response.[37] In *Drive*'s elevator scene, for example, there is barely any spoken dialogue, and sound editing is used to deliberately cut out the real and everyday noises of the mechanism as a tense and gory confrontation begins to unfold inside the claustrophobic space.

Since an absence of dialogue deprives the audience of a conventional means of following filmic narrative, the audience are also frequently presented with alternative visual cues to decipher meaning. In Chapter 3, I will focus on the use of gesture, particularly facial expressions and hands, to cultivate meaning. Twenty-first-century films such as *Blade Runner 2049*, *Drive* and *Only God Forgives* use hands as an expressive means to articulate emotional states (Figures 8 and 9). As well as frequent use of facial close-ups, both Villeneuve and Refn regularly focus on hands as signs of discovery and physicality. For example, Refn himself has given several interviews where he discusses hands in terms of masculinity, and I will include and analyse his theories, as I believe they provide an interesting perspective on the typical masculine archetype of the silent hero. This is a figure that film critic Kim Newman notes is summarized by his 'mysterious past. Something has happened to him',[38] yet we never find out what this 'something' is, and the audience are offered histories they will never fully understand. Kermode also acknowledges this essential mysterious element of the silent hero and asserts that 'it's what he does rather than what he says that becomes the mythical archetype'.[39] Action takes precedence over speech. Drawing upon comparisons with earlier expressionist films, facial expressions will also be a central part of

---

[36] Shilina-Conte, 'Silence as Elective Mutism in Minor Cinema'.
[37] Murch, 'Preface', *Audio-Vision*, xiv.
[38] Epton, Interview with Kim Newman, 9 March 2021.
[39] Epton, Interview with Mark Kermode, 10 February 2021.

FIGURE 8 In Drive, *Benicio gives Driver the bullet he received from gangster Cook. Familial understanding between the child and Driver's father figure is reinforced through this corporeal close-up, where no faces need to be shown.*

FIGURE 9 *Julian stares at the hands that have killed his father, which are rendered as static and powerless as those of the stone statue behind him due to the influence of his mother.*

my analysis; these contemporary silent heroes rarely speak, yet their faces remain a frequent focal point of the camera's attention. Characters emote through still expressions and, again, the audience is forced to supply meaning and interpret action. I will discuss such film production techniques as the Kuleshov effect during my analysis, where a visual chronology is established to create heightened emotional response.

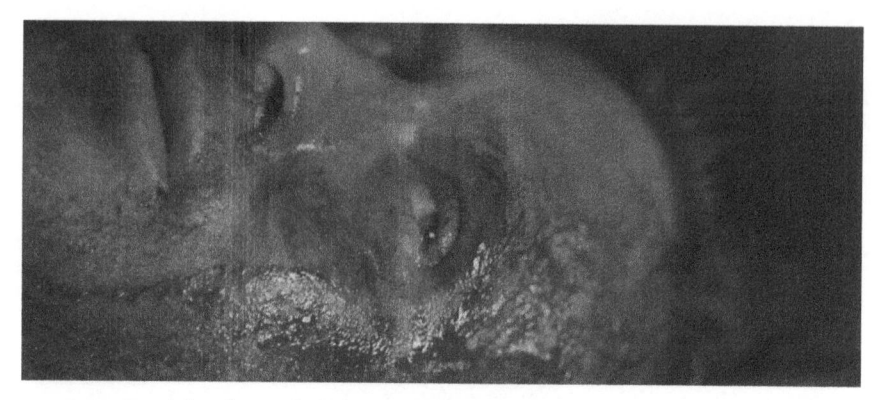

FIGURE 10 *After being left for dead by Luv, K directs a soulful, pained stare towards Mariette, one of the rebel replicants who has saved him. The pure, unbridled angst and disillusionment on display in the extreme close-up of K's bloodied facial expression represents one of the quintessential images of contemporary expressionist cinema.*

In 'Media, Affect and the Face: Biomediation and the Political Scene', Maria Angel and Anna Gibbs acknowledge the face of the silent hero as an essential affective focal point: 'An indispensable element in suturing the human into forms of visual communication, and in mediating forms of "inner" and "outer" expression'.[40] The face is an essential tool with which to decipher emotion and thus gain emotional reaction from an audience in exchange, emphasized in my films through numerous lingering close-ups, and sometimes extreme close-ups (Figure 10). Silvan Tomkins, an influential figure in affect studies, cites the face as the primary site of affective expression,[41] noting its significance in visual communication, and Angel and Gibbs describe its ability to bypass 'more temporally cumbersome forms of communication, such as speech' with the more immediate nature of facial expression.[42] They note the origins of affect in evolutionary fields with Charles Darwin's *The Expressions of Emotions in Man and Animals*. Darwin observes how 'most of our emotions are so closely connected with their expression that they hardly exist if the body remains passive'.[43] This presents an interesting challenge in the context of my chosen 21st-century films, most of which contain silent heroes with inscrutable facial expressions, and who are often decidedly passive in their bodily

---

[40] Angel and Gibbs, 'Media, Affect and the Face', 24. https://www.academia.edu/273221/Media_Affect_and_the_Face_Biomediation_and_the_Political_Scene.
[41] Tomkins, *Affect, Imagery, Consciousness*, 204.
[42] Angel and Gibbs, 'Media, Affect and the Face', 25.
[43] Darwin, *The Expressions of Emotions in Man and Animals*, 234.

movements. The audience are encouraged to interpret these expressions by utilizing their imagination and coming to their own subjective conclusions and interpretations.

As I explore the expressive opportunity that is available in both facial expressions and hands, I will use these ideas as a way to analyse the acting techniques of Ryan Gosling, who has worked with both Refn and Villeneuve. While the Canadian actor, like Refn himself, has remained secretive about the methods of his profession, there is nonetheless sufficient evidence of the importance of his role in contributing ideas to many of the productions he has featured in. We can observe the development of a strong silent hero type that makes an increasingly regular appearance in Gosling's later career and that draws heavily upon earlier expressionist genres. I will also briefly discuss the critical reactions that Gosling's performances have received, which intriguingly seem to divide critics as being either 'robotic' or 'emotionally intense'. This critical divide is key to the way expressionism itself is often perceived and received by audiences when heightened emotion is frequently combined with a stylized aesthetic. To this end, I have interviewed film critics Mark Kermode and Kim Newman to provide an overview of contemporary responses to the 21st-century silent hero as well as his links to earlier genres of film noir and the Western. I have also interviewed the actor Felix Granger to analyse the role of gesture and movement as part of his training in contemporary acting techniques, as well as eliciting his theories on the acting style of Ryan Gosling.

Feeling Theories: The Silent Hero as Affective Vessel

These ideas of audience response, and how affective reactions are cultivated, are particularly important in relation to silence in film. Sontag's theories, for example, provide intriguing perspectives on the way in which narrative is advanced through the absence of speech. However, throughout my work, to create a broader outlook on the productive nature of silence, I will also refer to a number of contemporary affective theories concerning film in order to detail the ways in which silence functions productively alongside speech and sound. Rather than focus on traditionally negative connotations of silence as absence of sound, I will try to move towards a position where the two play equally important roles in the soundscape. Drawing on the influential writings of Gilles Deleuze, Shilina-Conte notes how these moments of silence are able to transform themselves into 'an affirmative and empowering (dis)order that inspires creative experimentation in cinema'.[44] She also notes the essential role of the 'empty square' in narrative comprehension, describing this as the open space 'into which the spectator's horror pours, as the absence of words provides no guidance, identification, or critique of judgement'. This active, subjective task takes place in the minds of the audience. In *The Influence of Film Music on Emotion*, Alyssa d'Artenay relates this process to the affective power of catharsis in Greek tragedy, which she defines as 'the process of releasing, and thereby providing relief from, strong or repressed emotion'.[45]

The numerous silent heroes in my study, particularly those portrayed by Ryan Gosling, thereby act as affective vessels. That is, their performances, whether silent or verbalized, create a space into which, as Shilina-Conte explains, the audience can *pour* their emotional responses. Confronted with laconic dialogue and little expository information, the silent hero's reactions and emotional state become a key focal point for cultivating understanding. Again, adopting the terminology of Deleuze, Shilina-Conte notes how these techniques turn these silent figures into 'spiritual automata',[46] a fascinating phrase which aligns with similar ideas explored by Matthew Hawkins in *The Concept of Affective Tonality and the Role of the Senses in Producing a Cinematic Narrative*.[47] Hawkins emphasizes the affective importance of Robert Sinnerbrink's concept of autonomous mood, which 'occurs when mood is favoured over narrative progression or engagement with character'.[48] Both of these affective studies link with many of my debates about Gosling's 'robotic' acting style, as well as with ideas of the silent hero as ghost, a mysterious, seemingly invincible presence that appears out of nowhere and disappears back into nothingness.

In 'Taciturn Masculinities: Radical Quiet and Sounding Linguistic Difference in Valeska Grisebach's *Western*', Hannah Pavek employs Eugenie Brinkema's *Critique of Silence*, specifically her affective concept of 'radical quiet', which challenges traditional negative notions of silence as absence and which rejects the Western assumption that silence ever reaches a definite end point.[49] Pavek aligns with Brinkema's theories about silence 'as a tension within form itself' which acts as 'a sustained state of quiet that puts pressure on audible form',[50]

---

[44] 'Silence as Elective Mutism in Minor Cinema'. https://www.euppublishing.com/doi/10.3366/film.2021.0165.
[45] D'Artenay, *The Influence of Film Music on Emotion*, 4.
[46] Shilina-Conte, 'Silence as Elective Mutism'.
[47] https://repository.uel.ac.uk/download/983013beab892a8bb051711b30ec7454168963a6ea84eca32bb4cdc5dac6dc4f/7445538/__DLSTAFF1_USERS_D22_nazmin_DESKTOP_ROAR_Matthew%20Hawkins_Ammended%20Thesis.pdf.
[48] Sinnerbrink, 'Stimmung', 161.
[49] https://www.euppublishing.com/doi/full/10.3366/film.2020.0128?role=tab.
[50] Ibid.

intensifying the focus on the audience who have to work hard to actively listen to every layer of sound around them. Pavek cites the example of the film *Western*,[51] describing the ways that elements such as radical quiet work 'to destabilise ... the spectatorial experience, shifting the spectator towards a mode of Nancean listening that invites defamiliarizing encounters'.[52] Pavek's emphasis on the philosopher Jean-Luc Nancy's 'listening' is particularly important in encouraging an active audience response, and how it highlights the way sound is capable of taking them out of their sonic comfort zone. Very much distinct from the more passive activity of hearing, listening involves attuning the audience's ear to every nuance of the soundscape in order to fully appreciate how sound is configured in relation to encouraging audience response. This cultivation of audience activity plays a vital role in the opening examples of *Drive* and *Under the Skin* discussed earlier, where the audience are presented with the inscrutability of the black screen and are forced to orientate themselves through sound alone.

This is important in considering the appeal of the silent hero. It helps to explain how silence is used to draw the audience in. The character of the loner or the 'other', who stands outside of human society, is often presented in direct opposition to the talkative bad guy, or the confines of the language of the system they are protesting. A prime example of this scenario can be found in the controlling nature of the verbal baseline tests that K must participate in to avoid being 'retired' in *Blade Runner 2049*. Newman notes how 'fists and bullets' are the traditional Western silent hero's weapons of choice rather than 'words', remarking how the audience doesn't trust talkative characters because of their deceptive nature, concluding: 'don't we prefer heroes who are better than everyone else but don't rub it in? And fast-talking heroes rub it in. Whereas men-of-few-words heroes don't'.[53]

The Sound of Music

While my work centres on silence and its productive capabilities, it is impossible to discuss these elements without acknowledging its counterbalance, sound. Even when I analyse the early 'silent' German Expressionist films in Chapter 1, these works would not have been experienced as truly silent. As well as the use of intertitles, there would have been music to accompany the images on screen – often expressly written or arranged for a particular film – to evoke

---

[51] Valeska Grisebach, dir. (2017, Piffl Medien), DVD.
[52] Pavek, 'Taciturn Masculinities'.
[53] Epton, Interview with Kim Newman, 9 March 2021.

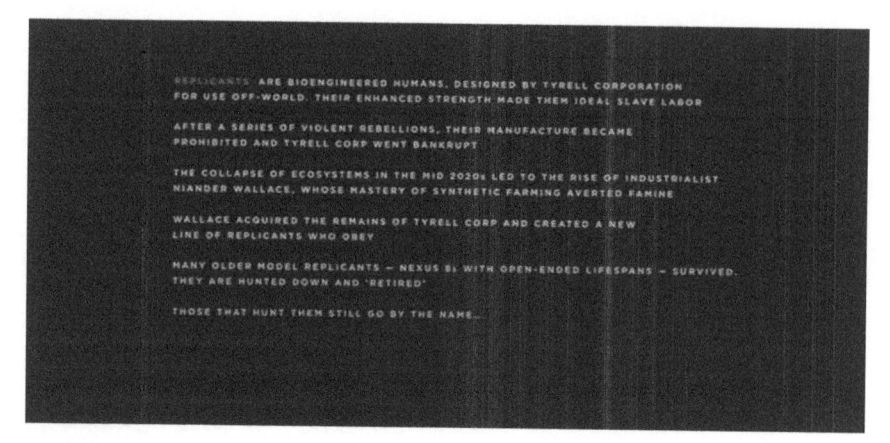

FIGURE 11 Blade Runner 2049's *opening text. While more detailed and expository than Expressionist intertitles, the principle of using the written word (as opposed to voiceover) alongside music to cultivate dread nonetheless evokes a similar atmosphere to silent film. The first word* 'Replicants' *is in stylized red, drawing the audience's attention up and to the left in much the same fashion as* 'defunct' *replicants are ordered to do in the film itself.*

mood and to describe the action. We can see a similar example of this in the opening of *Blade Runner 2049* (and its original), where text and music are used instead of speech to evoke the doom-laden environment of a dystopian future (Figure 11). In Chapter 4, referring specifically to the use of music, I will discuss many of the films that I have already mentioned and will focus on their use of musical motifs and sound design to forge heightened emotive responses within the audience.

One of the key works of scholarship I draw upon in my discussions of sound in film, particularly with reference to the use of music within film production, will again be Michel Chion's *Audio-Vision*, where he argues for an integral link between images and sound, and the idea of a trans-sensory space. Central to this argument is his concept of '*added value*' as 'the *expressive* and informative value with which a sound enriches a given image so as to create the definite impression … that this information or expression "naturally" comes from what is seen and is already contained within the image itself'.[54] This is very similar to the idea put forward by Susanne K. Langer in her article 'A Note on the Film', where she concludes that 'Music is a tonal analogue of emotive

---

[54] Chion, *Audio-Vision*, 5. Emphasis added.

life.'[55] D'Artenay also points towards music's distinctly sensual character when she notes how it can be employed 'as a way to provide texture to the overall narrative'.[56]

By analysing the expressive spaces opened by sound and silence in film, particularly with reference to the device of a silent hero, my work asserts the importance of reviving emotional and active responses in an audience that is too often subjected to empty noise and expository narrative.

---

[55] Langer, 'A Note on the Film', 27.
[56] D'Artenay, 'The Influence of Film Music on Emotion', 3.

1
Mythologies of the Silent Hero

The advent of silent film brought with it both detractors and supporters, and this ideological conflict is on full display with the observations made by two key artistic figures of the era:

> This is all strangely silent. Everything takes place without your hearing the noise of the wheels, the sound of the footsteps or of speech. Not a sound, not a single note of the complex symphony which always accompanies the movement of a crowd. Without noise, the foliage, grey as cinder, is agitated by the wind and the grey silhouettes – of people condemned to a perpetual silence, cruelly punished by the privation of all the colours of life – these silhouettes glide [over the grey ground] in silence. (Russian poet Maxim Gorky, 1896, considering the Lumière brothers' films at a fair in Nizhni-Novogrod, quoted by Emmanuel Toulet)

> The producers [of silent films] had in their hands a medium that was international, one in which screen performers while silent were able to talk to any country in the world. It is to be hoped that this [new] combination of shadow and sound will not destroy all interest in the silent picture, for after all is said and done there is something gentle and poetic in the idea of animated shadows that flit across the screen. (Samuel Goldwyn, 1928, quoted by Mordaunt Hall)

Gorky, not yet able to witness the marriage of sound with accompanying images on screen, is unnerved by the film's lack of audiovisual harmony. Likely commenting on the Lumière brother's famous train footage, he suggests that the people and surroundings which might otherwise gain vibrancy through noise are, with the absence of sound, instead rendered 'grey' and therefore lifeless. Gorky perceives the figures as silent, ghostly 'silhouettes', figures who 'glide' over the grey ground instead of walk. Without noise, for Gorky, authentic human life seemingly cannot take place, despite the power of the Lumières's cinematograph. Importantly, the Greek translation of cinematograph reads as 'writing with motion'. For Gorky, however, sound – speech and all the background noises of everyday life – is vital to animate the figures he witnesses on screen.

By the time the era of silent film was reaching its close, however, Samuel Goldwyn, despite accepting the move towards the 'talkie' within his studio MGM, notes the incomparable universality at the heart of the silent film. His remark that silent actors could 'talk to any country in the world' exemplifies the inclusive opportunities provided by non-verbal communication. Murch, in his introduction to *Audio-Vision*, notes that silent films 'rose above the particular and spoke to those aspects of the human condition that know no national boundaries'.[1] To illustrate this point, he cites how Charlie Chaplin 'was adopted as a native son by each of the countries in which his films were shown'.[2] The moment when the actor audibly 'talks', however, linguistic barriers are formed and only a select number of the audience can understand the narrative. The universal language is lost. Goldwyn, like Gorky, addresses the ghost-like 'animated figures' that possess the screen. However, rather than grey apparitions, he sees these moving images as 'gentle and poetic' – harmless, even beautiful entities that risk being lost to the noise of increasingly popular 'talkie' films. Whereas the poet Gorky views silent images with apprehension and estrangement, Goldwyn ironically chooses to use the word 'poetic' precisely to highlight the imaginative possibilities of these images.

When approaching the element of sound in German Expressionist silent films, it is important to reiterate that these works were never truly silent. Screenings would always be accompanied by musicians, who often used cue sheets that were commissioned by the film studios. By the early 1920s – when the key German Expressionist films were produced – these cue sheets had become what Rick Altman calls 'an independent entrepreneurial product',[3] with successful companies such as Winkler's and Berg's Belwin, Inc. sourcing their specialized cue sheets to seventy theatres across the country.[4] However, Altman's assessment that these musical aids were 'at the heart'[5] of the 1920s film-music system is diminished by Wierzbicki,[6] who cites Charles Berg's

---

[1] Murch, *Audio-Vision*, x.
[2] Ibid.
[3] Altman, *Silent Film Sound*, 353.
[4] Wierzbicki, *Film Music: A History*.
[5] Ibid., 354.
[6] Ibid., 65.

claim that 'many music directors felt their own musical tastes superior to the [cue sheet] arranger's and therefore chose to compile their own scores'.[7] The range of music played at these screenings could be very interchangeable, with composers frequently using their imaginative capabilities to complement and shape the narrative and to encourage critical emotional audience response.

Similarly, the common practice of using intertitles to indicate dialogue or to set a scene was not fixed. Murch, in his introduction to Chion's *Audio-Vision*, notes that they were rather considered as a 'necessary evil' and were 'routinely switched according to the language of the country in which the film was being shown'.[8] Some films, such as *The Last Laugh*,[9] whose screenplay was written by Carl Mayer, used no intertitle cards at all. Mayer's intertitles in *The Cabinet of Dr. Caligari* are not directly expository or narratively linear. In the opening scene, for instance, the audience witness two men sitting on a park bench. The man on the right, eyes adorned with Expressionist shadowed make-up, is briefly shown in close-up speaking words that cannot be heard. An intertitle swiftly appears on screen in Expressionist artist Walter Reimann's distinctive uneven, disjointed white font, foregrounded by a jagged selection of cut-out shapes. The intertitle reads, in translated English: 'There are spirits – they are all around us – They have driven me from hearth and home – From wife and child'. Aside from the deliberate stylized aesthetic of the intertitle itself, the audience are also unsettled by the lack of expository dialogue. As Marc Silberman notes of intertitles such as these in *Caligari*, 'They do not serve the story's narrative progress or even mark a rhythmic alternation for the editing, rather they intensify the uncanny atmosphere and frightful anticipation at the heart of the narrative'.[10] When the camera returns to the image of the two men, no such ghostly apparitions can be seen, just shadowed, indistinguishable tree branches and a dark path. The audience are invited into a world of subjective imagination.

In this opening scene of *Caligari*, ghosts – real or imaginary – take centre stage. One wonders how Goldwyn and Gorky might have reacted to such a scene. If sound technology had been available at the time, perhaps hearing the spoken words about these all-pervading spirits alongside the images would have injected Gorky's sought-after 'colours of life' into the picture. But as the short moment stands, only the intertitles provide any semblance of narrative coherence, and Goldwyn's ideals of silent cinema are preserved here in the dark landscape that is symbolic of an even darker inner turmoil.

---

[7] Berg, *An Investigation of the Motives*, 156–8.
[8] Murch, *Audio-Vision*, ix.
[9] F. W. Murnau, dir. (1924, UFA), DVD.
[10] 'Soundless Speech, Wordless Writing: Language and German Silent Cinema' (2010). *Imaginations*. http://imaginations.glendon.yorku.ca/?p=181.

Since the musical elements of German Expressionist screenings varied in their accompanying scores and the intertitles provide minimal guidance, it is more productive to look at films such as *Caligari* through concrete elements that all audiences would have experienced. These include dramatic chiaroscuro lighting, stylized sets and narratives concerning morally ambiguous characters, all of which are central elements of Expressionist film that feed into the aesthetics of many of the 21st-century works in relation to the silent hero. As Kurtz explains, 'The expressionist film sets up a living space which is fundamentally different from that of the experienced world' because it is 'decisively influenced by psychological means.'[11] In other words, the emphasis is on engendering a critical, emotional response within the audience rather than depicting a merely photographic surface reality. Referring to his idea of affective tonality, Matthew Hawkins acknowledges this pivotal relationship between audience and film, referring to 'a collision between the physical make-up of the film and the physical make-up of the film's spectator(s)'.[12] The environments of *Caligari* are so evocative in their design that many critics have focused primarily on the film's sets rather than the actors or the plot. It is also important to note that *Caligari* is one of a very narrow selection of films that can be called purely Expressionist, with later works often combining more romantic and impressionistic styles of filming with Expressionist atmospheres and aesthetics. As Francis (Friedrich Fehér) – the man sitting on the left in the film's opening image – first walks through the unnamed town, the audience witness a painted drawing of the town's houses, squeezed tightly together and rising into a spiral that appears on the point of bursting (Figure 12).

Not a single shape in the town is even. Buildings tilt precariously at various angles, looming over the already tight path. Shadows oppress the environment, and objects as natural as a blade of grass are distorted into a sharp, threatening shape. Each individual intertitle is given its own unique, jagged form behind the text. The audience is bombarded with distorted, unnerving stimuli in both visual and textual form.

The commercial practicalities of *Caligari*'s production are also important in their contribution to the film's Expressionist style. The light seen on the buildings was painted on by Wiene himself, as electricity was strictly rationed during the film's production. The shadows were also painted on walls, with the sets formed out of paper. These dark shapes dominate the set design, adding visual ambiguity to a world that is already difficult to decipher in terms of its morally ambiguous characters. Such sharp contrasts between dark and light are described by German film critic Lotte Eisner as 'Helldunkel', representing

---

[11] Kurtz, *Expressionism and Film*, 120.
[12] Hawkins, 'The Concept', 24.

FIGURE 12 *In* The Cabinet of Dr. Caligari, *this painting of a town with claustrophobic, uneven houses appears as Francis begins to describe where he was born, with the image devoid of reality or natural perspective.*

'a sort of twilight of the German soul, expressing itself in shadowy, enigmatic interiors, or in misty, insubstantial landscapes'.[13] For Eisner, the shadow represents spiritual, internal turmoil and not simply a realistic portrayal of light. Similarly, Robert Sinnerbrink utilizes the term 'Stimmung' in his 2012 work *Stimmung: Exploring the Aesthetics of Mood*, employing the early film theory of Béla Balázs to envision the soul as the affective heart of the film. Hawkins describes how, for Sinnerbrink, audiences engage aesthetically with the mood of a film, where a narrative is constructed 'that is not principally goal orientated but instead focused on the emotional experience of the central characters'.[14] *Caligari* was filmed solely in a studio and contained no exterior shots, creating a dark and claustrophobic Expressionist environment. The areas that are most exciting are those that cannot be easily discerned – the audience is drawn to what the camera does not reveal. If Wiene had been provided with a higher budget, or greater access to electricity, then it is unlikely that *Caligari* would retain the same influence that it continues to have on contemporary films. By

---

[13] Eisner, *The Haunted Screen*, 8.
[14] Hawkins, 'The Concept', 17.

having fewer materials at his disposal, Wiene was able to create a much more visually startling and enduring film.

Feelings of alienation and dread created by the sets were central to Expressionist ideas of chaos and nightmarish imagination. Screenwriters Carl Mayer and Hans Janowitz both identified as pacifists following the First World War, with the former feigning madness to avoid military service. Everything in the town of *Caligari* is out of place and disordered, from its buildings to its inhabitants. When it is finally revealed at the film's end that the story related by Francis is an illusion, the audience is forced to question reality itself. They have been given the limited perspective of Francis's psyche, and have viewed the warped town and its characters as he has seen them. This idea of the flashback, and the unreliability of human memory, is a central element of Expressionism, in which the whole nature of narrative objectivity is brought into question. Gosling's K in *Blade Runner 2049* similarly draws the audience along with him on his quest to follow the trail of his (ultimately) unreliable memories.

Wiene's more experienced background in German Expressionist theatre also lent a particularly distinctive framework to the style of pantomimic acting and gestures he encouraged within the cast. Both Werner Krauss and Conrad Veidt were well-versed in this style of acting and they both distorted their actions and facial movements to mirror the film's exaggerated sets. Vincent LoBrutto remarks that the behaviour of the characters 'represents the actors' emotional responses to the expressionist environment and the situations in which they find themselves'.[15] Internal feelings of angst and disillusionment are articulated through the use of gestures. The horror-themed narrative of *Caligari* made these melodramatic actions particularly effective, allowing actors to accentuate the distortion and terror of their environment (Figure 13).

The intrusive iris shots of actors, for example, allowed filmmakers to emphasize these intense facial expressions. The shot of Veidt's disturbed expression as he is displayed in front of a captivated audience articulates horror without the need for a single intertitle (Figure 14).

His slow, concentrated movements also reflect the acting style Wiene wanted his actors to achieve, asking them to model their movements on dance, with only Veidt and Krauss managing to fully achieve these controlled actions.[16]

The exaggerated sets and costumes of *Caligari* are not present in F. W. Murnau's seminal Expressionist film *Nosferatu*,[17] yet a similarly disturbing

---

[15] LoBrutto, *Becoming Film Literate*, 64.
[16] Thomson, '*Have You Seens...?*', 139.
[17] F. W. Murnau, dir. (1922, UFA), DVD.

FIGURE 13 *The wide-eyed, crazed expression of Dr Caligari, a typically Expressionist gesture, is on display within an irregularly tilted window outlined with ominous black shadow as he attempts to hide his evil acts from society.*

atmosphere is crafted through techniques of light and shadow, while the stylized appearance and actions of his central villain, Count Orlok, played by Max Schreck, represents the archetypal madman in German Expressionist film, composed of controlled, exaggerated facial expressions and displaying similarly unsettling slow movements to Dr Caligari. Schreck only blinks a single time. While *Nosferatu* is regarded as one of the first examples of horror film, this is not the horror of jump scares, gore and screams that the audience are accustomed to today. All the feelings of dread and unease involved in audience response are founded in image and sound, and what is *not* shown. For example, the minimalist concept of *Caligari*'s cheap sets is reflected in *Nosferatu*'s approach to how long the filmmakers let the malnourished vampire occupy the screen. Schreck is only visible for nine minutes of *Nosferatu*'s ninety-four-minute running time, and he doesn't appear until twenty-one minutes into the film.

Feelings of terror are created through anticipation. If Schreck was shown in the film's opening scene, for example, or featured heavily throughout the events that take place, then no intense build-up of emotion could be cultivated. The audience is scared by what they do not see. *Nosferatu* clearly achieved

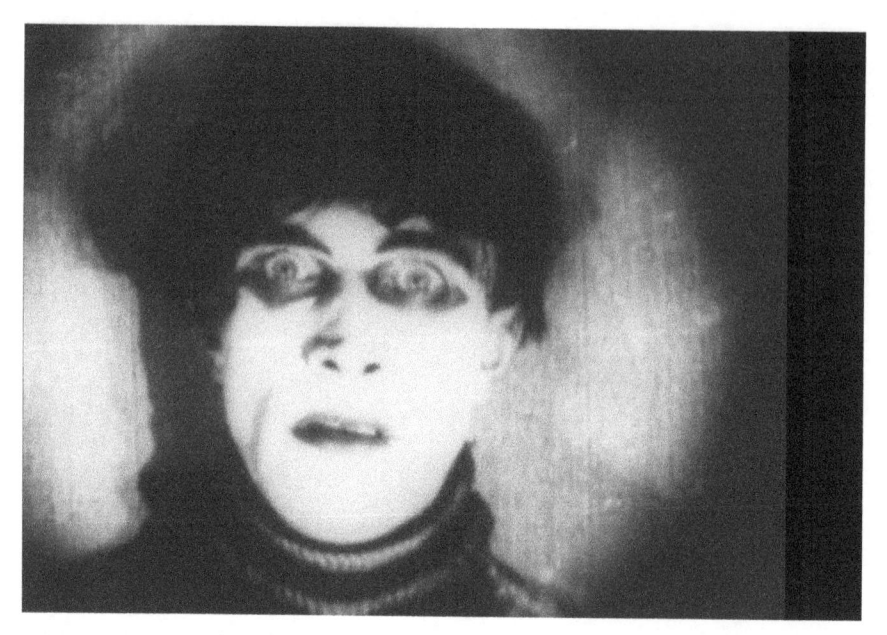

FIGURE 14 *On the orders of Dr Caligari, the sleeping somnambulist Cesare slowly awakes, twitching his nose and mouth before gradually opening his shocked, wide eyes.*

its desired effect of terror in Sweden, which banned the film for fifty years. This was not because of the various legal issues that haunted the film with its plagiarism of Bram Stoker's *Dracula*, but rather due to its 'excessive horror'.[18] No violence or gore is ever shown, yet the mere suggestion of violence was enough to cause such strict censorship. The audience is forced to pour their deepest and darkest fears into the unknown.

The 'vividly dreamlike and nightmarish'[19] atmosphere that Styan identifies as key to Expressionist theatricality is at its most powerful in the famous staircase scene, where the Count ascends to the bed, but his figure can only be seen in shadow (Figure 15). Eisner's 'Helldunkel' is now manifested in physical form. Schreck's naturally exaggerated features are accentuated further, with his nails transforming into animalistic talons. The shadow becomes even more frightening than his actual figure. No dialogue or intertitles are required to provoke unease; the image of the Count's shadow conjures all these feelings of dread by itself.

---

[18] IMDb, 'Trivia'. *IMDb*. https://www.imdb.com/title/tt0013442/trivia.
[19] Styan, *Modern Drama in Theory and Practice 3*, 4.

FIGURE 15 *The iconic shadow of Nosferatu. The straight, orderly bannisters are contrasted with the unnatural features of Shrek's figure, with the slim body, clawed hands and pointed nose suggesting a more animalistic, primal creature.*

William Burns notes how 'the shadows in *Nosferatu* are like another character. Hidden in the darkness, alongside the vampire, lurks the paralysing fear of disorder, uncertainty, upheaval and the unknown'.[20] The shadow in this scene is both an aesthetic element and a metaphor for internal dread. The deathly pale, diseased complexion of the Count is often highlighted with intense light, while his dark shadows convey a distinct, ominous spirit. Stylistic elements become central to a narrative that is predominantly articulated through imagery. Hawkins notes how the formal elements of 'light, colour, sound and movement are not solely sites of representation, but are affectual characters of varying intensity acting across a filmic plane'.[21] The Count's shadow is a direct instigator of the cultivation of fear and unease within audience response. In the following chapters, I will show how the influence of these stylistic techniques feed into both the aesthetic and symbolic narratives of my 21st-century case studies, such as the use of shadows and lighting

---

[20] Burns, 'From the Shadows', 4.
[21] Hawkins, 'The Concept', 32.

to cultivate intimidation in *Drive*, and the heightened, angst-inducing use of colour in *Only God Forgives*.

Since the Count's screen time on *Nosferatu* is so limited, the way in which Murnau frames the gothic character is essential to the cultivation of emotional audience response. The frequent low-angle shots of the Count grant a menacing viewpoint of the monster, whose diabolical figure often dominates the shot, creating further unease. The character is rarely shot outside his gothic abode – he is positioned very clearly in a world of the audience's imagination. However, as Murnau did not work exclusively in studio settings like Wiene, he was also able to film in outside areas of forestry and nature. Here the Count's malign influence is spread to local citizens as a coach carries his body around the town in a coffin. Dread is externalized through the deaths the creature's presence causes. The greatest moments of tension are nonetheless kept within the dark, claustrophobic shadows of the house itself, where the disordered aesthetic of Expressionist chaos manipulates narrative coherence.

Visual symbolism continues to dominate narrative in one of the last films of the Expressionist era, Fritz Lang's *Metropolis*, which also borrows heavily from Futurism in its style and creation of dystopian architecture. As Eisner notes, *Metropolis* combines a blend of artistic styles with Expressionism, describing the mechanical imagery of wheels and pistons 'as a fusion of surrealist-expressionist vision with the technological achievements of the avant-garde', and notes that the city itself is 'the encounter of Expressionism and Surrealism'.[22] Lang's sets were far more expensive to build than Wiene's structures,[23] with the buildings symbolizing the oppressive, claustrophobic nature of the ruling upper city and the enslavement of humanity through industrialization. Much like Kurtz's observations on Expressionist ideas of 'getting away from the time-bound',[24] the futuristic narrative has no fixed date. Eisner placed the settings roughly in 2000,[25] the official Paramount US release specified the year 3000,[26] while the 2010 release gave no year at all.

An obvious key Expressionist influence on the film *Metropolis*, whose themes align with later discussions of my 21st-century films, is George Grosz's 1917 painting *Metropolis*, particularly with reference to its hellish, heightened saturated reds (which become such a prominent aesthetic feature in *Only God Forgives*). Nothing is in order. Despite the presence of numerous, supposedly human figures, nobody stands on a definable, solid surface. Perspective is

---

[22] Eisner, *The Haunted Screen*, 83.
[23] Minden and Bachmann, *Fritz Lang's Metropolis*, 19.
[24] Ibid., 11.
[25] Eisner, *The Haunted Screen*, 83.
[26] Hall, 'Movie Review *Metropolis* (1927) A Technical Marvel'. *New York Times*, 7 March.

distorted. With Grosz producing the work shortly after his expulsion from the German army due to a mental breakdown, his anxiety is on full display, as is his vision of the world as an apocalyptic dystopia. The man in the bowler hat appears skeletal and ghostly despite being dressed in formal wear. This dreamlike or, more accurately, nightmarish visual palette plays a central role in many of the films I will discuss.

Lang was also rumoured to have taken inspiration from the dull, suffocating landscapes of Paul Citroen's photomontages of the New York Metropolis, which depicted a hellscape of buildings superimposed together. Citroen's dystopian images are frequently referenced throughout Lang's film in similar Expressionist montages, where huge numbers of eyes and faces are superimposed closely together as the Machine Man (Brigitte Helm) incites the workers into rebellion. The shifting perspectives of the images confound audience understanding, forcing them to interpret claustrophobic hellscapes with limited narrative signifiers. Channing Pollock, an American playwright charged by the distribution company Parufamet with creating a simplified cut of the film, noted that the original *Metropolis* was 'symbolism run such riot that people who saw it couldn't tell what the picture was about ... I have given it my meaning'.[27] Pollock's assessment reveals the power of Lang's act of symbolic expression over narrative exposition, an issue which Nicolas Winding Refn will later highlight in relation to his own and his father's filmmaking approaches.

Lang's use of new technology also created a wider range of visual aesthetics. The Schufftan process, where a section of the camera is obscured with a mirror, was first employed in *Metropolis* and made miniature models appear much larger by placing the mirror between the metropolis and the camera. By standing further away from the camera, actors would appear smaller, but would also look the correct size proportionally to the effect of the large building made by the mirror, thus creating an illusion. This technique is used during the Eternal Gardens scene, and again in the Moloch sequence in the lower city, where the audience sees the stylized 'MOLOCH' intertitle that is similar to many of the monosyllabic intertitles of *Caligari* (Figures 16 and 17). Lang renders a small object into a terrifying spectacle of oppression as Freder (Gustav Fröhlich), with typically Expressionist overwrought features, hallucinates the beast ingesting workers into its mechanical mouth. These practical illusions represent psychological illusions within the protagonist's mind.

A similarly exaggerated emotional display is seen from Freder when he first witnesses the Machine Man in the office of Joh Frederson (Alfred Abel). The camera rotates and flashes, including swift edits of jagged shapes that

---

[27] *Metropolis*, 'Release and Reception', *Wikipedia*. https://en.wikipedia.org/wiki/Metropolis_(1927_film).

FIGURE 16 *The dramatic intertitle that appears in* Metropolis *when Freder envisions the demonic monster ingesting workers. Letters are not evenly aligned, with some stretched and overlapping other characters.*

resemble the distorted forms behind *Caligari*'s intertitles. These quick edits articulate the immediate shock of Freder's experience. Freder puts his hands over his face in an effort to wipe what he has just seen from his memory, and the hazy focus of the following image is blurred, mirroring Freder's own obscured vision (Figure 18).

The black rings around the Machine Man's eyes reflect the exaggerated Expressionist make-up that was employed in *Caligari*, and the crazed appearance and gestures of the villainous Rotwang (Rudolf Klein-Rogge) recall the Frankenstein-like figure of Dr Caligari himself (Figure 19).

Although *Metropolis* begins to diverge from traditional German Expressionist film techniques, it remains rooted in the stylistic traditions of its forebears.

While previous German Expressionist films such as *Caligari* used a limited number of intertitles, Lang attempted to reduce them to an absolute minimum.[28] The nature of silent film presented audiences with the opportunity

---

[28] Roger Ebert, 'Urban Renewal on a Very Large Scale' (2010). *Roger Ebert*. https://www.rogerebert.com/reviews/great-movie-metropolis-2010-restoration-1927.

FIGURE 17 *While the intertitles in* Caligari *are more decorative in terms of their jagged shapes than* Metropolis, *similarly stylized font is employed to create an atmosphere of disorder and unease.*

to follow plots through means of music and intertitles and Lang challenges the audience even further by forcing them to focus primarily on the performances of actors and their surrounding stylized sets. Lang proclaimed his fascination with 'fear, horror, and death' and his wish to 'show my preoccupation with violence, the pathology of violence'.[29] *Metropolis*' opening images depict the workings of gargantuan, repetitive machinery, with the endless drudgery of time symbolized in the clock, and no human can initially be seen. These images and the accompanying dramatic music (understood here as the music used in the film's most comprehensive, 147-minute version; several versions of the film survive with various accompanying tracks) depict central themes of Expressionism (stylized sets, alienation, tyranny), and Lang's desire to analyse the pathology of violence rather than the simple act of violence itself suggests a wish to penetrate the inner, subjective workings of the human psyche. This preoccupation is perhaps best articulated after the Machine Man

---

[29] n.d.

FIGURE 18 *The image of Jon Fredersen and the Machine Man becomes blurred after Freder wipes his eyes in disbelief, with the blurred image imitating Freder's own unclear vision and dwindling sense of reality.*

has successfully encouraged workers to revolt against the machines. A statue of the grim reaper comes to life and starts playing a leg bone, at which point the sounds of a flute resound from the object and statues of the seven sins disperse to enact tyranny on mankind. With just a few notes and gestures, the audience is shown the horrifying nature of human suffering. In Chapters 3 and 4, I will discuss how both gesture and music play a pivotal role in creating meaning in the 21st-century case studies I discuss, particularly during scenes that contain no verbal communication.

Film Noir

The visual and metaphorical darkness depicted in German Expressionist film proved to be hugely influential in many films and film genres that followed. The central themes of angst and disillusionment, however, were particularly prevalent in the development of film noir in America, and it is here where

FIGURE 19 Metropolis' *devious inventor Rotwang, exhibiting Expressionist features through his wide eyes, dramatic eyebrows, and unkempt white hair. Visual exaggeration is key in evoking his villainous aesthetic.*

the gradual emergence of a laconic, cynical, masculine yet strangely romantic hero can be seen. When Billy Wilder, a Jewish Austrian filmmaker emigrating to the United States to escape the horrors of the Nazi regime, was asked whether the angst following the First World War fostered a darker attitude to his work, he made the claim that 'the dark outlook is an American one'.[30] Like so many fellow European refugees at the time, Wilder himself came to embody the movement of key German Expressionist themes and styles into mainstream American culture. It is also important to note that it was once again a reaction to war – this time the Second World War – and the social and economic repercussions of that war which cast such a lasting gloom over the American populace and its film industry.

These themes of disillusionment and alienation are present throughout Wilder's 1944 film *Double Indemnity*.[31] In the opening image, a mysterious

---

[30] Porfirio, 'Interview with Billy Wilder'.
[31] Billy Wilder, dir. (1944, Paramount Pictures), DVD.

silhouetted figure hulks slowly through the mist, his shadow eventually covering the entire screen in darkness. While the audience no longer have the jagged, distorted buildings of *Caligari*, the same unnerving darkness and sense of claustrophobia are conveyed through the small offices of Walter Neff (Fred MacMurray) and Barton Keyes (Edward G. Robinson). Rather than just using clear open windows to allow sun into these rooms, filmmakers use blinds to split light and shadow into bars; the windows themselves are never seen. This lighting choice is not a simple matter of style. The strips of dark and light cast doubt on the moral integrity of characters. Blinds are featured on the train as Neff fakes Mr Dietrichson's 'accidental' death and are frequently seen when Neff converses with the mysterious Phyllis Dietrichson (Barbara Stanwyck) in her shadowy mansion. The strips of light and dark sit particularly ominously across Neff's figure in Keyes's office as he attempts to hide his actions from his boss (Figure 20). The blinds are a visual signifier of moral corruption; no character can be seen as entirely heroic in their actions.

FIGURE 20 *A guilty Walter Neff holds a speech-blocking cigarette to his mouth in* Double Indemnity *as his figure is overlaid with ominous shadows from an unseen window blind.*

Like the atemporal nature of the silent hero, critics have no decisive dates on the precise start and end of film noir. American director Paul Shrader asserts that it began with *The Maltese Falcon*[32] and reached its climax with *Pickup on South Street*,[33] existing exclusively within a twelve-year period.[34] Foster Hirsch initially set the boundaries of film noir between Wilder's *Double Indemnity* and *Sunset Boulevard*,[35] shaving Shrader's time period by half.[36] However, Hirsch later revised his opinion, stating that 'noir never died', citing *L.A. Confidential*[37] as one of many continuing examples.[38] Kim Newman sets out the archetypal features of the genre, describing Wilder's *Double Indemnity* as a story of 'a desperate dame and a greedy man, of murder for sordid profit and sudden, violent betrayal'.[39] The moral natures of film noir protagonists are often just as dark and ambiguous as their shadowy settings, and the cynicism in these characters that Newman describes is often a direct reflection of the distrust felt by individuals and nations following the economic fallout of the Second World War. Bernard Dick also notes film noir's fluid nature as an aesthetic style of filmmaking as well as a genre, describing its 'high-contrast photography ... disorientating camera angles, and a sense of entrapment'.[40] Film noir's claustrophobic atmospheres and dramatic camera techniques both resonate with the German Expressionist films that came before it and provide aesthetic and thematic influences for many of the films that followed.

Although the ultimate heroism of Neff is highly debatable, the audience can nonetheless begin to observe the awakenings of a silent hero archetype in *Double Indemnity*'s first scene. The central character is framed from behind in a tracking shot as he walks through a building, as opposed to being filmed face-on. Intrigue is instantly created from this shot, as the audience are forced to follow the character from behind. They cannot read his face to discern his intentions or emotions. When a concierge notes the late hours Neff is working, the salesman provides the blunt response: 'Late enough', and soon wields the cigarette that will become a staple of speech-blocking masculinity in the silent hero. Instead of talking, this item becomes a substitute for speech, embodying an external calm and control that is not expressed in words. The less he says, the more powerful and intimidating his silence – and perceived masculine

---

[32] John Huston (1941, Warner Bros.), DVD.
[33] Samuel Fuller (1953, 20th Century Studios), DVD.
[34] Schrader, 'Notes on Film Noir', 58–9.
[35] Billy Wilder, dir. (1950, Paramount Pictures, 1950)
[36] Hirsch, *The Dark Side of the Screen*, 199.
[37] Curtis Hanson, dir. (1997, Warner Bros.), DVD.
[38] Hirsch, *Detours and Lost Highways*, 164.
[39] Schneider, *1001 Movies You Must See Before You Die*, 196.
[40] Dick, 'Columbia's Dark Ladies and the Femmes Fatales of Film Noir', 155.

'toughness' – becomes. Mark Kermode notes this common film noir trope, which is 'full of people not telling you things'.[41] Even when a figure might deign to open their mouth to provide a pithy comment, this speech is unlikely to provide any enlightening, expository information. In Hawkins's theories of the affective tonality of film, he clearly specifies that 'dialogue should not be used to give information concerning plot or narrative, nor should it be used for an expository function'.[42] As he nears death, Neff apologizes to Keyes, puts a cigar in his mouth and smokes it – and this is *Double Indemnity*'s final image. Instead of blurting out an extensive, emotional monologue, Neff enjoys a few final puffs of sobering nicotine.

Wilder's claim that the 'dark outlook' is wholly American does not entirely ring true. It is rather a combination of the European and the post-war American experience. The haunting shadows of the mansion's staircase in *Double Indemnity*, for example, evoke both the chaos and distortion of *Caligari* and the sense of dread created by the Count as he slowly climbs the stairs in *Nosferatu*. The close-up of Phyllis's satisfied facial expression when she knows Walter will kill her husband is also similar to the icy smirk of *Metropolis*' Machine Man as it encourages the workmen towards anarchy (Figures 21 and 22). In the same way, the shot of Neff speeding through the streets of a chaotic Los Angeles echoes the tumultuous crowd of vehicles that infest Lang's dystopian cityscape. Angst, disorder and fractured realities are seminal themes in Wilder's film and in German Expressionist cinema. The darkness that pervaded the American consciousness after the Second World War fed into the cynicism of the films that followed, as well as the outlook of the many directors who fled Nazi Germany and who ultimately built their careers in Hollywood.

A product of this pervasive cynicism, clearer characteristics of the silent hero can be identified in Michael Curtiz's *Casablanca*. It is still debated by critics as to whether *Casablanca* can be considered a true film noir, largely due to its hopeful conclusion. However, its shadowy aesthetic, atmosphere of moral corruption and the quiet, brooding main figure of Rick Blaine (Humphrey Bogart) justify *Casablanca*'s position in the genre. Cafe owner Blaine shares Neff's cynical outlook while participating in a similar world of expressionist shadows and sleaze, superficially uncritical of the actions of the German officials who have overrun the area and freely enter his bar. He also has the same non-existent past. When asked by Captain Renault (Claude Rains) if his choice not to return to America is related to theft, adultery or murder, Blaine sardonically replies that 'It's a combination of all three.' His

---

[41] Epton, Interview with Mark Kermode, 10 February 2021.
[42] Hawkins, 'The Concept', 54.

FIGURE 21 *Femme fatale Phyllis Dietrichson smirks inside her car, knowing she has successfully coerced Neff into committing an act of murder.*

origins and moral compass are unclear, allowing him to simultaneously cultivate both a sense of fascination and distance within those who meet him, including the audience. The film attempts to engage the audience in a backstory that is never fully explained. This sense of mystery is only intensified with the arrival of old flame Ilsa Lund (Ingrid Bergman), as the film encourages the audience to question Blaine's tough masculine exterior and individualism.

Unlike the relationship between Neff and Phyllis, the entrance of the central female character in *Casablanca* ultimately erodes Blaine's cynicism and reignites his heroic character. When Ugarte (Peter Lorre) is taken away by German soldiers, Blaine announces that he will stick his neck out for nobody and informs Ilsa that he is 'not fighting for anything anymore except myself'. Blaine is initially determined to keep his ordered life in balance. However, once Ilsa needs his assistance, Blaine undertakes a heroic sacrifice by helping her escape. When Ilsa tries to make a final attempt to stay with him, Blaine nobly states, 'Where I'm going you can't follow. What I've got to do you can't be any part of.' The hero cannot fully integrate with society if

FIGURE 22 *The Machine Man performs a similarly satisfied smile, having driven the workers to commit acts of tyranny. The deceiving roles of both figures are coded through distinctive make-up, cold glares as well as thick, commanding garments.*

he wants to retain his heroic status. In his role as a silent hero, he maintains his laconicism up to the very end, undercutting the dramatic nature of the romantic action with the casual 'here's lookin' at you kid'. Blaine simply disappears into the mist.

The deep cynicism of the post-war era is an integral backdrop to film noir and permeates the atmosphere of Carol Reed's British production *The Third Man*. The cosmopolitan nature of the film's production with Hungarian co-producer Alexander Korda mirrors the diverse nature of *Casablanca*'s cast and crew with Hungarian director Michael Curtiz, while many refugees were also included among *The Third Man*'s extras. Reed's film also presents a similar moral ambivalence between financial profit and human loyalty, but is even more damning in its cynical world view. The shadowy staircases of *Double Indemnity* are exchanged, significantly, for winding sewer steps and tunnels, whose ends the audience rarely see (Figures 23 and 24).

The haunting, repetitive chords of Anton Karas's zither in the famous 'Harry Lime Theme' are heard and are constantly played against the bleak

FIGURE 23 *Neff's shadow is in clear view as he looks upward, with the ominous patterned shadows asserting Neff's moral ambiguity in visual form.*

realities of war-torn Vienna. The much-discussed, legendary figure of Harry Lime (Orson Welles) is only seen in the film's final act, where he is stripped of all the heroism that Holly Martins (Joseph Cotton) thought he possessed. Holly visits the hospital of the babies that Lime's drugs have mutilated, but the filmmakers never show the audience their bodies; the last image the audience sees in the scene is an upturned teddy bear, and the horrors are left to the imagination. When Holly confronts Lime about the deaths he has caused, Lime informs him that 'the world doesn't make any heroes.' Holly's moral compass upon realizing this truth is shattered. Appearing and disappearing in darkness, Lime is a literal and metaphorical shadow of the man Holly wished him to be.

The clearest strand of the silent hero archetype in film noir figures such as Neff, Blaine and Martins is their essential romanticism – be it actual or imagined. In common with many earlier expressionist films, the audience are presented with inscrutable men of few words, positioned in dark, alienating, fractured environments, into whom the audience and other characters must

FIGURE 24 *Harry Lime attempts to escape his pursuers as he climbs up tunnel steps, his face lined with dirt that externalizes his true, morally grimy nature.*

pour their emotion and imagination. Neff naively believes he can both help a woman by committing murder and yet hide this fact from his closest friend and colleague. Blaine maintains a hard surface of cool cynicism whilst undercutting this with his heroic actions. Lime emerges as the very darkest version of these heroes, having previously been built up by Martins as the best friend he ever had and incapable of wrongdoing. Neff dies, Blaine saves and Lime kills. In the following chapters, similar themes of death, sacrifice and murder are embodied in many of my 21st-century case studies and their respective silent heroes.

The Western

A man utters four words to an undertaker ('Get three coffins ready'). He continues walking, gives a brief lecture to four men before dispatching them, and indulges the audience with another four words as he tells the funeral director that he will require an extra coffin, before walking off into the distance.

FIGURE 25 *The Man takes a moment to part with his precious cigar and inform the undertaker of his imminent duties. This terse moment has become so ingrained in popular culture that these few seconds have been immortalized in a GIF (Graphics Interchange Format), a short looping image on the internet that – significantly – contains no sound at all.*

In one short scene from Sergio Leone's A Fistful of Dollars,[43] a microcosm of a Hollywood silent hero is illustrated. Laconic, slow-moving and boundlessly confident in his gestures, Clint Eastwood's nameless figure epitomizes cool as he wields his Toscano cigar like a sword, just like the speech-blocking cigarettes used by the morally ambiguous male heroes of film noir (Figure 25).

While the Man with No Name (hereafter referred to as The Man) represents the most recognizable example of the silent hero archetype, this is but one of many which continue to inspire films today, standing alongside the earlier examples noted in film noir. In order to decipher the contemporary silent hero, it is essential to analyse his earlier cinematic iterations.

The laconic romanticism of the classical Western hero shares many of the cynical yet decidedly romantic traits of his film noir counterparts. Will Wright summarizes these Western narratives as 'a lone stranger who rides into a troubled town and cleans it up, winning the respect of the townsfolk and the love of the schoolmarm'.[44] The expressionist concern with individual struggle in a violent world is a common factor within this silent hero mythology, with many film directors reflecting on the hero's position as an outsider within society. Loneliness is therefore an essential trait of the silent hero. He can have no previous connection to any citizen of the town, and so is able to

---

[43] Sergio Leone, dir. (1964, Unidis), DVD.
[44] Wright, *Sixguns and Society*, 32.

depart from the town just as easily once he has performed his noble action. A non-existent past is a necessary part of the mythological allure.

This lone stranger narrative is embodied in the classical Western *Shane*.[45] Alan Ladd's hero never reveals his surname and is quickly referred to by the Starrett family he assists as Mr Shane. The less society knows about him the easier it is to maintain distance from this society and retain his mythical status. In his first conversation with Joe (Van Heflin), he tersely remarks that he is 'headin' north'. After Shane is invited into the Starrett's family home, Joe asks Shane where he is going, to which he replies: 'One place or another', then 'some place I've never been'. Like the film noir figures seen previously, this masculine laconicism is an essential characteristic of the silent hero. By saying less, Shane is able to keep his past hidden. Even after he has dined with the family and has been allowed to spend the night in their home, he still avoids the question of his ultimate destination when Joey (Brandon De Wilde) attempts to press him. Shane can only help the family and the surrounding community by remaining outside it. Barbara Will summarizes this essential expressionist struggle within the silent hero as 'the seeming conflict between the individualistic striving ... and a world of stable and unchanging values'.[46] Shane is willing to help tidy up the chaos that plagues the community and tries to integrate within it, but ultimately must return to the same wilderness from which we see him emerge. The filmmakers acknowledge this cyclical necessity by focusing on the exact same shots in the film's opening and closing images. The silent, unknown figure entering the scenic pastures on a horse is the same one that returns to the mountains after carrying out his heroic act.

Lonely Are the Brave,[47] a Western adapted from Edward Abbey's *The Brave Cowboy*, sits at an interesting crossroads in the genre and distinctly positions itself in the contemporary world (the hero is a veteran of the Korean war) whilst deliberately drawing on the mythologies of earlier, more traditional notions of the Western. Like Shane and the silent heroes before him, Jack Burns (Kirk Douglas) is rootless and without means of legal identification; he positions himself on the fringes of human society. He defines his loner perspective when he states: 'A Westerner likes open country. That means he's got to hate fences.' But as the film develops, it becomes clear that Burns is also representative of a very specific kind of masculinity that is bound up with the idea of a contemporary silent hero – it is an uneasy, more complicated iteration of the archetype. Articulating a similar brusque explanation for his isolated position as

---

[45] George Stevens, dir. (1953, Paramount Pictures), DVD.
[46] Will, 'The Nervous Origins of the American Western', 295.
[47] David Miller, dir. (1962, Universal Pictures), DVD.

Rick Blaine before him, Burns gruffly challenges Jerry (Gena Rowlands) with the revealing rhetorical question: 'Know what a loner is? He's a born cripple. He's a cripple because the only person he can live with is himself.' Like the loners before him, Burns has no place in the modern world, which is depicted as claustrophobic and violent – roads, cars and helicopters become objects of death and destruction with the police and prison system there to trap and confine. Equally, he recognizes that he has no place in the human society that is represented in the domestic warmth of Jerry's home. Like the loners before him, Burns resorts to violence and literally heads for the hills, just as Blaine disappears into a cloud of mist. It is this precise expressionist contradiction that Gosling will have to articulate with his 21st-century iterations of the silent hero, the romantic push for self-discovery and individual freedom that sits so uneasily with an ability to live a 'normal', human life.

As the film reaches its crescendo, the action becomes increasingly tense and chaotic, with the natural landscapes that Burns exists in used to reflect his inner turmoil and conflicts. The romantic West of mythology is being squeezed out of existence. In a similar fashion to the uneven, paranoid paths of *Caligari*, the zig-zag mountainous path Burns ascends to escape his pursuers becomes ever narrower and more dangerous. His beloved horse, an archetypal symbol of an earlier, more elemental existence, struggles against the machines of the contemporary world. The affective use of music is key here in eliciting audience response. Extradiegetic music is constantly used to create mood and atmosphere, locating Burns in the natural wilderness of traditional Westerns and particularly escalates tension in the final dramatic scenes of the film. His pursuers are frequently linked with the diegetic sounds of the modern world of helicopter rotors and car engines. As d'Artenay notes, music provides the audience with 'descriptive cues' which 'boost our emotional response to the visuals on screen and therefore interpret the specific emotions that are being inferred',[48] which works particularly effectively during scenes with minimal dialogue or no dialogue at all. The final scene sees the pair plunge back down to the border road only for the horse to be dazzled and terrified by the lights and fast-moving vehicles. The symbolism is unbearably crushing. The pair are hit by a lorry carrying toilets, perhaps the ultimate metaphor for the dirt and corruption of modern society. Burns doesn't get to walk away into the wilderness. Instead, his horse is shot and he is taken away in an ambulance, his ultimate fate unknown.

Two very different interpretations of heroism can be seen in the Western through the films of John Wayne. The actor's early, pre-Second World War career epitomized the light-hearted type of films that Sergio Leone appeared

---

[48] D'Artenay, 'The Influence of Film Music on Emotion', 10.

to dislike. In *The Big Trail*,[49] Wayne's first starring role, a band of strangers attempt to pass through the Oregon Trail, with Wayne's Breck Coleman trying to find the men responsible for killing his friend. Unlike Shane and The Man with No Name, Wayne's hero is fully named, allowing no room for mystery. He is a man instantly at ease with the society around him; when he arrives in Missouri, he casually informs a man that he has 'been down Santa Fe way' and must return there to avenge his comrade. Wayne's hero is far from silent, particularly when he gives a loud rallying monologue to a group of downtrodden settlers. Lopez (Charles Stevens) is already aware of his talents with a knife, and Coleman ends up getting the girl after beating the baddies rather than riding away into the distance. Breck Coleman has none of the angst-ridden, conflicted and complicated traits of later Western heroes like Shane and The Man. His lack of anonymity leaves little room for mythical status, as everything concerning his character is black and white. *Stagecoach*,[50] Wayne's first major hit, fits into Wright's category of the vengeance variation, where the hero ultimately integrates into human society.[51] The film has the same vengeance set-up as *The Big Trail*, with villainous Native Americans and a romantic sub-plot. No real threat – either literal or metaphorical – is present in either film; Coleman informs Ruth (Marguerite Churchill) that he is about to go scalping Indians, but also reminisces about 'the water smiling all day long'. The brutality of the hero's actions is underwritten with romantic and artificial whimsies about an ungoverned country that the 'noble' white Americans will soon conquer and reform.

Post-Second World War, however, there is a major change in the type of hero Wayne portrays – particularly evident in his role as the world-weary marshal Rooster Cogburn *in True Grit*.[52] Like *Shane* and particularly *The Good, the Bad and the Ugly*[53] (as well as the protagonists of earlier film noir), the flawed nature of the hero is dissected, and simple notions of good and evil are complicated. The disillusionment and chaos of the Second World War feed into the character of cinematic heroes that followed. Like *The Good, the Bad and the Ugly*, *True Grit* also fits into Wright's category of the professional plot, noting that 'the fight itself, divorced from all its social and ethical implications, become[s] of central importance'.[54] Moral motivations in the professional hero are secondary, and violence is a necessity. When Mattie Ross (Kim Darby) enquires about the best marshal to track down her father's killer, she ignores

---

[49] Raoul Walsh, dir. (1930, Fox Film Corporation), DVD.
[50] John Ford, dir. (1939, United Artists), DVD.
[51] Wright, *Sixguns and Society*, 69.
[52] Henry Hathaway, dir. (1969, Paramount Pictures), DVD.
[53] Sergio Leone (1966, United Artists), DVD.
[54] Wright, *Sixguns and Society*, 86.

the well-meaning recommendations of the straightest men and the best trackers, and instead chooses Cogburn, who is described as both a 'pitiless man' and 'double-tough'. A lack of moral integrity is instantly linked with brute strength. As Newman remarks, in the cut-throat environment of the Western, 'you don't trust people who talk a lot because they're lying to you. Whereas people who aren't saying anything aren't lying'.[55] When Ross enters Cogburn's home, he is not the lively, free-talking cowboy of *Stagecoach* or *The Big Trail*, but a gruff, whisky-slugging old man. It is Cogburn's taciturn abruptness that appeals to Ross as opposed to any kind of clear-cut moral virtue. Newman goes on to explain how this type of masculine performance is 'all wrapped up in the code of the West, which rather like the code of chivalry in the Arthurian romance, it's nothing to do with how people actually behaved in the relatively brief period of the Wild West'.[56] Newman highlights the mythological element that lies at the centre of these Western narratives.

Wayne clearly could not have conveyed Cogburn's age and physical presence in his younger roles, yet Cogburn's cynical attitude reflects a post-war hero similar to film noir heroes, one that is separate from the earlier character and world view of Coleman. After four decades of acting, Wayne had the ability to portray a far more nuanced individual. When Ross asks what family Cogburn has, he sardonically replies that Chen Lee (H. W. Gim) is his father and General Sterling Price – a cat – is his nephew, echoing the amusement of Carl (S. Z. Sakall) in *Casablanca* when he informs an intrigued gambler that Rick Blaine's father is 'the bellboy'. Neither Cogburn nor Blaine have any wish for their past to be known to a wider society – both are notoriously monosyllabic – even though both their occupations require them to function within society's confines. The audience experiences the pure expressionistic concept of the lone, romantic individual positioned against society.

Although Cogburn begins to open up to Ross about his ex-wife, he remains silent about any other figure or event in his past. He carries out his agreement with Ross and remains a man of his word when he dispatches a quartet of villains in precisely one minute. By fulfilling his promise and returning Ross home, he retains the moral code of the hero, exhibits more selfless heroism than The Man, and avoids the constraints of society by riding back into the wilderness. He does not get the girl and accept domestic life like his earlier Western heroes. The final static image of Cogburn joyfully riding a horse with hat in hand epitomizes the mythical, rugged hero in his element within the Wild West, a place distinctly positioned outside the boundaries of civilization.

---

[55] Epton, Interview with Kim Newman, 9 March 2021.
[56] Ibid.

The emergence of the Spaghetti Western in the 1960s pushed the mythology of the silent hero even further, into even darker, more cynical places, where the brand of heroism was, like film noir, rarely black and white. Wright refers to this strand of Western as the professional plot, which retains the classical concept of the lone hero outside of society, but now contains 'men willing to defend society only as a job they accept for pay or love of fighting, not from commitment to ideas of law and justice'.[57] Any sense of moral righteousness in the individual's actions is now void. The audience no longer witnesses the white and black hats representing good guys and bad guys and are instead presented with characters trying to find a role in darkly corrupt and abusive societies. Sergio Leone (another non-American) was the foremost figure of this new approach to the Western genre, which is epitomized in *The Good, the Bad and the Ugly*, the final part of Leone's *Dollars Trilogy*. Where previous Westerns often only touched on the impact of the American Civil War, if they discussed it at all, Leone brings this conflict into full focus to discuss the futility of violence and its impact on the film's three central characters. Looking at the ravaged fields of conflict with Tuco (Eli Wallach) at his side, The Man remarks that he has 'never seen so many men wasted so badly', while Angel Eyes (Lee Van Cleef) simply continues to abuse those around him in search of gold and profit. Much like the impact that the First and Second World Wars had on expressionist artists, the suffering in the American Civil War provides outsiders like Leone with a powerful framework to articulate his discontent. As Harry Lime cynically observed, the Borgias experienced 'thirty years of warfare, terror, murder, bloodshed but they produced Michelangelo, Leonardo Da Vinci and the Renaissance', whereas Switzerland's brotherly love and '500 years of democracy and peace' produced little more than the cuckoo clock. War is presented as both the dark backdrop and the catalyst for creative expression.

The use of hyperbolic violence was a key addition to the Spaghetti Western and led to heavy criticism of *The Good, the Bad and the Ugly* upon its original release. Renata Adler commented in the *New York Times* that Leone's film 'must be the most expensive, pious and repellent movie in the history of its particular genre'.[58] Financial expense and a religious devotion to violence evoked disgust. Like Fritz Lang before him, Leone was interested in the pathology of violence, and he defended his use of it as a satire on earlier Westerns, whose depictions of early America painted a glamorous picture of morally pure heroes and luscious landscapes that were bereft of true evil. As

---

[57] Wright, *Sixguns and Society*, 85.
[58] 'The Good, the Bad and the Ugly' Begins Run: Brutal Italian Western Stars Clint Eastwood' (1968). *New York Times*. https://www.nytimes.com/1968/01/25/archives/the-screen-zane-grey-meets-the-marquis-de-sade-the-good-the-bad-and.html.

Newman acknowledges, 'The whole point about the Western hero is that he *expresses* himself through violence.'[59] His gun does the talking. Despite Clint Eastwood's character being labelled as 'The Good' in the film's title, we first witness him killing a trio of bandits purely to gain his half of a £2,000 bounty, working entirely for himself and exhibiting no signs of heroic behaviour. It is significant that Spaghetti Westerns were international affairs with multilingual casts, and were often originally released in Italian. Sound, including dubbed dialogue, was added in post-production and this increased the audience's reliance on facial expression, gesture, sets and props, automatically lending the films a more universal appeal. Rather like earlier silent films, they were less hamstrung by an over-reliance on the spoken word. Newman reveals that 'I always think of those amazing close-ups in Sergio Leone's films, Clint Eastwood's eyes, where he's squinting.'[60] The stylized aesthetic has become so iconic that it has become fundamentally linked to the concept of the Western silent hero.

When The Man initially addresses one of the bandits with the confident claim that that man won't be the one collecting Tuco's bounty, the audience do not even see Eastwood's face, only the reaction of the bandit and other characters hearing it. The Man is such a recognizable figure from Leone's *Dollars Trilogy* at this point that the audience does not need to see a face to recognize his voice, and are not surprised by the stunned silence that follows as the characters watch him smoke a cigar and are obliged to obey his orders. Still filmed from the back, Eastwood laconically says 'couple steps back'. Angel and Gibbs stress the importance of 'affective display' in 'establishing a social position',[61] with the camera here asserting The Man's superior ranking in the audience's affections, not through the obvious emotional signifier of the face or expository dialogue, but rather with a focus on the inscrutable slab of his back. The bandit instantly gets the message from this short phrase and moves back several times more than requested. Filmmakers then provide the audience with a series of Leone's famous close-up shots, focusing on the expressions of each character as they size up The Man. Already prepared, The Man whips his gun out before the bandit has a chance to shoot. Leone only shows his hand casually retrieving the weapon from his coat pocket. This scene reflects Styan's identification of the 'staccato telegraphese' of so much expressionist dialogue, which he sees as being 'made up of phrases of one or two words or expletives' rather than traditional, realistic 'conversation'.[62]

---

[59] Epton, Interview with Kim Newman, 9 March 2021. Emphasis added.
[60] Ibid.
[61] Angel and Gibbs, 'Media, Affect and the Face', 25.
[62] Styan, *Modern Drama*, 5.

Kermode uses very similar wording when he comments on the acting style of Ryan Gosling, as 'telegraphing a lot of what is going on'.[63] Both Eastwood and Gosling are able to cultivate strong affective responses in the audience by employing subtle physical actions and minimal dialogue. Through laconic speech, deliberate movement and tight framing, masculinity is asserted. It is interesting to note at this point that whilst Eastwood's is a version of masculinity that feels utterly invulnerable, Gosling frequently portrays one which is decidedly more complicated and fragile. Whilst presenting an outward impression of cool dominance, Gosling's characters often appear to mask an extremely repressed and troubled inner psyche.

Eastwood's whole figure is represented by the gun he wields. Physical skill and superiority are emphasized by the filmmakers not through filming Eastwood's full body, but by focusing solely on his weapon of destruction. As Martin M. Winkler notes in his study of the Western and its relation to classical mythology, 'Only he [the hero] can wield his sword or gun, and his arms are often of divine origin or endowed with supernatural powers.'[64] The Man never loses his gun to another individual and the gun never misses its target. Like Achilles's spear, the gun follows the commands of its master and always delivers violence and death. The Man's mouth does not have to be seen moving to know that he is a force of nature who commands the attention of those around him, and only his hand and the gun need to be shown to appreciate the swift brutality of his actions. As Pavek asserts, 'Silence in the classical Western is coded masculine, embodied by the central protagonist: the taciturn hero who holds discursive authority. In its association with the taciturn hero silence is instrumental in shaping the genre's specific form and performance of white heroic masculinity: the "strong, silent type" '.[65] Referring to the famous characters played by Eastwood and Wayne, she also significantly notes that 'the taciturn hero is not mute but reticent: a man of few (well-chosen) words who speaks through action, often involving physical and gun violence'.[66] The Man's sparse, carefully chosen dialogue allows the filmmakers to create intrigue by focusing primarily on his physicality, and on the physical landscape and visual signifiers that envelop and define him.

---

[63] Epton, Interview with Mark Kermode, 10 February 2021.
[64] Winkler, 'Classical Mythology and the Western Film', 520.
[65] Pavek, 'Taciturn Masculinities'.
[66] Ibid.

2

Silent Heroes in 21st-Century Film

When I analyse the characteristics of the silent hero in contemporary film, it is essential to delineate my precise use of the term 'silence'. What I am primarily interested in is the idea of *non-verbal* sound, where characters are silent (not speaking), but where meaning is conveyed instead through Sontag's 'surrounding environment' of both diegetic and extradiegetic sound as well as through gesture and imagery. Even without dialogue, as in the opening of *Blade Runner 2049*, a filmmaker may encourage the audience to form a critical response – in this case Villeneuve uses distinctive dystopian imagery and an accompanying unsettling score to engender a sense of dread and doom (Figure 26).

Synthetic farms roll out symmetrically before the audience, positioning them within the spinner, and the music pulses ominously, reminiscent of the waves of an atomic bomb, wheeling to a menacing crescendo. Villeneuve describes the sequence as 'the ultimate dystopian film opening of all time', notes its 'claustrophobic' atmosphere and declares that, with this plastic expanse, 'Mother Nature is dead'.[1] Devoid of any natural features, the collection of artificial shapes represent a doom-laden expressionist hellscape.

Even if there is a just a black screen and the audience is denied any visual clues (as in the opening of *Drive*), filmmakers can employ sound to direct the audience toward meaning. Despite the inherently passive nature of cinematic viewing, especially regarding what Chion defines as the 'vococentric'[2] nature

---

[1] Lapointe, *The Art and Soul of Blade Runner 2049*, 45.
[2] Chion, *Audio-Vision*, 5.

FIGURE 26 *A derelict structure can be viewed in a dystopian vision of California. As in* Metropolis, *gargantuan, ordered geometric structures are used to cultivate feelings of oppression within the environment.*

of a lot of sound in cinema where expository dialogue is used to move the story along, directors like Refn and Villeneuve instead use laconicism, gesture and imagery to encourage an active emotional and critical reaction from the audience. In his analysis of expressionism in drama, Styan highlights how the 'characteristic use of pause and silence, carefully placed in counterpoint with speech and held for an abnormal length of time'[3] are part of the expressionist tradition. As Sontag declares, 'Silence never ceases to imply its opposite and to depend on its presence; just as there can't be "up" without "down" or "left without right", so one must acknowledge a surrounding environment of sound or language in order to recognise silence.'[4] Silence can never truly be realized unless the audience accepts that it takes place in conjunction with and juxtaposed against noise. By recognizing the paradoxes that silence entails, and looking at Sontag's theories of silence more precisely, the expressive capabilities of saying less become far more productive.

Writing in 1967, Sontag specifies that her analysis of silence takes place in an era experiencing a lapse in religious fervour, noting that 'though no longer a confession, art is more than ever a deliverance, an exercise in asceticism'.[5] As stated previously, Sontag's use of the term 'ascetism' is detached from the word in its religious sense, and rather points towards the emotional punch that can be achieved through stripping down art to its most fundamental elements, gaining freedom through reduction. This matches with what Villeneuve says about the production of *Arrival*, where he and cinematographer Bradford

---

[3] Styan, *Modern Theatre*, 4.
[4] Sontag, 'The Aesthetics of Silence', 11.
[5] Ibid., 6.

Young were obsessed with the idea of 'going away from the scope of the huge movies' and instead tried to 'make something delicate'.[6] Sontag goes even further when she presents the relationship between artist and audience as a fruitful tension, pushing the audience to actively experience, critique and engage with art, observing that 'the ultimate weapon in the artist's inconsistent war with his audience is to verge closer and closer to silence'.[7]

It is important, however, to explain the complexities that are involved in silence itself. Sontag asserts that 'silence doesn't exist in a literal sense ... as the *experience* of an audience. It would mean that the spectator was aware of no stimulus or that he was unable to make a response'.[8] There will always be stimuli that will be seen or heard, with silence framed in relation to sound and image. When Julian stares mutely at a door in *Only God Forgives*, the audience is compelled to focus on both the heightened colour of the environment he occupies and to imagine what he is too concerned to voice. Sontag notes that silence cannot exist on its own but rather can only exist interdependently with sound; if there is no dialogue, for example, other stimuli will necessarily always be present: 'Something is neutral only with respect to something else.'[9] For silence to be recognized, the 'surrounding environment' of sound must be equally acknowledged and appreciated. As Sontag contends, 'A genuine emptiness, a pure silence is not feasible – either conceptually or in fact.'[10]

Compare the two baseline test scenes from *Blade Runner 2049*, for instance, where sound, silence and image play essential roles in character development and audience response. The film centres on Ryan Gosling's K, a blade runner and replicant forced to carry out the orders of his human superiors or face death (coldly referred to in *Blade Runner*[11] as 'retirement'). The face-to-face Voight-Kampff test used to identify replicants through emotional response in Ridley's Scott's original film is replaced by a faceless, questioning voice monitor in its sequel. K is subjected to baseline tests to confirm his emotional stability after completing traumatizing and violent assignments. The test's language (taken from Vladimir Nabokov's *Pale Fire*) is used as a weapon to verbally control K and the interplay between silence and sound is emphasized in the very first baseline test the audience sees. While flying back to the LAPD (an oppressive building that bears a resemblance to the structure in *Metropolis*) to undergo the test, both K's and the monitor's

---

[6] FilmIsNow Movie Bloopers and Extras, 'Arrival: On-Set Visit with Denis Villeneuve 'Director' (2016). *YouTube*. https://www.youtube.com/watch?v=qzKLJ4GeFto&t=0s.
[7] Sontag, 'The Aesthetics of Silence', 8.
[8] Ibid., 9.
[9] Ibid., 10.
[10] Ibid., 11.
[11] Ridley Scott, dir. (1982, Warner Bros.), DVD.

FIGURE 27 *The brutalist LAPD building towers over its surroundings, representing the omnipotent role of the police over the citizens on the ground. Like the towering building in* Metropolis, *its autocratic purpose is exemplified by its domineering size.*

voices are heard speaking, yet the image remains focused on a mute K in his spinner vehicle (Figure 27).

Image and sound are not synched. The audience continues to hear this conversation as the image cuts to a still-wordless K walking towards the test inside the building, not yet inside the room from which this sound is already emanating. When the image finally synchs to the voices the audience have been hearing, K is sitting and framed from the back. He is not even seen speaking. First the audience is deliberately disorientated and bombarded with unsynchronized voices and images, and when they are finally shown both elements linked together, the audience still does not get to witness K's facial expression. Sontag's 'asceticism' is on full display. By refusing to initially align speech with images, the filmmakers challenge the audience to experience K's troubled psyche through the confusing, disruptive stimuli of non-linear sound design and imagery (Figure 28).

During this first baseline test, K's repressed psychological state is represented through the speed of his responses. Many of these repeated answers are tightly phrased, single words. The most repeated word, 'cells', stretches no further than a single syllable. K's responses are laconic, yet this laconicism is not the 'tough', masculine phrasing of the Western heroes seen before. By responding obediently and swiftly to each individual word uttered from the speaker, K relinquishes any power that might have been gained from silence. Sontag points towards this historical 'fallenness'[12] of language

---

[12] Sontag, 'The Aesthetics of Silence', 14.

SILENT HEROES IN 21ST-CENTURY FILM 59

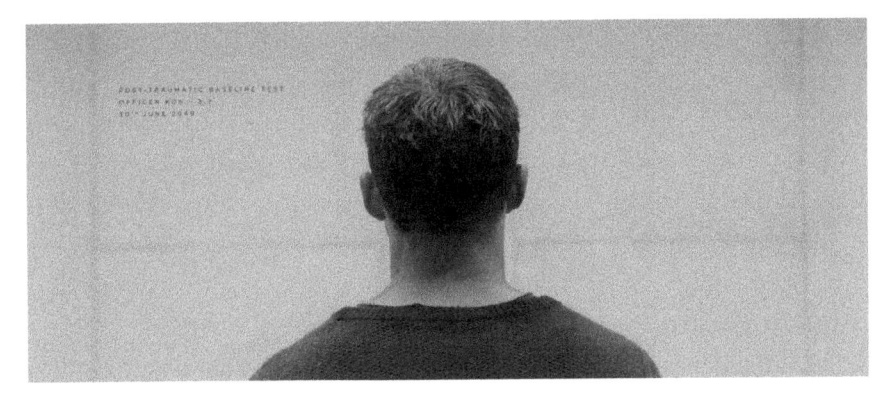

FIGURE 28 *During the first baseline test, K is robbed of any sense of identity through the severe commands of the unseen speaker and the filmmakers' focus on K's back until the moment the speaker has stopped the test, only deigning to focus on K's front after he is given a patronizing 'promotion' for his work, an emanator for his virtual girlfriend Joi.*

through its excessive use in human communication. The scene also serves to neatly dehumanize K in the eyes of his superiors and thus the film forces the audience to immediately engage with the entire AI debate about what it means to be human; his name, K, is designed to strip him of an essential humanity. It fits with Styan's definition of so many expressionist characters who 'were merely identified by nameless designations, like The Man, The Father, The Son'.[13] When the monitor in *Blade Runner 2049* asks questions that might normally elicit an emotional reaction, such as 'How does it feel to hold the hand of the one you love?', K mutely replies with the prescribed answer 'interlinked'. In this first test, contamination of language remains rife through the repetitive yet apparently unconnected nature of the questions and K's subservient responses.

In the second baseline test, however, after K has convinced himself that he is the replicant-human child he has been tasked with eliminating, the entire framing of the test room reflects his newfound awareness (Figure 29). As in the expressionist films seen before, music and camera angles are manipulated to convey emotional states. K is now shot from the front, and the invasive, diegetic beeping noise of the monitor in the previous test is replaced by extradiegetic synth sounds. K has discovered a new sense of identity and purpose that is expressed through this musical alteration. By changing from diegetic to extradiegetic sound across these two baseline

---

[13] Styan, *Modern Theatre*, 5.

FIGURE 29 *In the second test, the change in power is not only communicated in the change of camera angles, but also in the removal of the expository text in the top left corner of the screen. By no longer listing K's assigned name KD6 – 3.7 or the time stamp on which the test takes place, the audience are presented with a subtle metaphor of K's growing identity (and escape from the time-bound) through what is not shown.*

tests, the filmmakers articulate K's development from passive servant to active fighter. The audience can also now clearly see his expression as he answers the same questions as before. However, when K is confronted with the question 'What's it like to hold the hand of someone you love?', which appears slowed down and phrased in a more taunting tone than before, the audience can hear a pause before K gives his prescribed answer, at which point his boss Joshi (Robin Wright) detects an anomaly. As Timothy Shanahan asserts, K 'fails and is forced to flee. He has found himself, or has chosen to become, intimately interlinked with others, and that profound internal change cannot elude detection'.[14] During this moment of silence, however short, the filmmakers intend to produce intense emotional reaction in the audience through the 'surrounding environment' of sounds that have been heard before. After repeatedly using Sontag's 'contaminated' language, 'the most exhausted of all the materials out of which art is made',[15] to complete his baseline tests without displaying emotion, his silence provides a 'less contaminated, less distracted'[16] mode of expression. K's pause represents a powerful, silent act of rebellion.

Sontag raises important issues about the nature of audience response, as well as the creative potential inherent in the process of stripping back

---

[14] Shanahan, 'Do You Long for Having Your Heart Interlinked?', 10.
[15] Sontag, 'The Aesthetics of Silence', 14.
[16] Ibid., 13.

language: 'The notions of silence, emptiness, and reduction sketch out new prescriptions for looking, hearing, etc. – which either promote a more immediate, sensuous experience of art or confront the artwork in a more conscious, conceptual way'.[17] As in the earlier expressionist films I have discussed, these empty spaces created by silence present the audience with a range of possible critical interpretations. These 21st-century silent heroes that the filmmakers have created are similarly complicated, angst-ridden and morally compromised.

21st-Century Expressionist Film

Film noir and Westerns have articulated some of the central characteristics of the silent hero, particularly in post-Second World War films. His mythical status is established by the fact that he is an outsider within the society he occupies. His past is a mystery, and he frequently maintains his anonymity with laconic responses and long silences. He must leave the society he saves by the film's end. Some of these heroes yearn to exist within the fractured worlds they have entered, but few are able to do so after they have cleansed the communities of evil by either committing murder or, at the very least, crossing the boundaries of accepted civilized society. They are morally ambiguous, conflicted figures. The 21st-century silent hero further strains the relationship between society and the individual, often questioning – and making the audience question – the very nature of humanity itself. Many characters struggle to seek meaning in their own world while attempting to navigate the trials of the people surrounding them. Themes of unreliable flashbacks developed in German Expressionist films like *The Cabinet of Dr. Caligari* are revisited in works such as *Blade Runner 2049*, a film I shall discuss in detail alongside *Only God Forgives* and *Drive*. The plots and structures of these films often reflect Styan's definition of expressionist drama as being 'disjointed and broken into episodes, incidents and tableaux'.[18] The audience must follow characters' journeys of self-discovery and expression – often having to rely on gesture, music and sound rather than expository dialogue. They are forced to accompany the hero on their journey as they piece together the clues. The audience experience the heroes' insecurity, angst and disillusionment with their fractured worlds as they move towards acts of heroism, restoring balance to societies of which they can never be a part.

---

[17] Ibid.
[18] Styan, *Modern Theatre*, 4.

Alongside the use of diegetic and extradiegetic sound, the lack of speech in film provides directors with a variety of opportunities to articulate the mindsets of characters visually. As in earlier Expressionist works like *Metropolis* and *Caligari*, landscape and architecture – the set itself – plays a major role in the works of directors such as Villeneuve and Refn. This focus on utilizing aesthetic to evoke mood is on display in the very first scene of Refn's *Valhalla Rising*, a film in which Mads Mikkelsen's brooding One-Eye does not utter a single word. The audience are presented with a shallow focus shot of a hill, and are compelled to engage their imagination and look closely at the scenic details which the filmmakers refuse to make clear. While the green foreground is sharp and vivid, the misty background is blurred as an obscured boy walks down the slope. The pagan men are not introduced in words but through a panning shot; no spoken words or narrative voice are provided for the viewer to interpret their characters. The film's main focus, the mute One-Eye, has yet to even appear in the first images, remaining unseen behind obscuring, noir-like mists.

Echoing the traditions of many silent films and reflecting the disjointed, episodic nature of expressionist drama, *Valhalla* employs numerous title cards to divide the narrative into sections. These details are incredibly brief and non-expository, with only a single word or phrase summing up each 'section'. However, they perfectly mirror the story arc of the classic silent hero: 'Wrath', 'The Silent Warrior', 'Men of God', 'The Holy Land', 'Hell' and 'The Sacrifice'. They draw on the mythological, archetypal qualities associated with the hero such as the use of violence, the almost superhuman powers he wields, the operating in dystopian societies and the sacrificing to save others within those societies. The violence of the silent figure is on full display in this first chapter as an enslaved One-Eye silently slaughters other men as spectacle for his captors. Shilina-Conte notes how, traditionally, 'silent male protagonists in cinema have been addressed far less frequently than female characters',[19] and One-Eye provides a particularly engaging example of a truly silent hero; he remains Refn's only study of an entirely mute character in his career at the time of this writing. Shilina-Conte is highlighting the traditionally vococentric nature of a lot of films, where it has often been the male voice that has dominated the expository narrative and dialogue. The silences have been more traditionally assigned to female characters, boosting the sense of the 'other' and productively encouraging the audience to fill in the gaps. In her analysis of these silences, Shilina-Conte highlights the apparent omniscience that is granted to a mute figure, noting that 'as silent spiritual automata of life, mute protagonists in cinema often see, hear, and observe everything around

---

[19] Shilina-Conte, 'Silence as Elective Mutism'.

them, like a camera, but are unwilling to react'.[20] In her acknowledgement of the passivity that often goes hand in hand with this almost supernatural omniscience, Shilina-Conte draws attention to the fascinating, inherent contradiction that lies at the heart of many of these male iterations of the silent hero. Alongside their all-powerful traits and the frequent resort to physical violence lies a mysterious quality of numbed robotic-ness, the idea of the hero as empty vessel into which an audience can pour their own emotions and interpretations.

One-Eye's mutism goes hand in hand with his omniscient, god-like nature. Refn's dark and brooding portrayal of Odin harks back to early Norse representations of the god as a violent figure who carries out his actions in a blunt manner – in Old Norse, Odin translates significantly as The Furious One – and contrasts with noisier, morally shinier interpretations of Norse mythology and Odin in recent texts and films. With its sparse use of dialogue and lack of clear plot, *Valhalla* forces the audience to create meaning from the elemental natural world depicted. One-Eye's environment is composed of muddy earth, brooding skies and waters. An evocative musical score accompanies various shots of the bleak landscape, and characters are positioned theatrically, often symmetrically, within this huge backdrop. At the start of the film, the human figures rolling in the mud are almost indistinguishable from the earth itself. Despite the generally monochromatic colour scheme of the film (the sun only comes out halfway through the film), the events on screen are suddenly laden with a saturated red at various points (an aesthetic that will make frequent appearances in *The Neon Demon*, and particularly *Only God Forgives*), acting as a visual representation of One-Eye's omniscient foresight. One of these 'red' shots takes place as One-Eye bathes in a body of water, and this event occurs later in 'real time', signified by a return to the film's standard colour palette. Hawkins describes these moments of colour saturation as 'affective elements of mood' which 'go beyond narrative function'.[21] These are intervals for the audience to bask in a narrative void and pour their emotive responses into these abstract images. As all sound is withdrawn, One-Eye dives into the water and the camera provides a lingering shot of him retrieving a discarded spearhead from the floor. While the spearhead is ultimately used as an instrument of violence against the pagans, the intense close-up of One-Eye as he retrieves the item provides the audience with an aural and visual respite from conflict.

As with the Expressionist sets of *Caligari* which employ the stylized, dramatic use of light and shadow, so the use of mist is employed so frequently

---

[20] Ibid.
[21] Hawkins, 'The Concept', 18.

within the narrative of *Valhalla* that it becomes a character in its own right, and this is illustrated most powerfully in the scene where One-Eye embarks on a boat to the Holy Land with the boy and the Christian Vikings, and the boat stops due to a complete absence of wind. Shallow focus shots of the mist enshrouding the boat create a distinctly and deliberately unsettling sensation for the audience, as if they are literally and metaphorically 'at sea'. Helpful signifiers of boundary and time have been withdrawn. Instead of flashing lightning, the sounds of pounding thunder or the voices of men, the pathetic fallacy of the enshrouding mist evokes the doom-laden atmosphere of dread all by itself. Unlike more glamorous portrayals of the king of the gods in literature, Mikkelsen's One-Eye remains mute as he watches the other men in stony silence while their paranoia increases, with unease cultivated by the tense stares of the men as well as several close-ups of disturbed expressions. Silence here is equated with power as the other men are forced to back down. The camera never zooms out from the boat except to focus on mist, and the distinct lack of human movement within the vessel creates a particularly claustrophobic atmosphere. Apart from a moment where one of the men unwisely tries to kill the boy, the majority of the scene proceeds in silence, and the audience is left to negotiate meaning from the shots of still faces.

With the minimal use of dialogue in the film, imagery and music become central components to cultivate meaning. Even when snatches of dialogue are heard, they are never expository and the human voice is frequently reduced to primal yells and grunts. Just as the audience are presented with visual and metaphorical symbols (such as the tattoos on One-Eye's back), so they must also glean meaning from a soundscape that is made up of disjointed bursts of diegetic and extradiegetic sound. Heightened effects of the wind howling go hand in hand with sinister synthetic drones and taut, violent sounds of strings. This unsettling effect is only increased by the way sound and image are often not synched. For example, when the audience hear the voice of one of the pagans describing how One-Eye is 'driven by hate', so they also see One-Eye sticking his head on a spike. The process of building narrative coherence is also frequently obstructed by One-Eye's abstract 'vision' scenes, some of which appear to have no relevance to or place within the chronology of other events. One of these depicts a large statue head of One-Eye on the left, and a mountain on the right. The image may refer to the film's opening quote, which states: 'In the beginning, there was only man and nature.' It could also relate to the god-like origins of One-Eye, and the creation mythology of the human and natural world springing from his own design. But, as with all good silent heroes, his past life is not explained, thus encouraging the audience to decode the symbolism for themselves.

A key insight into One-Eye's nature occurs when he arrives in the green pastures of the supposed New World with the Christian Vikings. Although they had intended to arrive in Jerusalem to fight in the Crusades, the mystical mists have driven them to this seemingly unpopulated island. Perspective and viewpoints change suddenly as the camera often tracks characters from behind, with the audience frequently as confused and disorientated as the Vikings themselves. As the men slowly lose sanity and fast cuts are used to emphasize the ensuing chaos, One-Eye sits alone on a small island and begins to build a cairn. Although the structure might simply be built as landmark, it is more likely that One-Eye is building up the stones as a memorial to himself, as if anticipating an imminent sacrifice. The cairn falls apart on his first attempt and only stands solidly on the second. Having witnessed his own death in a vision, he silently accepts his fate as he builds the stones as a pre-burial remembrance. The vision happens exactly as he predicted, and the audience are left with the strange final shot of One-Eye's statuesque face confronted with images of elemental nature. Nothing is spelt out for the audience. The rest of the image fades, leaving an ominous portent that this mute deity will return to earth again after giving his life to save the boy. Filmmakers leave the audience as they began, with nature at the forefront of the image and the audience in deep contemplation. The constant mutism of One-Eye allows the audience to form a wide variety of theories on the significance of each individual shot, which links back to Refn's interest in the multi-layered nature of myth-making. He acknowledges that *Valhalla* is a 'mythology film' and that One-Eye is a 'combination of all folklore',[22] but refuses to be pinned down to a precise analysis of the narrative. Warren Buckland, in *Puzzle Films*, discusses such works which 'blur the boundaries between different levels of reality, are riddled with gaps, deception, labyrinthine structures, ambiguity, and overt coincidences'.[23] The audience must work hard to decipher each individual 'piece' of a film's formal aesthetics in order to cultivate a more comprehensive individual interpretation.

Aesthetics play a similarly integral role in *Drive*, particularly through the film's coding of the classical Western hero. The film has frequently been defined as a neo-noir,[24] and does contain typical elements of dark, corrupt environments and morally ambiguous characters. However, the film can

---

[22] Museum of Cinema, 'Valhalla Rising Interview with Nicolas Winding Refn' (2009). *YouTube*. https://www.youtube.com/watch?v=HH06a3Y4lgw&t=211s.

[23] Buckland, *Puzzle Films*, 6.

[24] David Thomson, ' "Drive," a Cool, New Noir That Degenerates Into a Bloodbath' (2011). *The New Republic*. https://newrepublic.com/article/95110/drive-ryan-gosling-refn-noir; Ben Sherlock, 'Drive & 9 Other Ultraviolent Neo-Noirs' (2021). *ScreenRant*. https://screenrant.com/drive-similar-bloody-violent-neo-noir-movies/.

be read more accurately as a 21st-century iteration of *Shane*, which Wright describes as 'the classic of classic Westerns'.[25] The hero enters a society, rids it of evil, then returns to the wilderness from whence he came. Newman asserts the universality of the genre when he states how the Western 'is almost the defining genre of cinema. It's a form that was really invented at the same time movies were invented'.[26] One might argue how a film based entirely outside the traditional environment of the iconic American Wild West can be described as a true Western. During an interview about his film *Valhalla Rising*, Refn points to the inherently malleable nature of mythology in relation to the silent hero and his geographic location, stating thus: 'All folklore has the hero. The silent hero, he appears everywhere, be it the gunslinger or the Viking or the samurai'.[27] The silent hero is, as in the expressionist style outlined by Kurtz, outside of time, and therefore open to a variety of Protean forms across the atemporal spectrum of mythology.

Refn has frequently referred to *Drive* as a fairy tale, listing Driver as one of his recent characters 'of mythological proportions that have no past, and they live in a heightened reality and almost have a distinction that they're fantasy figures'.[28] Newman also notes that, during his interview with the director, Refn admitted that Mikkelsen's character in *Valhalla*, and Gosling's ones in *Drive* and *Only God Forgives* are 'the same man. Because the Viking in *Valhalla* is immortal, and he says that, it's sort of the same guy'.[29] Notions of subjective reality and multiple viewpoints that are linked to the fluid, timeless nature of mythology also lean towards distinctly expressionist concepts of chaos, episodic narrative, violence and shifting moral values.

The malleable nature of the silent hero can be seen throughout *Drive* in the way it deliberately draws upon traditional Western symbolism to create a new iteration of the form. The corrupted desert lands of *Shane*'s Wild West and its horse-riding heroes and villains are exchanged for the corrupt streets of modern-day Los Angeles and its getaway drivers and gangsters. The saloon which the bad guys occupy in *Shane* is also neatly exchanged for a pizzeria in *Drive* (Figures 30 and 31). However, it is important to note that Driver's vehicle (the 21st-century take on Shane's horse) is rarely framed externally in swift cuts designed to emphasize the nonchalant, action-based events that might be seen in a *Fast and Furious*-style film. Instead, the audience

---

[25] Wright, *Sixguns and Society*, 34.
[26] Epton, Interview with Kim Newman, 9 March 2021.
[27] Refn, '*Valhalla Rising* Interview'.
[28] Kermode and Mayo, 'Nicolas Winding Ref Interviewed by Zoe Ball' (2013). *YouTube*. https://www.youtube.com/watch?v=taNev9I5Xzs.
[29] Epton, Interview with Kim Newman, 9 March 2021.

SILENT HEROES IN 21ST-CENTURY FILM 67

FIGURE 30 *Baddie Rufus Ryker (Emile Meyer, left) converses with his minions within the safe environment of the saloon, a housing for Shane's corrupt evildoers.*

FIGURE 31 *Driver's POV shot as he spies on villain Nino (Ron Pearlman, right), his next kill. As in* Shane, *business carries on in the background, with the primary bad guy shielded – temporarily – by his goons as they nonchalantly converse or joke with their familiars.*

frequently witness Driver *inside* his vehicle, where the camera focuses on Driver's hand or still face (Figures 32 and 33).

Like Shane, Driver is a master of his mode of transport; even when faced with the threat of pursuing villains, he is never driven off the road, just as Shane is never removed from his trusty steed. Driver's peerless, god-like skill

FIGURE 32 *Driver disappears into the night, with his hand resting on the wheel. This shot features frequently in the film, representing Driver's constant control and mastery of his craft.*

FIGURE 33 *In* Drive, *profile shots and colour are frequently used to articulate the laconic Driver's thoughts inside the car; in this example, his face is shot in a symbolic angry red after he has berated Shannon for telling the gangsters about Irene. This is a rare shot of Driver from this angle within his car. He subsequently places his hands over his face in frustration, breaking his typical stoic stillness and displaying vulnerability.*

is articulated particularly well during the opening scene; a taciturn Charon, he transports his passengers efficiently to their final destination and ensures their safety during the journey, but only on his terms. If the passengers arrive even one minute outside his allotted time, he'll disappear with his vehicle into the fog, never to be contactable again. Driver and Shane are heroes with an almost supernatural element of skill and prowess, existing in heightened, fantastical realities where neither can be defeated. Both heroes retreat into

FIGURE 34 Shane *rides into the distance, having saved the society he can never be a part of. Like classic film noir heroes, he disappears into the darkness, with his mystery and myth still intact as a result of his laconic and solitary nature.*

FIGURE 35 Drive *switches the imagery of the dark wilderness to the golden light and urban setting of Los Angeles as Driver rides into the distance, leaving behind the body of Bernie Rose as well as the stolen one million dollars in a particularly chivalric act.*

the wilderness in the final scenes, with the societies they leave behind having been purged of evil (Figures 34 and 35).

This contrast between wilderness and civilization, between an individual and society, that runs through many expressionist films – where a central figure is often positioned against a diabolical or corrupt system – can be seen in the way family dynamics and ideas of masculinity are represented through plot and visual coding in both *Drive* and *Shane*. When Driver first meets Benicio, a spiritual successor to *Shane*'s Joey, Driver offers him one of the toothpicks that he constantly chews – a symbolic nod to the speech-blocking cigars wielded by Clint Eastwood's The Man and various film noir figures. This exchange represents a foreboding sign that Benicio will become the man of the house once his father Standard (Oscar Isaac) is killed – the fact of his father's death neatly sidelining any need for Driver to remove him from the action (as Shane knocks out Joey's father). As Wright notes, the classical hero 'joins society because of his strength and their weakness',[30] and no other individual, be they man, woman or child, is allowed to interfere in the hero's acts of bravery. Driver's position as alpha male is secured through violence and constancy; he is enduring and unchanging, endlessly dependable. Masculinity is cultivated here through Driver's fragile desire to belong to society combined with an inability to remain within its confines due to his aggressively solo nature.

The climactic scene between Driver and Albert Brooks's arch-villain Bernie Rose (where Driver, like The Man, utters a grand total of four words) also transposes the geographical location of *Shane*'s famous final duel from its desert saloon setting to the interior of a Chinese restaurant and tight framing of facial expressions is a feature of both films' showdowns. Newman describes how, in the traditional Western, 'the point of it is not so much how uncommunicative or silent or man of few words [the silent hero] is, it's the contrast with the bad guy in the story, who talks a lot'.[31] When Bernie methodically lists the deal he is willing to offer Driver, Driver listens in stony silence, thereby emphasizing Bernie's villainous nature as he carries on talking regardless. In *Drive*, the restaurant scene is intercut with scenes in a car park as Driver retrieves the stolen money from his vehicle. The editing in this scene represents a visual power play between two men who are equally matched. The camera first cuts to the car park before subsequently switching to Rose's profile in the restaurant, positioned to the extreme right of the frame, followed by Driver positioned to the extreme left. It then switches back to Driver getting the money out of the car, followed by Rose back in the restaurant instructing

---

[30] Wright, *Sixguns and Society*, 59.
[31] Epton, Interview with Kim Newman, 9 March 2021.

FIGURE 36 *Driver's shadow dominates the image in the centre as his dying prey is framed at the edge of the shot. Even the shadow of an object in Driver's pocket is shaped like a tail as Driver employs his primal instincts to dispatch his enemy.*

him to retrieve it, again followed by Driver's apprehensive expression. The camera now cuts to Driver being swiftly stabbed by Bernie, but this shot is quickly followed by the image of Driver offering a rare, knowing smile back in the restaurant, with his face now fully in view on the left, followed by another shot of Rose framed on the right. The filmmakers' deliberate upsetting of chronology and focus on gesture and movement over speech reflect Sontag's 'strategies for improving the audience's experience',[32] removing the need for oversaturated expository dialogue. The filmmakers aim to stimulate the audience's imagination and critical faculties. The next image in the car park is of the injured Driver defiantly stabbing Rose through the neck in retaliation, before quickly returning to the image of Driver's apprehensive face in the restaurant. *Drive*'s final image of the showdown only shows Driver's shadow on the ground as the metaphorical scorpion dispatches his prey, leaving the audience to imagine the full nature of the killing in a similar fashion to the murder scene in *Caligari* (Figures 36 and 37). Feelings of dread are elicited by filmmakers in these examples through heightened violence (both shown and unshown) and stylized aesthetic.

In *Only God Forgives*, however, the audience are offered very different examples of both masculinity and the silent hero. Refn described the film he was planning to make as 'a Western in Bangkok',[33] decisively moving the genre from its ancestral origins towards the other side of the world. The 'hero' Julian (whose full name – like Shane, Driver and the symbolic figures in German

---

[32] Sontag, 'The Aesthetics of Silence', 12.
[33] Refn, '*Valhalla Rising* Interview'.

FIGURE 37 *Cesare kills Alan with an unknown instrument. As in* Nosferatu *and* Drive, *terror and intrigue are cultivated by not witnessing the physical figures themselves, with the audience forced to imagine the violence that takes place.*

Expressionist film – is never revealed) initially seems to a be a picture of silent hero masculinity with his laconic demeanour and intense facial expressions, as well as his outsider status as an American expatriate living in Bangkok. As the narrative develops, however, the audience realizes how the Oedipean undertones of his relationship with his mother Crystal (Kristin Scott-Thomas) emasculate his whole character. Kenneth J. Munden argues that the whole Western myth can be viewed through the lens of the Oedipus Complex itself, where conflicts are based on 'the decisive, universal, emotional relationships that exist between every child and its parents, no matter what variable environmental factors be introduced'.[34] Similar to Refn's ideas on the Protean, malleable nature of mythology in relation to the silent hero, Munden frames the 'universal' appeal of the Western, the conflict between the individual and society, as the fundamental clash of a child coming up against parental authority.

---

[34] Munden, 'A Contribution to the Psychological Understanding', 144.

A pivotal example of this emasculation can be found in the fight scene between Julian and Chang (Vithaya Pansringam). Chang stands composed in the centre of the fighting arena, unmoving as Julian walks around him. Chang's control of the fight is clear even before it has begun, as the camera slowly circles him in an arc shot. He is the master of his environment and asserts his dominance through the simple act of standing still. By contrast, Julian is shot in slow motion as he rolls up his sleeves, suggesting that this movement before the start of the fight is a form of weakness. By doing less, as Sontag might argue, Chang conveys more menace and power by not moving at all. When the actual fight commences, Julian is not able to land a single blow with his fist and intruding cuts of Crystal in a separate room emphasize her emasculating influence. These cuts do not emphasize masculine superiority as in *Drive*, but rather the opposite. When Crystal finally arrives in the boxing ring, Julian lies beaten on the floor in a Christ-like position as Chang, untouched, walks away. Intrusive femininity has robbed Julian of his physical power. The audience is met with a hero that faces an unstoppable force in the form of (quite literally) an immovable object and is incapable of delivering the masculine physicality that the silent hero archetype traditionally demands.

Expressionist aesthetics play a major role in French-Canadian director Denis Villeneuve's sci-fi sequel, *Blade Runner 2049*. Rather than the futurist aesthetic of *Metropolis* or the stylized distortion of *Caligari*, however, Villeneuve defined the overall feel of his film as 'Post Neo-Brutalism'.[35] Production designer Dennis Gassner notes that 'brutality and chaos became the language pattern of the film' before any production had even taken place.[36] These two words at the heart of the film's subject matter articulate the same themes that concerned expressionist filmmakers before it – what Styan defines as the avoidance of reproducing naturalistic detail with the use of 'starkly simplified images ... bizarre shapes and sensational colours' and often aided by 'shadowy, unrealistic lighting and visual distortions in the set'.[37] After the first baseline test, K walks stoically across a barren Los Angeles cityscape, and the audience are not provided with any wide shots of these monolithic gargantuan structures but are instead only given the claustrophobic ground shots of the buildings as K himself experiences them – the audience are oppressed by spectacles they are not fully shown.

Echoing the morally murky steps of *The Third Man*, in the subsequent scene in *Blade Runner 2049*, K stoically climbs a series of seemingly endless stairs whose beginning the audience do not see. He ignores insults directed at him in verbal and visual form; a squatter shouts at him in Hungarian and the words

---

[35] *The Art and Soul*, 17.
[36] Ibid.
[37] Styan, *Modern Theatre*, 4.

FIGURE 38 *K's passivity at this stage as well as his power are emphasized by his refusal to respond to the various insults he receives. The Hungarian woman addresses the insult to him in high volume, yet K makes no response. Likewise, when he receives the numerous intimidating glares from squatters outside his room, he doesn't respond, with the human citizens knowing that responding to him with physical aggression won't end well for them.*

'Fuck Off Skinner' are crudely written on his flat's door, a direct echo of the insult spat at him in the previous LAPD scene. It is particularly important to note the words that are exclaimed by the Hungarian woman, as subtitles show the audience that she derides K as a 'beautiful tinplate soldier' (Figure 38).

Her insult points to three common tenets of the silent hero, particularly the type of silent hero that Gosling plays. 'Beautiful' refers to the rugged cool of his physical appearance, but most importantly his ability to elicit audience sympathy; 'Tinplate', in the context of *Blade Runner 2049*, clearly insults K's inferior social position as a replicant, thereby referring to him as a creature less than human, and is another example of the automata or ghost-like supernatural quality of the hero. It also links into the debates around the 'robotic' nature of Gosling's acting style. The final 'soldier' element of the phrase describes the inherently violent nature of the silent hero who struggles against bad systems and individuals but, in the case of K at this point in the narrative, remains a subservient, strangely passive figure with no identity of his own.

The role of miniatures, as in *Metropolis*, was central to achieving the film's mood. Weta Workshop, a studio specializing in miniatures based in New Zealand, meticulously recreated large models of the dystopian Los Angeles, some of which they referred to as 'bigatures'.[38] Villeneuve's preference for

---

[38] 'Weta Workshop – Blade Runner 2049 Miniatures' (2017), *YouTube*. https://www.youtube.com/watch?v=sLxxbfsj8IM&t=195s.

this older method of design over computer-generated technology emphasizes his love for traditional techniques of filmmaking, even though digital cameras and computer-controlled motion rigs were employed to film these scenes. In a similar organic fashion to *Caligari*, these buildings were 'meticulously hand-painted'.[39] The creative divergence from traditional Hollywood practices of excessive special effects aligns Villeneuve with outsiders like Leone, Wilder and Lang. Their 'immigrant' status has allowed these directors to revolutionize and rejuvenate American traditions.

In common with expressionist films and film noir in particular, shadows – and darkness in general – play a central role throughout *Blade Runner 2049*. They articulate feelings of desolation and confusion without the characters having to open their mouths. Like *Nosferatu*, these shadows become characters in themselves, constantly surrounding K as he tries to make sense of the replicant child's identity. In keeping with the original film, Los Angeles is mostly shown at night, and only the obtrusive, artificial advertisements provide any strong sources of illumination. Much like the artificial light of the underground in *Metropolis*, *Blade Runner 2049*'s neon adverts symbolize the oppression of the lower classes, enslaved to mass consumerism and huge corporations (Figures 39 and 40).

Similarly, it draws on earlier expressionist films in the way it uses dramatic lighting to contrast the worlds of the inhabitants of Los Angeles. In the character of Niander Wallace (Jared Leto), for example, we see the archetypical Expressionist madman reincarnated in the 21st century (Figure 41). His megalomaniac personality is represented by both his headquarters' gargantuan size and by the reams of golden light and wood (both precious materials in the film's deprived world) within the temple-like structure. Like the original *Blade Runner*, the utopian Off-world colonies also remain tantalizingly out of sight, inviting the audience to ponder what an alternative society might look like. *Blade Runner 2049*'s sets, like the expressionist films before them, serve as characters in themselves.

Key elements of expressionism continue to be emphasized through this heightened contrast of light and dark. Assistant production designer Camille Verhaeghe asserts that *Blade Runner 2049* has far more film noir elements than science fiction, and that the design is 'all about shadows and light'.[40] As a replicant, K has no real memories of his own (appropriately for the silent hero archetype, he literally has no past) and is provided with manufactured memories to stabilize his personality. After knowingly describing Ryan Gosling's role as 'a Man with No Name but K', Brian D. Johnson notes that

---

[39] Lapointe, *The Art and Soul*, 31.
[40] Ibid., 64.

FIGURE 39 *The lower-class workers change shift as they move in robotic synchronization. The towering, curved roof over their heads acts as a metaphorical reminder of their subservience to the upper classes, who are literally higher in the world than they can ever hope to be.*

FIGURE 40 *K is pictured in the centre of a suburban area of Los Angeles, seemingly more free than the workers in* Metropolis *as he walks in the outside environment. However, a similarly curved roof sits above both himself and lower-class citizens, a visual reminder of his slavery to the LAPD, with the high class off-world citizens never even seen.*

FIGURE 41 *Although lacking white hair or gloved hands, the frowning eyebrows, intense facial expression and maniacal inventor persona of Wallace provide distinct similarities to the archetypal Expressionist antagonist. Instead of manipulating somnambulists or creating a single robot, Wallace invents millions of human-like replicants who (supposedly) obey.*

K is 'a stranger in a strange land', and thus highlights the essential outsider persona and the besieged lands of silent hero films as well as Westerns.[41] When K learns that he is not the prophesied child born of man and replicant and is instructed to kill the man he hoped to be his father by rebel leader Freysa (Hiam Abbass), his silent figure is enveloped in shadow, emphasizing the literal darkness of the setting as well as his own emotional and moral torment. As in *Caligari*, only near the end of the film does the audience realize that the central character's memories have not matched actual events. The audience shares in the disorientating experience of having their own sense of 'reality' shattered.

The intrinsic linking of masculinity with laconic dialogue and violence that is key to earlier expressionist iterations of the silent hero is brilliantly illustrated in the confrontation scene between K and Sapper (Dave Bautista) at the start of the film, where verbal dialogue quickly breaks down into physical aggression. When Sapper enters his apartment after sighting K's spinner, he walks over to the sink to start cooking, apparently oblivious to K's silhouetted figure in the window. K then coldly states: 'I hope you don't mind me taking the liberty' (Figure 42).

K's deliberate use of a statement rather than a question begins a calculated verbal power play. Having already decided to enter Sapper's home without permission, the statement simply acts as a teasing ruse to alert Sapper to his

---

[41] Brian D. Johnson, 'How a Pair of Canadians Infused Their DNA into Blade Runner 2049' (2017). *Macleans*. https://macleans.ca/culture/movies/how-a-pair-of-canadians-infused-their-dna-into-blade-runner-2049/.

FIGURE 42 *K's confrontation with Sapper Morton epitomizes film noir aesthetics, especially with the scene's terse dialogue. While most of Sapper's silhouette can be viewed against the bright window, K's body is far more obscured in darkness, a metaphor for his current state of naivety. While 'sapper' refers to a soldier in military jargon, Sapper refuses to be defined by any general designation ascribed to him by his manufacturer.*

presence. It is also intriguing to notice K's specific use of the word 'liberty' in his taciturn address; he has literally violated and stolen Sapper's freedom by entering his home without invitation. However, when K coldly identifies Sapper by his serial number – a deliberate dehumanizing strategy – Sapper provides a verbal counter to K, assigning himself humanity by clearly defining himself by his profession as 'a farmer'.

The taut verbal exchange begins to increase in tension when K refuses Sapper's offer of food and delivers the hard-boiled line: 'I prefer to keep an empty stomach until the hard part of the day is done.' The audience is then provided with a visual signifier of this rising unease when the camera cuts to a close-up of Sapper's boiling pan. Hawkins refers to shots such as these as 'moments of heightened affective resonance' which occur outside the narrative flow of film.[42] In his refusal to respond to K's questions about his history as a medic, it is Sapper who is able to wield silence as power. K places his blaster on the table as a visual threat when he states his intention to take Sapper in peacefully if he complies with his orders. In a nod to the gun battles of the Western, the audience is shown K readying his scanner as the camera provides a close-up of his hand before swiftly cutting back to Sapper's hand removing a knife from his bag in preparation for the duel. K monotonously asks him to look up and to the left, just before Sapper lunges at him. The two

---

[42] Hawkins, 'The Concept', 87.

engage in physical combat before K finally manages to scan Sapper's eye, at which point he politely asks Sapper not to get up. Sapper taunts K that he has never seen a miracle before standing up in a last-ditch effort to attack K. K shoots him dead with two bullets. When words fail, violence becomes the only viable form of communication. However, in terms of a portrayal of masculinity, it is important to note that in this scene it is Sapper who retains the emotional upper hand – and therefore audience sympathy – both in terms of his refusal to speak and through his careful choice of words when he does. Like the precious flower that K later finds lying under the tree, a splash of bright colour in a grey and barren landscape, Sapper's talk of life-affirming miracles leaps out at the audience and engages their sympathy and curiosity.

A similarly bleak picture of masculine communication is conveyed in the eventual meeting between K and Deckard, where fighting, for Deckard at least at this point, becomes a necessary ritual that must be performed before any meaningful verbal communication can be exchanged. After the first attempt at talking has ended, with Deckard shooting K off the first floor of the decrepit Las Vegas casino, leaving K's bloody outline adorning the carpet, the ensuing conflict takes place in relative darkness in similar fashion to the fight scene in Sapper's house. However, the light in this scene does not enter from a single window, but rather from an artificial source of projections depicting a series of moving figures, including broken, surreal sequences of dancers and Elvis Presley. Image, lighting and particularly sound, are employed here to distract and disorientate K – and thus, the audience – from discerning Deckard's location. Cinematographer Roger Deakins revealed that the scene was originally so expensive it was going to be cut. Instead of investing in a large set, however, he decided to use simple black drapes around the edges of the space, employing a music company in Budapest to create what he describes as a 'rock and roll lighting scheme' comprised of 'different lighting that goes with different characters'.[43] Formal elements are essential in framing – and literally highlighting – central characters. Also, as with *Caligari*, the use of cheaper materials creates a more lasting impact.

K cautiously walks towards an image of Elvis singing, although Elvis's voice is not heard in synch with the moving image. This image briefly distorts into a projection of Marilyn Monroe before flickering back to the singer. As K moves closer, sound suddenly aligns with image in fractured form for a few seconds, before both image and sound disappear. The flickering lighting highlights a clearly disorientated K with his hands over his face, again staring as the

---

[43] Brady Entwistle, 'One Blade Runner 2049 Scene Was Almost Too Expensive, Details Cinematographer' (2023). *ScreenRant*. https://screenrant.com/blade-runner-2049-scene-too-expensive-cinematographer-response/.

singing Elvis momentarily re-emerges, before hiding as a bullet sound from Deckard's gun is heard. Holograms of burlesque dancers perform on tables, while brazen trumpet sounds are heard in the background.

K suddenly emerges out of this visual and aural chaos, disabling Deckard. The two stare at each other following a quick tussle before Deckard takes the opportunity to punch K repeatedly (Harrison Ford even managed to accidentally punch Gosling on the nose during earlier takes of the scene). Significantly, K stands passively throughout this attack. The two are then framed together in medium shot between the singing Elvis as 'Falling in Love With You' starts playing, with Deckard offering, with a weary irony, that they continue to listen to the song or go off and get a drink. Violence is diffused with amusingly romantic cliches as Deckard realizes he's met his physical match. As in K's earlier confrontation with Sapper, lighting, sound and sets play key parts in cultivating the atmosphere of the scene, as well as progressing K's narrative arc by highlighting his ultimate refusal to carry on fighting Deckard.

Villeneuve's dedication to traditional production effects as opposed to overused green screen and CGI also evokes many of the hands-on techniques employed in earlier expressionist films. Referring to the hulking creatures in *Arrival*, Villeneuve remarked, 'I wish I had the chance to do my Aliens in animatronics' and praises how cinematographer Roger Deakins 'was able to create landscape with tricks'.[44] Despite the visually impressive alien ship we see in the film, Refn's admission that he would have rather spent the film's substantial $47 million budget on a far cheaper mode of set design is intriguing; one might wonder what the film would have ultimately looked like if it had been provided with a similarly meagre budget in comparison to *Caligari*'s. Likewise with *Blade Runner 2049*, the director stresses how 'we tried our best to do as much as possible in-camera, building everything ... I think I can count on one hand how many times I saw a green screen in all those months of shooting'.[45] Despite a few necessary uses of CGI, the emphasis of Villeneuve's recent filmmaking is very much grounded in organic sets. As with *Caligari* and *Metropolis*, homemade settings are often employed to emphasize powerful visual aesthetics that symbolize mood and emotional atmosphere, which contemporary technologies cannot fully convey. This echoes Kurtz's earlier definition of German Expressionist film as deliberately and distinctly moving away from naturalistic 'photographable' everyday life.[46]

---

[44] 'Blade Runner 2049 Will Be Almost Entirely Free of Green Screen Effects' (2017). *Radio Times*. https://www.radiotimes.com/tv/sci-fi/blade-runner-2049-will-be-almost-entirely-free-of-green-screen-effects/.
[45] Ibid.
[46] Kurtz, *Expressionism and Film*, 11.

FIGURE 43 *Driver's figure looms in the mirror, spectre-like, as he converses with Irene, with his facial features obscured. Although he is merely staring at the ground, the angle presented by the camera suggests he is surveying the photo, as if he is preparing to eliminate the competition presented by Standard.*

Both Refn and Villeneuve have shown a strong interest in aesthetics to convey narrative across their works, particularly through the medium of colour. Refn – who as well as being dyslexic is also colour-blind – uses strong contrasting colours in many of his films. As Styan notes, 'sensational colours' were a common feature of expressionist theatre and contributed to the deliberate dreamlike or nightmarish aesthetic.[47] This heightened colour coding is used symbolically throughout *Drive* to contrast the crime-ridden city of LA (depicted in cool blues) with the innocence of Irene and Benicio (portrayed in warm oranges). Vicari acknowledges how, 'in classic hero-myth structure, there is always a toxic or dangerous environment, a literal area of land or realm of existence which has been invaded or always-already occupied by forces hostile to fragile life'.[48] Instead of the plains of the Wild West, *Drive* has the congested streets of Los Angeles. When Driver talks to Irene (Carey Mulligan) inside her apartment for the first time, Irene smiles, framed to the left in front of a wall of orange tiles. To the right we see an image of Driver in the blue-tinted mirror, with a smaller picture of Benicio and Standard in the corner. The audience is presented with a visual metaphor of Driver – and his criminal connections – taking over from Standard as the alpha male of the family (Figure 43).

In *Only God Forgives*, Refn again utilizes blue to encourage emotional critical response from the audience. This time, however, the colour is far more saturated and is employed to suggest moments of brief respite from the

---

[47] Styan, *Modern Theatre*, 4.
[48] Vicari, *Nicolas Winding Refn*, 181.

extreme reds that dominate the claustrophobic, geometric halls of interiors. Like *Caligari*, sets are used to represent the troubled psyches of characters. What Refn himself is ironically unable to see through his heightened use of colour ultimately results in far more striking visual motifs for the audience.

Discussing the visual palette of *Blade Runner 2049*, Villeneuve noted that he 'intentionally didn't want any [colour] in this harsh world of survival. What he did want was a dark and bleak storyline with occasional pops of colour and bright lights'.[49] Since darkness is such a dominant aesthetic throughout the film, these 'pops' become all the more significant through their rare appearances. Take the colour yellow, for example. Describing the yellow door which the replicant Sapper Morton walks through and the yellow flower which K later finds by the tree Villeneuve remarks, 'That story you feel is linked with the idea of creation and childhood and mad desires. Slowly, it becomes red when he goes to Vegas, but the edges are still yellow.'[50] The director's focus is on feeling, and how this single colour can evolve to have numerous meanings across the film's epic narrative. But, as with Refn, a colour does not always retain exactly the same symbolic resonance across his filmography. Throughout Villeneuve's *Enemy*,[51] for example, yellow pervades whole environments, making the audience question the sanity of the film's main characters. This use of the colour yellow to convey madness is remarkably like many of the early tinted prints of *Caligari*, in which the disturbed Francis is often framed in a sickly yellow tone. Colour becomes an essential form of narrative expression in plots that do not rely on excessive expository dialogue.

Ideas of silence and the silent hero are also integral to both directors, both in terms of laconic speech and the visual symbols that are used to fill this narrative space. As Refn observes in a personal note, 'All my films are about transformations' and 'Driver transforms himself from a human being to a real hero',[52] hinting again at the idea of the silent hero as a supernatural, unbeatable force of nature. Likewise, Villeneuve, commenting on his creative approaches in *Blade Runner 2049*, states, 'There's a kind of research of trying to be as simple and monosyllabic as possible that I deeply love. I'm hypnotized by this approach, I deeply love it.'[53] Villeneuve's reference to silence and its

---

[49] Lapointe, *The Art and Soul*, 26.
[50] Bill Desowitz, '"Blade Runner 2049": The Most Difficult Craft Challenges for Director Denis Villeneuve' (2017). *Indiewire*. https://www.indiewire.com/2017/11/blade-runner-2049-roger-deakins-denis-villeneuve-1201900768/.
[51] Villeneuve, dir. (2013, Entertainment One), DVD.
[52] Koehler, 'Nicolas Winding Refn and the Search for a Real Hero' (2011). https://cinema-scope.com/cinema-scope-magazine/interview-nicolas-winding-refn-and-the-search-for-a-real-hero/.
[53] Vice, 'Inside the Making of 'Blade Runner 2049 – Created with Blade Runner 2049' (2017). *YouTube*. https://www.youtube.com/watch?v=T0kobbjpdUg.

hypnotic effects emphasizes the power of the reduction of language. As Sontag remarks, 'The tendency is toward less and less. But never has "less" so ostentatiously advanced itself as "more"'.[54]

One of *Drive*'s most prominent symbols of heroism is embodied in the scorpion jacket. Whenever Driver participates in an act of violence, the scorpion symbol is always in clear view. Refn remarked of Gosling: 'Whenever we were in doubt, let's just shoot his back, because that's just the ultimate enigma.'[55] The mystery already inherent in a character that says little and moves economically is furthered by filming from behind; as in *Drive*'s opening scene, the audience is fascinated by what they cannot see. Whenever Driver converses with Irene, the clothing is notably absent as he tries to fit into everyday society, in a similar fashion to Shane when he buys a new shirt in an attempt to fit into the local community. Yet both attempts are futile, as violence and aggression are inextricably linked with the garments. However, as Vicari asserts, despite Driver's masculine symbol of authority, 'passivity is at the heart of the Refn hero, no matter how violent he may be'.[56] Driver is destined to perform heroic actions which no one else can, but he can only perform these acts with the knowledge that he cannot ultimately be a part of the wider community. Driver wears the iconic clothing as he taunts Bernie with the prophetic tale of the Scorpion and the Frog, and he wears it at the film's conclusion when it is covered in blood as he rides into the distance. Vicari remarks that 'in general, a hero becomes exceptional only after he or she has accepted that his or her identity no longer matters'.[57] This idea of the sacrificial hero is a central characteristic in Refn's heroes, as well as Villeneuve's, and I will discuss this concept in more specific detail in relation to gesture in the following chapter. Like the symbolic scorpion itself, it is in Driver's nature to kill, even if it ultimately causes his own death.

Clothing also plays a central role in *Blade Runner 2049*. In the same way that colour comes across as particularly meaningful in a world full of darkness, garments become more symbolic in revealing the internalized psyches of monosyllabic characters. As with Driver's scorpion jacket, K's coat became similarly iconic upon *Blade Runner 2049*'s release. Gosling notes that while initial designs for the coat were 'longer and sleeker, it was changed to tell a clever story about the harsh world he lives in'.[58] Props are utilized in a similar aesthetic fashion to sets, reflecting the moods of characters while also

---

[54] Sontag, 'The Aesthetics of Silence', 14.
[55] 'Drive – Interview with the Cast at Cannes 2011' (2011). *YouTube*. https://www.youtube.com/watch?v=Y0AGBO7w7dA.
[56] Vicari, *Nicolas Winding Refn*, 187.
[57] Ibid.
[58] Lapointe, *The Art and Soul*, 59.

FIGURE 44 *K's collar completely obscures his mouth as he walks towards Sapper's house, filmed from the back and still subservient to his LAPD superiors. In later scenes such as his slow walk through the dystopian Las Vegas, however, the visor has completely disappeared. Visual signifiers (and the subsequent lack of them) are used as subtle metaphors for K's increasing autonomy.*

emphasizing the laconic – and ultimately lonely – nature of the silent hero archetype. The top section of K's coat is significantly tailored to incorporate a high collar which he frequently wears up, serving not just as a practical way to keep warm, but also to symbolize his own repressed, gagged mindset at the start of the film; as the narrative continues and K gradually gains a sense of identity, this mouth guard is no longer seen (Figure 44). Gosling also noted that 'since K has very little by way of objects to call his own or to reflect his inner landscape, his coat was one of the only opportunities to try to reflect the utilitarian nature of his existence'.[59] Through the coding of props as simple as a coat or a jacket, the audience can witness a silent hero's inner emotional turmoil and angst.

While the interpretations of the 21st-century silent hero discussed so far have focused exclusively on male iterations of the form, and primarily on their portrayal by Ryan Gosling, I also wish to look at examples of the female silent hero in film, in order to gain a useful comparison of the two and to analyse representations of masculinity and femininity on screen. An interesting starting point, since it is by one of the key directors I have been discussing, is the character of Louise Banks (Amy Adams) in Villeneuve's 2016 film *Arrival*. Despite her unspecified past and outsider persona (coded both through her gendered position as a woman surrounded by men in her work, alongside her own initial unwillingness to open up to many of her co-workers), it might

---

[59] Ibid.

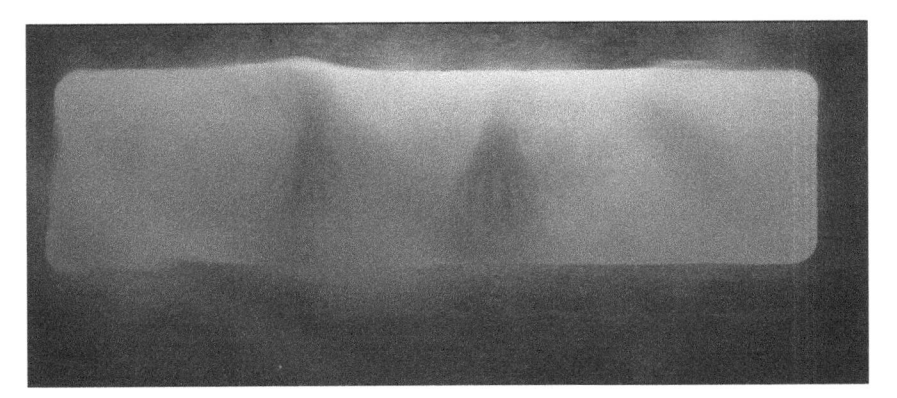

FIGURE 45 *The claustrophobic, unclear POV shot of Louise as she witnesses the aliens behind her equally claustrophobic safety suit. Through this heightened shot, the audience experiences Louise's doubt and fear alongside her.*

seem counterintuitive to label Banks as a silent hero. Unlike the male silent heroes already mentioned, as a linguist, Louise achieves her objectives and her very identity through language and communication; she has been brought in by government forces to decipher the language of an alien species that has recently occupied Earth. However, her reticence in daily human communication and interaction and the ways in which her character is filmed emphasize her withdrawn, troubled psyche. During her first contact with the aliens, for example, we see Louise anxiously repeating the word 'human' to try and establish understanding. After witnessing her external figure and hearing her strained breathing, the camera cuts to Louise's claustrophobic point of view inside the suit, with the image of the aliens behind the glass screen smudged and vague. The audience sees, hears and feels Louise's fear and confusion, in a similarly obscured fashion to Freder in *Metropolis* after he witnesses the Machine Man with his father (Figure 45). Emotive responses are encouraged through these stylized and claustrophobic points of view, as the audience is forced to experience events alongside the characters themselves.

As *Arrival*'s plot develops and the audience gradually begin to learn more about the events that are unfolding, it becomes increasingly clear that the film's story aligns with expressionist ideas about atemporality and Kurtz's idea of Expression as 'away from the time-bound ... and toward creation'.[60] By the end of the film, the audience discovers that the 'flashbacks' in the opening

---

[60] Kurtz, *Expressionism and Film*, 11.

scene when Louise discusses the death of her daughter Hannah are actually flash-forwards. As Louise learns the atemporal language of the aliens, she begins to witness the non-linear nature of time itself, fulfilling the concept of the Sapir-Whorf hypothesis that she mentions to her colleague (and future husband) Ian (Jeremy Renner). In the future, we see images of a book Louise has written about the symbols she has learned, which is titled *The Universal Language*. By learning from the outsider figures of the aliens, Louise is able to provide humanity with the ability to communicate and avoid conflict. Ideas of universal understanding through silence (or in *Arrival*'s case, symbols – the ultimate reduction of language) are explored in this film primarily through the narrative of a female protagonist.

Notions of the silent hero are represented particularly strongly during the scene where Louise enters the centre of the alien ship towards the end of the film. After communications between countries have broken down during negotiations concerning the alien presence, Louise abandons the tent of her warring male colleagues, walks outside and is met by a miniature vessel that transports her to the remaining alien. At this point, Louise has literally moved outside the boundaries of human civilization. As in her very first entry into the alien vessel at the start of the film, the audience are again as disorientated as Louise when perspective shifts under her feet; it is significant that the final space she enters has no clear boundaries at all and is enveloped in mist. A visual form of pathetic fallacy is used to reflect Louise's confused state of mind and the mystical awe she experiences on first approaching the gigantic alien creature floating before her (Figure 46).

FIGURE 46 *Louise's feelings of doubt are again highlighted, this time using the pathetic fallacy of mist alongside the intimidating wide shot of the alien's huge figure which is contrasted with that of Louise.*

This is not the type of mist or fog that we might find surrounding silent heroes in film noir. No darkness or shadows pervade the scene, and Louise's moral compass is not corrupted. In deliberate contrast, the following scene cuts to a silhouetted Louise within her dark home, in an arc shot. This serves both to highlight her heightened emotional state and to suggest to the audience that the human world has now become more mysterious and more disturbing to her than the alien – she is positioned firmly as a silent hero outside of the confines of society and time itself. Styan notes how expressionist drama often moves away from traditional linear narrative, what he calls 'the dramatic conflict of the well-made play', towards an emphasis on 'a sequence of dramatic statements made by the dreamer'.[61] Upon embracing Ian after the aliens have left, Louise's joyous comment that 'I forgot how good it felt to be held by you' is laden with tragedy for the audience who know Ian will not understand the true meaning of her words. Through non-linear narrative, the audience's whole sense of chronology and reality is brought into question.

Just as Shane and Driver are the only people capable of ridding their societies of evil and chaos, Louise is the only individual capable of restoring peace. Subverting the traditional masculine silent hero tropes, the weak society is not the civilized world of women and children, family and community, nor is *Arrival* Will Wright's straightforward classical plot of 'a lone stranger who rides into a troubled town and cleans it up, winning the respect of the townsfolk and the love of the schoolmarm'.[62] Rather, the 'society' in the film is represented by weak male leaders who are ultimately incapable of democratic negotiation. Louise is one of the few voices of reason and comfortably fits the 'lone stranger' stereotype. However, in the epic narrative of science fiction, she does more than simply clean up 'a troubled town', as her final conversation with fictional General Shang (Tzi Ma) directly saves the whole of humanity from conflict and destruction. Louise gets the boy, but does so knowing the tragic consequences of this decision. This subversion of the typically masculine silent hero archetype adds elements of both pathos and scale, where the world is saved through the actions of one individual at the personal cost of both husband and daughter.

Another intriguing study of female silent heroes which also revolves around issues of family and conflict and is also told in non-linear narrative can be found in Villeneuve's earlier work *Incendies*. It tells the story of twins Jeanne (Mélissa Désormeaux-Poulin) and Simon (Maxim Gaudette), who, following the death of their mother Nawal (Lubna Azabal), are sent on a mysterious task to find a father they believed dead and a brother they never knew they had.

---

[61] Styan, *Modern Theatre*, 4.
[62] Wright, *Sixguns and Society*, 32.

FIGURE 47 *By opening with this all-encompassing wide shot, the prominence of landscape in framing the journeys of its central characters is emphasized. Rather than a mere backdrop, these wide shots express nature's elemental and enduring presence despite the human chaos that takes place within its boundaries.*

Based on Wajdi Mouawad's 2003 play of the same name, landscape becomes a pivotal signifier to evoke the emotional journey of its taciturn central female character Jeanne, as well as her mother in flashback. *Incendies*' opening image focuses on a vast, all-encompassing wide shot of land with a single tree in the foreground (Figure 47), and slowly pans in on a building with young boys being converted to child soldiers as their hair is shaved. The unspoken horror that takes place is given a heightened, nightmarish unreality as the extradiegetic angst of Radiohead's 'You and Whose Army?' plays during the scene. While the audience are initially presented with the confused and angry figures of the children as Thom Yorke's moody vocals articulate their unspoken trauma, the camera begins to slowly pan across their feet. This tight framing deliberately forces the audience to disengage with the boys as individuals by reducing them to dehumanized body parts as balls of shaved hair fall on the ground. This alienating imagery is subsequently heightened as the camera focuses on a foot in extreme close-up, with three dots on the skin's surface.

The use of such intense synecdoche in this editing choice suggests this foot, and therefore this individual, must be of great importance to the film's wider plot. The next image shows the boy who this foot belongs to as dramatic piano chords enter the soundscape, with his shaved head already stripping him of identity as he stares grimly back at the camera – and therefore the audience. Yorke's vocals likewise become louder and more ethereal as the camera zooms in on the boy until his face dominates the screen. The audience might expect some explanation of who this individual is by this stage, but the camera simply cuts away to images of a bland office room. The significance of the boy – and his foot – will not be fully realized until the film's closing scenes. Landscape is employed in this example to emphasize the sublime, elemental force of nature that continues to endure despite the human indignities that take place on its soil.

Environments are also employed to highlight the contemplative silences shared between mother and daughter. The audience watch Nawal, a Christian Arab, silently move through an unnamed landscape, which is shortly followed by the camera cutting to a similar image of Jeanne silently walking through a city. These lands are not traversed by gun-toting, cigar-wielding men of few words, but earnest, determined women seeking knowledge about lost family. Locations are never explicitly named; although set in clearly recognizable established human societies, the fact that these places are never specifically titled nonetheless lends the plot a fairytale-like, heightened reality. Filmmakers frequently juxtapose lingering shots of Jeanne in the film's narrative present and Nawal in flashback to link their emotive experiences in the narrative. The pieces of the puzzle are not aligned chronologically or in an expository fashion, but must be assembled affectively in the minds of the audience.

Landscape plays a particularly important role during a flashback scene where Nawal is on a bus journey with Muslim refugees, with the camera providing a lingering close-up of her sleeping face. The bus is stopped and attacked by a group of Christian nationalists who slaughter most of the passengers, with Nawal's fear only heard (rather than shown) in her breathing as she hides. When she manages to leave the bus as she tries to save a woman's daughter, she shows her necklace as evidence of her faith and is allowed to escape, but the daughter is forced by the soldiers to stay. As Nawal walks away, sound design cuts out the noise of gunshots as the daughter is shot and the bus is set on fire with the passengers inside. Nawal's heavy breathing is heard again as she lies on the ground in despair and the men walk past her as the billowing smoke and fire rages, providing a desolate wide shot of human atrocity within an unsympathetic environment, with the image of Nawal's anguished face in close-up at the front of the screen becoming the film's central promotional poster (Figure 48).

It is also intriguing to analyse the introduction of Jeanne and Simon, who the audience first witness filmed from behind in silhouette talking to

FIGURE 48 *Landscape and human suffering remain intrinsically linked. The emotive close-up of Nawal's facial expression is combined with the atrocity that is taking place behind her to evoke a similar horror and shock within the audience with imagery and sound alone.*

another individual. They subsequently walk into the screen still in silhouette, with the words 'Les Jumeaux' (The Twins) appearing on the screen in bright red as their walking bodies fill most of the frame. The stylized nature of the introductory text serves a similar purpose to the intertitle cards of silent films, not providing us with expository narrative, but simply identifying them by their familial relationship rather than their names.

During the next sequence with the man they have been talking to, revealed to be the notary for their mother's will, the audience watch the twins being talked at. The camera provides a close-up of Jeanne's face as she listens to details of the will being read out, but she remains reticent. The man's methodical descriptions are eventually interrupted by Simon's frustrated statement, 'I've heard enough.' Jeanne calmly and briefly tells the notary to continue reading the documents, and he does so. When the two are outside the building, Simon talks angrily about the revelation of their still living father and of the existence of a brother that their mother never talked about while Jeanne remains silent, not bothering to respond when Simon patronizingly declares that 'We'll take care of her, then you.' Jeanne walks to their car, then turns around, exclaiming: 'Do you realize what we just heard?' Jeanne's first sudden outburst carries more affective weight because of her previous refusals to respond. Discussing the use of defiant silences in film, Shilina-Conte notes that examples of lingering silence followed by speech in film are 'not a powerless paralysis but a potent protest',[63] boosting their effectivity – and affectivity. In highlighting Simon's inability to listen and his frustrated verbal outbursts which dominate the soundscape, filmmakers encourage the audience to actively 'listen' to and engage with the contrast between the siblings' approach to language.

When Simon slowly puts the pieces together about their unknown relatives, he presents Jeanne with the bleak rhetorical question: 'One plus one … can it make one?', acknowledging that their father and their brother are ultimately the same individual. Jeanne stares at her brother for several seconds as she puts his words together in her mind, then takes a huge, anguished inhale of breath as she understands his meaning and covers her face in despair. The pause that Jeanne takes to work out the full implication of Simon's question is mirrored in the space the audience also needs to fully realize the situation. Her dramatic inhaling acts as a diegetic bond of trauma to the heavy breathing of Nawal that the audience listens to during earlier flashback scenes; instead of vocalizing the horror they experience in words, pain is expressed by mother and daughter through non-verbal breaths that evoke primal states of being both in their pathos and heart-rending volume. The audience experiences cathartic pain alongside Jeanne as the dots of the mystery are finally drawn together, with the camera cutting away to the sublime landscape of mountains and cold forests, reinforcing how nature endures despite the tragic human discoveries that take place within its confines (Figure 49).

In Jonathan Glazer's *Under the Skin*, The Woman (perhaps a sly reference to Eastwood's iconic cigar-wielding hero) undergoes a similar episodic, unsettling journey of self-discovery and transformation, gaining newfound purpose and sense of identity here on Earth as she interacts with the human beings around her. The audience never witness, or know anything about, the world The Woman arrived from; she appropriately fits the silent hero archetype as the ultimate loner in her lack of expository backstory. She is literally an alien in a human world. The screenwriter Colin Herber-Percy also reveals a key sacrificial trait of many of the silent heroes I discuss in his study of the narrative arc of The Woman in this particular film, stating how she gradually 'recognises herself as a subject among subjects. In short, she chooses (or cannot fail to choose) to become human, to empathise, to be weak as flesh'.[64] Like the contemporary male silent heroes I have discussed, The Woman seeks to make connections with some of the humans she meets on her mysterious

---

[63] Shilina-Conte, 'Silence as Elective Mutism'.
[64] 'The Flesh Is Weak. Empathy and Becoming Human in Jonathan Glazer's Under the Skin' (2020). *Aesthetic Investigations*. https://doi.org/10.58519/aesthinv.v3i2.11943 https://zenodo.org/record/4415711#.Y9kFRi2l24I.

FIGURE 49 *The dark, unknown landscape with its entangled branches mirrors the dark, complicated secrets that Jeanne has uncovered in all their bleak and remorseless truth.*

journey within the human world. Like them, she is positioned outside of this world (she is literally an alien) and the audience are compelled to join her in questioning the fundamental idea of what it means to be human.

It is interesting to note how filmmakers depict The Woman's journey through acts of looking (exemplified through the film's narratively jarring opening scene with the close-up abstracted image of The Woman's eye); there are frequent still shots of The Woman's face juxtaposed with point-of-view shots that cause the audience to actively and affectively experience the known human world around her as alien. Herber-Percy remarks how, 'along with Johansson's alien, we are thrust into the pre-existing middle of things',[65] relying primarily on image and sound for narrative guidance (Figure 50).

In his review of the film in *The Guardian*, Leo Robson also significantly highlights how, 'just as Sergio Leone said that he looked through Clint Eastwood's face and saw a block of marble, so Glazier gets something boulder-like – impassive, abstracted – from Johansson'.[66] Here again, the silent hero is an affective vessel for audience emotion and insight. In a similar fashion to Eastwood's iconic performances, Johansson's movements are coded

---

[65] Ibid., 352.
[66] 'Scarlet Johansson in Under the Skin: "Prick Her and She Doesn't Bleed"' (2014). *The Guardian*. https://www.theguardian.com/film/2014/mar/15/scarlett-johansson-under-skin-extraterrestrial.

FIGURE 50 *The Woman stares as the misty environment surrounds her. This is not The Woman as she stared unemotionally at the girl below her and the ant crawling across her hand in the opening scenes within an area of blank white, but The Woman actively engaged and intrigued by the human life she witnesses.*

masculine through the Western genre's traditions of rigid, rarely moving features and taciturn dialogue.

In a reversal of the traditional role of Man as Predator and Woman as Prey, The Woman is shown prowling through the surrounding area in her van and trying to pick up lone men in the streets (although filmed around Scotland, no specific location is ever mentioned). Her first point of communication occurs through sound as she beeps her horn at her first potential victim. Once she has the man's attention, she proceeds to roll down the van's window and engage him in banal conversation, exhibiting a vague smile as extra bait. The dialogue is disjointed and 'learnt'. The audience are given brief snatches of conversation made up of practiced phrases and responses with repetition of key words, notably 'alone' and 'family'. Once her target refuses to bite, however, the studied trappings of humanity fall away instantly as she drives off, her face returning to a cold blankness.

Under the Skin's preoccupation with looking (in this instance, a strong employment of the female, albeit alien, gaze) is interesting to note in terms of the film's production, where hidden cameras were employed to secretly film members of the public who accepted lifts from Johansson, seemingly not recognizing her identity as one of the most successful actors in Hollywood. The audience are presented with the idea of a double ontological deception: just as the male victims don't suspect The Woman to be an alien entity, so too do these same involuntary actors not suspect that they are in the presence of Scarlett Johansson. Herber-Percy observes how 'the star, whose role it is to be noticed, becomes unnoticed',[67] with the academic Duane Dudek intriguingly describing how Johansson 'allows herself to be transformed into a design element'.[68] This deliberate, mechanical style of acting allows Johansson to portray this alien creature particularly expressively. The audience witness frequent shots of Johansson looking in a mirror, applying make-up, taking off and putting on clothes as she tries to navigate the human world around her.

While the use of untrained actors in *Under the Skin*'s production might suggest a certain degree of cinematic realism, the unsettling sequences in which The Woman 'digests' them is very much positioned in a world of nightmarish unreality. Production designer Chris Oddy describes this area as 'that black world, that threshold, the transitional place', explaining how a tank was used as the mechanism in which victims sink to their demise, also noting how the reflective glass used in the scenes was entirely 'painted black', evoking similarly artistic creation methods to those used in the production of *Caligari*.[69] Oddy explains how, later in the film, instead of using artificial CGI methods to solve problems with lighting in the dark forest scene, he 'took about twenty of the trees' tops off to let more light flood into the woodland'.[70] Visual dread is cultivated in audience response primarily through practical, formalist means. At one point, the audience experience The Woman's disorientated state through the use of a *Metropolis*-like collage of images, and they are frequently presented with flashing lights, quick cuts and bursts of sound combined with jarring, discordant music. Cuts to scenes of still nature are often the only point of visual and aural respite (Figure 51).

Although The Woman's key moments of self-discovery arrive through looking, they also occur through touch. When The Woman is first seen, she is standing within an inscrutable, featureless whiteness with the corpse of a dead woman. This is not the misty white space that Louise occupies as she engages in her newfound communication with an alien, but rather a space of cold silence and horror. As she extracts clothes from the corpse, she stares blankly at an ant crawling across her hand, which is shot in extreme close-up. At this point in the narrative, the haptic encounter telegraphs that The Woman

---

[67] Herber-Percy, 'The Flesh Is Weak', 353.
[68] ' "Under the Skin," with Scarlett Johansson, Confounding, Captivating'. (2014). *Milwaukee Journal Sentinel*. https://archive.jsonline.com/entertainment/movies/under-the-skin-with-scarlett-johansson-confounding-captivating-b99269582z1-259400161.html/.
[69] 'Behind the Scenes of Under the Skin' (2014). *Dazed Digital*. https://www.dazeddigital.com/artsandculture/article/19225/1/behind-the-scenes-of-under-the-skin.
[70] Ibid.

FIGURE 51 *As* The Woman *takes refuge in a forest bothy, her sleeping image becomes superimposed onto the forest itself, emphasizing her role as a creature of elemental nature.*

feels little more for this tiny insect than she does for the dead woman lying motionlessly below her.

The scene which most highlights The Woman's alienness, her lack of humanity, occurs when she, isolated, stares at a human family on a beach. As human tragedy unfurls, she stares on impassively. This emotional tension reaches a crescendo for the audience when a small child is left unattended and in danger, with its shrieking cries eliciting an intense emotional pain from the audience that The Woman does not feel. This scene sits in direct contrast to the narrative arc of nearly every other silent hero I have discussed where, classically, it is the vulnerability of a child or an innocent that becomes the catalyst for the silent hero's transformative sacrificial act. It is only when The Woman later encounters The Deformed Man (Adam Pearson, whose character is nameless, as are all characters in the film) during one of her prowls, that touch finally becomes the trigger for allowing The Woman to feel real human connection and empathy. Hands take on a powerful affective resonance. As they sit in the van, The Deformed Man's hand is framed in close-up as he pinches the skin on the back of his hand, as if to check that the situation he is in with this beguiling woman is really true. He then meekly hides his hand after considering the embarrassing nature of this gesture. The moment when The Woman decides to touch and hold his hand is pivotal not only in her abandonment of the stilted language that she has used with previous men, but also because of the way the scene is shot. Not only is the image of the two holding hands shot in close-up,

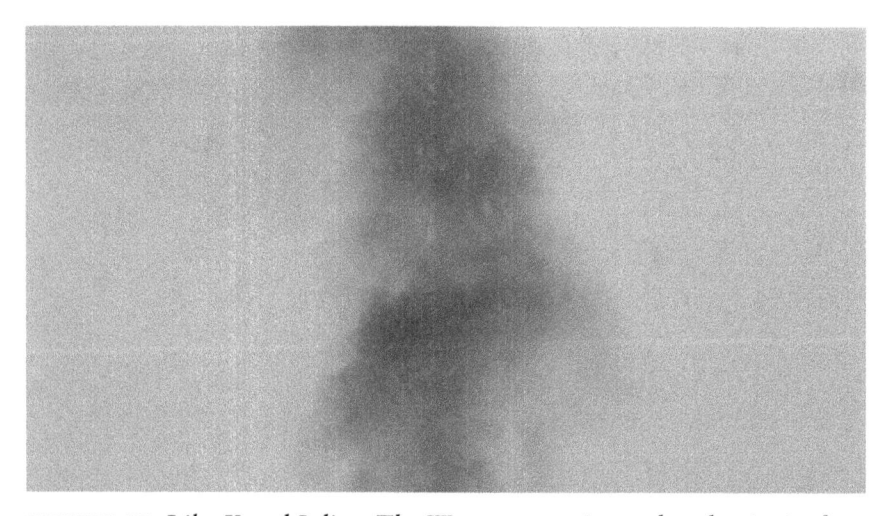

FIGURE 52 *Like K and Julian, The Woman experiences her demise in the natural world. While K feels snow and Julian resides within an unspecified forest area, The Woman literally becomes one with nature as she kneels and sacrifices her burning body to the air, becoming part of the world she desperately wanted to join in physical form.*

but both The Deformed Man and The Woman are framed together. During all the previous scenes with men, The Woman and her victims have been shot apart, in a sequence of quick cuts, evoking a cold disconnection that mirrors The Woman's alien lack of felt emotion. In this moment, however, touch leads her to a pivotal moment of sacrifice, choosing to save The Deformed Man while knowing it will ultimately result in her own demise. Herber-Percy notes at this point, during The Woman's moment of 'weakness' at refusing to attack her victim, that the film 'becomes a hymn to humanity'; The Woman becomes relatable 'because of a heightened emotional susceptibility which we ourselves, as audience, are prey to' and, when The Woman 'makes vain attempts to join human society, we are moved'.[71] It is significant that the more vulnerable The Woman is shown to be, the more human she becomes even though, as a silent hero, she is ultimately unable to enter this human society (Figure 52).

A similarly elliptical opening narrative (and a similarly bleak ending) occurs in Refn's *The Neon Demon*. While we don't begin with the oppressive black that dominates the screen in *Under the Skin*, the audience are presented with recognizably jarring imagery as a red, hellish tapestry appears and slowly changes colour as the credits gradually emerge. The dissonant violin

---

[71] Herber-Percy, 'The Flesh Is Weak', 361.

FIGURE 53 *Although the image of Jesse eventually reveals itself to be a photoshoot as opposed to the murder scene it initially looks like, this image nonetheless forebodes Jesse's grisly death, which the audience are never allowed to see; fear is cultivated through withholding.*

noises of *Under the Skin* are exchanged for similarly unsettling synth sounds, which again increase to a point of almost unbearable sound. The audience is assaulted with high decibel noise while being provided with no expository information through either image or speech. They receive their first image of a recognizable human space with a slow panning image of what first appears to be a bloodied corpse on a sofa. The camera cuts to a close-up of a man looking at something the audience are not yet aware of, with loud synth sounds only adding to the audience's sense of dislocation. The man is revealed to be a cameraman, presumably shooting the female model who the audience learn is just posing for a photo shoot in red paint (Figure 53). Here again, the act of looking is highlighted, this time through the means of the male gaze. When the camera switches back to the sofa, the woman is gone, with the sofa returned to its former pristine blue aesthetic and not a drop of paint in sight.

These opening images set up an idea of looking that essentially continues to construct the narrative coherence of the whole film. A 'plot' can be vaguely discerned in the way that the camera follows main character Jessie (Elle Fanning) as she tries to survive in the unsympathetic world of modelling, but the rest of the storytelling is left to visual and aural aesthetics. Again, it is the 'act of expression' itself that Refn is interested in.[72] The taciturn notions of the silent hero are quickly established in the audience's introduction to

---

[72] Brooks, 'My Father and I Disagree on the Purpose of Cinema'.

Jesse (Elle Fanning); as with many of these archetypes, only a single name is ever mentioned. When stylist Ruby (Jena Malone) introduces herself with her name and Jessie doesn't respond, Ruby sardonically asks: 'Do you have a name or do you want me to guess?' Jessie eventually provides her name in a one-word answer. When Ruby asks what Jesse's parents think about her chosen line of work, she laconically states: 'They don't, really. They're not around anymore.' No further information is provided about her parentage. It's not clear whether Jesse is a runaway or if her parents have died. Following silent hero traditions, she has no discernible past.

With the film's dark focus on the fashion industry and women's position within it, clothes and make-up become key physical signifiers to articulate characters' inner psyches. Again, like Glazer, Refn is intrigued by what is under the skin and what it means to be human. Costume designer Erin Benach notes the importance of clothing as visual symbols when she states, 'We knew from the start that we needed to find clothing that could carry a story on its own, not only to show Jessie's evolution as a character, but also to depict the world we wanted to depict, which is sort of this material reality.'[73] Clothing is 'carried' in the literal sense on the bodies of the woman we view throughout the film, but because of *The Neon Demon*'s minimal dialogue, it also acts as a device for the audience to cultivate narrative. Benach was also responsible for costuming on *Drive* (as well as Gosling's clothing in *Half-Nelson*[74] and *Blue Valentine*[75]), with Driver's iconic scorpion jacket becoming synonymous with the character.

While music is often chosen in Refn's films before the actual narrative is created (much of *Neon Demon*'s initial story outlining was discussed with regular Refn collaborator Cliff Martinez), the final scene of the film was constructed entirely through the aesthetic of clothing. After Jesse is killed, torn apart and literally consumed by jealous models Sarah (Abbey Lee) and Gigi (Bella Heathcote), the two pose outside a flashy apartment for a glamorous photo shoot. Drawing inspiration from designer Marina Hoermanseder's collection, Benach describes how the clothes possess 'such an intense quality as far as the human female form, because it's all pre-shaped to the female body, it's all sculpted'.[76] It was only after Benach showed the pieces to Refn that the scene was subsequently developed. Expression is created not through the conventional means of expository 'plot' (the linear action of

---

[73] The Chic League, 'The Neon Demon Analysis: High Fashion & Neuroaesthetics In Film' (2021). *YouTube*. https://www.youtube.com/watch?v=95FICC4M1_w.
[74] Ryan Fleck, dir. (2006, THINKFilm), DVD.
[75] Derek Cianfrance, dir. (2010, The Weinstein Company), DVD.
[76] Fernandez, 'The Neon Demon'.

writing down a screenplay on a piece of paper or on a computer), but rather through pieces of clothing.

This unconventional mode of storytelling is intriguing in the way that Benach worked backwards in her conceptions of Jesse's aesthetic. It is also reflective of the way women in society are so often judged by the way they look and the clothes they wear. The fashion industry prioritizes this above all else. Referencing fashion company Yves Saint Laurent's controversial spring 2015 ad campaign, Benach reveals how 'I had this idea that Elle [would transform] into something like that ad campaign'.[77] As with previous 21st-century silent heroes, transformation is key, even though Jesse's rise through the fashion industry ultimately results in her gruesome death, one which the camera never allows the audience to see (like previous expressionist films, the precise gory details are left to the imagination). Benach then went backwards to find clothing to express Jesse's more innocent character at the start of the film, 'one more partial to wearing long or loose-fitting Ulla Johnson dresses'.[78] At this early stage in Jesse's journey, 'her style is high-coverage, and carries more of an ethereal essence, that gives Jessie an otherworldly-type look'.[79] It is important to note the reoccurring idea of the silent hero as a creature that is not fully human, as something 'ethereal', ghostly and inherently different, or 'other' from the people surrounding them. Benach's backwards approach presents an intriguing technique that defies traditional narrative plotting. When Jesse makes her runway debut, her increasing rise in the fashion industry is again emphasized through her extravagant dress, with costume designers noting how the item was 'chosen to enhance the dramatics of the lighting in relation to Jesse, so it could cover all of her skin in order to envelop all of her being into the dress'.[80] The dress is described not merely as an item adorning an individual, but an item that becomes intrinsically linked with the character herself. Within a narrative where the central character says little and emotes primarily through outfits, these items become pivotal emotional signifiers for the audience to try and decode and interpret, leaving them with a dark commentary on the emptiness of human existence.

A fruitful analysis of the way notions of masculinity and femininity are coded and cultivated in 21st-century silent hero film is found in the interesting female characters within the dystopian world of *Blade Runner 2049*. This is particularly relevant in relation to the backlash that the film received for its supposed sexist and demeaning portrayals of women. One commentator

---
[77] Ibid.
[78] Ibid.
[79] Ibid.
[80] Ibid.

even accused the filmmakers of perpetuating traditional notions of the male gaze in their decision to channel narrative coherence and audience empathy through K's male perspective rather than the viewpoint of the real female replicant child Ana Stelline.[81] These female figures will be analysed from the point of view of the film's dystopian setting. As Villeneuve asserted in his defence: 'Cinema is a mirror on society. *Blade Runner* is not about tomorrow; it's about today' and he admits the bleak fact that 'the world is not kind on women'.[82] As such, it is worthwhile to decipher the stereotypically masculine and feminine behaviours that these female supporting characters adopt to survive in their patriarchal society.

One of these key female characters can be found in Sylvia Hoeks's Luv. The character is introduced by a close-up of her controlled hand, which slowly pours tea in a cup as she calmly describes a shipment of replicants to a potential buyer. The camera remains focused on her hands as she brings the saucer onto her lap, and switches to the buyer before panning to a shot of Luv from behind, holding her cup. An alarm sound is heard as one of her earrings lights up, at which point the camera cuts to a wide shot of the room before finally focusing on her face after she looks at the alert about Rachael's remains on the monitor. The editing choices create a visual power play for the audience by withholding traditional establishing shots in order to focus on other physical signifiers; the camera is able to emphasize the character's pristine calm while also suggesting a deadly precision beneath the surface (Figure 54).

Every last drop of water falls perfectly from the teapot to the cup, and not a drop is spilled as she carries it on the saucer, yet the lingering focus on these hands creates an unnerving sense of what they could do with a weapon instead of a standard household item. Returning to her seat after viewing the image, the audience watches a smiling Luv politely ask the buyer if they can reschedule the call. The camera cuts away to Wallace's archives before the audience has a chance to hear her answer, as if to suggest that the deal is done. Luv exudes and retains power through her still, calm and precise use of language. She has the last word.

When the clerk informs K that Rachael's data is unremarkable, the audience are provided with a quick image of Luv's blurred figure in the background

---

[81] Monique, 'Hollywood's Obsession with Toxic Masculinity, as Seen in "Blade Runner 2049"' (2017). *Just Add Colour.* https://www.colorwebmag.com/2017/10/16/hollywoods-obsession-toxic-masculinity-seen-blade-runner-2049/.

[82] Julie Muncy, 'Blade Runner 2049 Director Opens Up about the Film's Treatment of Women' (2017). *Gizmodo.* https://gizmodo.com/blade-runner-2049-director-opens-up-about-the-films-tre-182 0747134.

SILENT HEROES IN 21ST-CENTURY FILM 101

FIGURE 54 *Hands play a pivotal role in highlighting Luv's control here, like Driver's hands on the wheel, through their minimal movement. Her precision highlights a more cool, remorseless nature underneath. When she directs rockets at citizens in the trash mesa to protect K, for example, they are again motionless, and Luv is similarly unemotional while a worker decorates her nails.*

before she is framed from the back as she calmly asks: 'There must be something else we can find for him?' The clerk turns around at the sound of her voice, provides her with the card then walks away without a word. Again, it is what is *not* said or heard that cultivates a sense of unease in the audience. This is someone who wields authority in their profession, even though their profession is not yet specified. When Luv reaches out a hand for K to shake, she states that she is 'here for Mr Wallace' and provides him with her name. An intrigued K states that Wallace named her, and the camera switches back to her still facial expression as we hear K say that she 'must be special'. A momentary pause, then Luv calmly repeats that she is 'here for Mr Wallace'. The verbal battle is at a stalemate here as Luv ignores K's comments and K does not acknowledge Luv's double mention of her (and K's) revered creator. Taut, masculine-coded, noir-like language is shot back and forth between each player with no alpha emerging from either side.

Verbal altercations between Luv and K take an intriguing turn after Luv's brute strength is exhibited when she opens the door to the memory room. The two listen to the Voight-Kampff interrogation scene between Deckard and Rachael that takes place in the original film. When Luv asks K if there was anything unusual about where the body was found, K gives an evasive answer, then observes that Rachael likes Deckard and is trying to provoke him. Luv acknowledges the invigorating nature of being asked personal questions, then proceeds to ask K if he enjoys his own work, deliberately attempting to provoke a reaction in turn. K simply pauses and stares blankly back, then proceeds to tell her to thank Wallace for the appointment. Both have gone off track from their formulaic polite dialogue; K considers the nature of human emotion while Luv attempts to incite emotion herself, with neither coming to a satisfied understanding.

Luv's subsequent meeting with Wallace plays out in a much more subdued fashion, with the audience having to work hard to elicit meaning from Luv's still facial expression. Her welcomes are rebuffed with Wallace's patronizing statement that 'an angel should never enter the kingdom of heaven without a gift' and demands of her: 'Can you at least pronounce a child is born?' He simultaneously dehumanizes her and upbraids her for her inability to procreate. Luv does not respond, remaining silent as she looks down at the ground, then stares passively as she witnesses Wallace observing the new replicant model, blankly answering with a 'yes sir' as Wallace details his megalomaniac desires to discover replicant procreation. Before he angrily mutilates the model, however, at which point the camera swiftly cuts back to Luv's disturbed jolt, a single tear can be seen dropping from her eye. She offers Wallace another meek 'yes sir' as Wallace tells her to bring him the fabled replicant child and walks out of the room, leaving the camera focused on her tormented face. This tear also reoccurs following her murder of Joshi, a visual symbol of sadness (and thereby human emotions of desire and regret). On both occasions the tears appear when a fellow replicant has apparently been killed. However, like K, Luv must keep her feelings repressed at all times in order to preserve her robotic efficiency, or in her case to remain the 'best angel' that Wallace describes her as. Silence and these brief tears of woe allow the audience to imagine and feel the emotions, which are so often coded as feminine, that lie beneath an inherently violent surface. Luv murders an officer in one fell strike to retrieve Rachael's remains in the hopes of discovering the secret to replicant birth and dispatches Joshi in a similarly brutal fashion when Joshi claims the prophesied child is dead. Luv crushes the glass in her hand and stabs her, coldly using her corpse to retrieve the location of K before letting the body slam down on the table. An innate sense of injustice at the death of her own kind drives Luv, but this is never spelt out for the audience. They must glean this through the outward presentation of both calculated silences and intense violence.

Significantly, all of the weapons Luv employs throughout her narrative (the blade, the gun and even the visor she uses to target and destroy civilians in the trash mesa scene) were specifically designed to reflect her deadly characteristics.[83] Jared Leto, the maniacal Wallace himself, remarks that Luv

---

[83] Lapointe, *The Art and Soul*, 132.

is 'loyalty personified: a warrior, a soldier, an engineer'.[84] We again see the recognizable traits of the silent hero in a similar fashion to the Hungarian woman's description of K, but with key differences. The 'warrior' description describes her skill in the arts of warfare, which is particularly on display in her final battle against K by the sea wall. 'Engineer' suggests the prowess of one who is adept at the process of control, in that she acts as Wallace's right-hand woman, literally engineering meetings between clients and carrying out murders for her creator. 'Soldier', however, once again refers to the idea of servitude; she is unable to relinquish herself from Wallace's grasp. As Hoeks notes, she wanted Luv 'to be as human as possible ... crying revealed a sense of humanity, a sense of longing, a sense of her pain and conflict'.[85] Luv's tears act as a silent rebellion against the frequently vicious, inhuman and masculine-coded acts of violence and brutality that she is compelled to carry out on her employer's behalf.

Luv's violent acts and suppressed inner humanity identify her as a spiritual successor to *Blade Runner*'s Roy Batty (Rutger Hauer); when Hoeks auditioned for the role, she read the part of Batty in the scene where he demanded more life from Tyrell.[86] If Luv represents a female update of Batty, then Robin Wright's Joshi presents as a close companion to *Blade Runner*'s world-weary cop Bryant (M. Emmet Walsh). When K reports to her after nearly being killed by Sapper, Joshi looks at K for a moment before noting his injuries, but immediately remarks that 'I'm not paying for that', establishing herself as K's superior. K laconically replies, 'I'll glue it.' After Joshi orders K to kill the child, K leaves a pregnant pause as the camera lingers on his face. Joshi asks if he has anything else to say, and K notes philosophically that 'to be born is to have a soul, I guess', unsure about killing a being of this nature. Questioning if K is disobeying her, however, K blankly tells her he 'wasn't aware that was an option, madam', and Joshi calmly responds with a demeaning 'atta boy', informing K he's 'been getting on fine without one'. When K questions what she means, she specifies a 'soul', and K stares at her blankly then leaves the room. Joshi asserts power in the scene by employing noir-like deprecations and put downs. Both Joshi and Luv frequently refer to K using the demeaning term 'boy', with Luv even referring to him in the Las Vegas battle as a 'bad dog' when she kicks him to the ground. Patronizing insults towards K are used by both women to assert their dominance in a dystopian world where women remain second-class citizens themselves.

---

[84] Ibid., 133.
[85] Brian Hodges, 'Tears of a Machine: The Humanity of Luv in "Blade Runner 2049"' (2017). *Roger Ebert*. https://www.rogerebert.com/features/tears-of-a-machine-the-humanity-of-luv-in-blade-runner-2049.
[86] Lapointe, *The Art and Soul*, 130.

When Joshi is in K's apartment following the death of Coco, the audience don't even witness her entering the space; it is presumed that K lets her in with due, dog-like obedience. After providing Joshi with short answers about his progress with the investigation, K and his boss sit and partake in a noir-like conversation, with Joshi asking the questions. When K is reluctant to talk about his memories, Joshi rhetorically asks: 'Would it help you share if I told you it was an order?' K then proceeds to do as she commands, relating the memory of the horse. After relating the story, Joshi commands K to look at her. He does so, and Joshi states: 'We're all just lookin' out for something real. What happens if I finish that?', referring to the drink, and essentially propositioning him. As with Luv, K refuses to acknowledge the provocation, suggesting that he should get back to work. During K's admonishment for failing the second baseline, Joshi then switches back to the role of the 'hard-ass' masculine-coded superior. As the angry monitor voice informs an angst-ridden K that he isn't 'even close to baseline', the camera makes a sharp cut to K sitting inside Joshi's office as the loud sound of a door shutting is heard. Joshi sends the rest of her officers out of the room and throws a couple of f-bombs at K, stating that the scans told her he 'didn't look like [himself] on the outside, miles off your baseline', but in so doing, acknowledges that he is experiencing real, and therefore dangerous, human emotions. K placates her by telling her he found and killed the child, with distinct emotion heard in his voice as he bluntly states that 'it's done'. She backs down, swearing again before she thanks him for his efforts and grants him forty-eight hours 'to get back on track'. Loud, authoritative language is employed by Joshi to try and assert her position and establish dominance over K's quieter tones of supposed obedience. Yet K's direct lies about killing the child and his continuing silences undercut her power, highlighting the redundancy of her more extensive speech.

This deception comes back full circle during Joshi's first and final confrontation with Luv, which echoes the tense final scene between Shannon and Bernie in *Drive*. Just as Shannon realizes that Bernie is lurking in wait at his garage, Joshi ultimately knows that she isn't going to make it out alive, but puts up a front of tough confidence nonetheless. Luv turns on the light of Joshi's office, with the camera zooming in on Joshi's unphased expression as if to suggest she has been expecting the encounter. No polite hellos are exchanged. Luv gets straight to the point, stating: 'I like him. He's a good boy.' The audience already know who the 'good boy' is, as does Joshi. Luv directly asks Joshi where he is, but Joshi doesn't give a concrete answer, telling her to 'check around', just as Shannon vaguely speculates that Driver went to 'Mexico ... or maybe it was ... Belize', buying his adoptive son some time with his considered pauses.

FIGURE 55 *Joshi displays a similar attitude to film noir figures like Neff as she downs her drink, knowing that she is about die but refusing to articulate this fact in words, swapping Neff's nicotine for alcohol as her final choice of relief.*

Luv carries on questioning Joshi, asking if there is 'anywhere our good boy might go'. Joshi announces that K destroyed the child, drinking a sobering glass of whiskey as she prepares to receive death (Figure 55). Luv grabs her hand with the glass still in it, and admonishes her fear of change. Luv's cool demeanour finally breaks as she loudly demands to know where K is. As Luv watches Joshi suffer, she questions K's reliability, uttering the words 'because he told you' in an odd, songbird lilt, then changing to a high pitched childlike tone as she gloats: 'I'm going to tell Mr Wallace that you tried to shoot me first ... so I had to kill you.' Resigned, Joshi tells her to 'do what you gotta do', and Luv briefly switches back to politeness, addressing Joshi by her rank 'Madam' before stabbing her as the audience hear the sound of the blade and Joshi's short cry of pain. The camera then cuts to the rainy outside as the audience watch Luv stabbing her again through a window, with no sound heard of either the blade's second entrance or Joshi's body hitting the floor. The signature tear flows down Luv's right cheek, then she carries on with her work. This confrontation between Luv and Joshi, with its brute violence and acerbic, futile wisecracking, is as complex and unhealthy as the duels of their male counterparts.

The final key female figure to examine in this dystopian world is the character that received the most accusations of sexism in its portrayal of femininity, K's holographic girlfriend Joi (Ana de Armas). The audience are first introduced to Joi when K presses a button on his apartment monitor and Joi's surprised voice is heard along with Frank Sinatra's 'Summer Wind'. At this point they hear her, but they don't see her. She notes that he's early, and

THE SOUND OF SILENCE

K sardonically asks if she wants him to come back. Joi just tells him to 'go scrub', and he follows her orders. She asks about K's meeting, and he blandly responds: 'the usual'. He enquires about Joi's day, to which she responds that she's 'getting cabin fever'. Before the conversation continues, with Joi still not seen, the camera cuts to K's almost amusing, brutally short shower. K talks about an accident at work, saying he ruined his shirt, and Joi (still not seen) assures him she can mend it. K says he wants a drink, and she accepts one too on his invitation. Joi mentions that she's trying a new recipe, and K briefly tells her not to fuss. He pours alcohol into two glasses while Joi comments on the meal.

The audience can start to see that something is not right, however, when K clinks the second glass with his own and then proceeds to drink both without Joi. Further confusion is cultivated when K doesn't respond to Joi's fact about the song playing and sits down at a table with one seat with his back to the camera. Still no Joi. She talks about the meal more, but K still doesn't provide her with any verbal acknowledgement. The audience hear her arriving with a meal as K tells her not to fuss with a firmer tone. Finally, as we see K from the front, it becomes clear that Joi is a hologram, and all the dialogue previously exchanged between the two has just been a performative ruse, particularly as the audience watch Joi place an enticing holographic meal over K's less than enticing real grub (Figure 56). Even when K has a tender moment with Joi on the balcony after presenting her with an emanator, an update that allows her

FIGURE 56 *Sinatra's rendition of 'Summer Wind' plays when K 'activates' Joi, linking the relief of hearing Joi's voice with the music. Sinatra makes a second appearance in holographic form during the Las Vegas scene when an intrigued K puts a coin into a record player and watches the moving image sing 'One for my Baby (And One More for the Road)', which contains the line 'set 'em up Joe', as if the hologram is addressing K himself.*

to function outside K's apartment, she is brutally paused as K receives an incoming call from Joshi to return to the LAPD. Here, the audience literally see harsh reality disrupting fantasy.

Joi, deliberately fitting the archetypal feminine role as she switches costumes from the idealized 1950s housewife to a 1980s disco outfit to try and grab K's attention, could just as easily be a remodelled version of *Lonely Are the Brave*'s Jerry, bustling round the kitchen and rustling up a meal for the silent hero. But this unreality is the point; the domestic fantasy is not real. Joi is not real. The world of domesticity and human warmth and the promise of family it brings with it, these ideals that K craves, are a fantasy that, on some level, Luv desires too. It is significant that it is Joi – an emotional avatar through which K can articulate his otherwise outlawed emotional state – grants K his name, 'Joe' (which later signifies K's 'average Joe', regular status when he discovers he is not the prophesied 'chosen one' as he had hoped) and refers to him, Pinocchio-style, as 'a real boy'. The concept of 'real' is discussed throughout the narrative, whether by Joi's referral to Mariette (Mackenzie Davis) as a 'real' woman, Joshi's assertion that everyone, replicant or human, is searching for 'something real', or even K asking Deckard if his dog is 'real'. The fact that Luv is the one who destroys the soul of K's Joi with a violent stomp of her boot is decidedly ironic, as is her cutting line before the stomp itself: 'I do hope you're satisfied with our product.' At first hearing, it could be interpreted that Luv is directing this taunt at K before she destroys his beloved, having already made a similar comment during their meeting at Wallace's headquarters. However, it is also likely that Luv is directing the jibe at Joi, implying that K is just as much a manufactured product and slave of Wallace design as she and Joi are.

Throughout all these interactions, the drive and desire for the possibility of replicant reproduction is necessarily bound up with the notion of what it means to be fully human, and these fervent hopes are embodied in the discovery of the sanctified child. The hope is strong enough for K to give up his life for the child and for Luv to die in her efforts to try and find her, with both fighting for this singular ray of light in an otherwise meaningless, dark dystopian world. To this extent, the unreachable dream is frequently linked to either female silent heroes or female supporting characters, be they alien or human, navigating cruel and warring worlds or to male silent heroes conflicted by their place in a world where the resort to violence is often the only avenue of communication left open to them. For both men and women, however, silence becomes a means of power, linked to a sense of physical and emotional control, but also a sign of their essential outsider persona. No matter what the situation, the outcome of their existential journeys remains bleak.

3

Ryan Gosling and the Star System

All the 21st-century films I have discussed in the previous chapters in relation to the silent hero encapsulate expressionist aesthetics and the accompanying themes of chaos and disillusionment, both within the films' settings and the near-mythical status of their lead characters. An element many of them also share is the actor Ryan Gosling, who often performs the silent hero role. Refn has so far worked with Gosling twice (almost three times – Gosling dropped out of his *Logan's Run* remake) and locates him within a pantheon of earlier actors known largely for their charismatic masculine roles when he exalts that:

> He's like a mixture of James Stewart, Charles Bronson, Alain Delon, Lee Marvin, and a little bit of Marcello Mastroianni. If you look at him on screen, your eye automatically goes to him. Very few people are born with that. And very few actors who have that have the guts to pursue the movies they want to do. Rather than take the dream machine offered to them. It takes a lot of integrity to do the things he has done. He's like the Velvet Underground or the Ramones.[1]

Refn likewise praises his leading actor's daring film choices. Like Refn himself, Gosling has experienced a range of commercial successes and failures across his career. Finally, Refn compares Gosling's audacious choices with two rock bands who did not achieve initial commercial success but who grew to

---

[1] Anna Silman, 'The Complete Illustrated History of Ryan Gosling, From Child Star to Heartthrob to Movie Director' (2014). *Vulture*. https://www.vulture.com/2014/05/illustrated-comprehensive-history-bio-biography-ryan-gosling.html.

be hugely influential among fellow musicians and immensely popular with audiences. Gosling is lauded by Refn as an anarchic outsider, an actor more focused on building a career based on personal, creative choices over box office gains. Since Gosling is the main actor in many of the films I discuss, it is important to analyse his persona through the device of the star system, as well as briefly analyse how this persona aligns with his private personal life. It is also interesting to note that, like both the bands Refn mentions, Gosling has received most critical acclaim for performances in his later career, where his characters are particularly laconic.

Gosling's long career has undergone a variety of transformations. At the age of twelve, he successfully auditioned for The Mickey Mouse Club, where he worked until the show was cancelled in 1995. During his time on this famous American variety show, Gosling's popularity was cultivated through comedic sketches, show tunes and dancing. After returning to Canada, he landed roles in successful children's series such as *Goosebumps* and *Are You Afraid of the Dark?*, and also began to establish the teenage heartthrob persona in the Fox Kids series *Young Hercules* from 1998 to 1999, a persona which would reach its peak with the romantic drama *The Notebook*.[2] The film won him four Teen Choice Awards and numerous positions in the year's top movie kisses lists and remains one of Gosling's most financially successful works. Gosling's own celebrity persona was boosted at the time through his real-life relationship with on-screen star Rachel McAdams.

It was only with *The Believer*[3] (notably, a role in which Gosling's Daniel Blaint is so articulate in his vitriol towards Jews that he gets recruited by a group of fascists), however, that Gosling began to receive serious critical acclaim for his work. In a GQ article titled 'The Loner', Gosling noted that 'in everything else I'd seen or read up to that point, it was like the writer was trying to make sense of life'.[4] Gosling's intriguing observation emphasizes his desire to appear in films like *The Believer* that take a more unconventional approach to narrative and that reflect and accept the chaos and disorder of the human experience. Pappademas's article also articulates a theme that would continue to define Gosling throughout his later career: 'Ryan Gosling wants to hide from us. He plays weirdos and sociopaths in small-budget films. He guards his personal life fiercely.'[5] *Drive*, *Only God Forgives* and *Blade Runner 2049* all feature Gosling as a man outside society, where violence

---

[2] Nick Cassavetes, dir. (2004, New Line Cinema), DVD.
[3] Henry Bean, dir. (2002, Fireworks Pictures), DVD.
[4] Alex Pappademas, 'The Loner'. 2007. https://www.gq.com/story/ryan-gosling?currentPage=3.
[5] Ibid.

rather than dialogue is the main vehicle of his expression. It is tempting to read significance into Gosling's own documented personal experience with violence when, after watching *Rambo: First Blood*[6] as a young child (with Rambo himself representing a brand of tough, laconic and violent hero), he went into school the next day and threw knives at his classmates and ultimately had to be home-schooled. However, it is perhaps more interesting to focus on his refreshingly guarded approach to his personal life.

Bim Adewunmi attributes much of Gosling's star appeal to his fierce privacy, noting that 'there's something about withholding that increases desire'.[7] By not providing personal details about his relationship with *The Place Beyond the Pines* co-star Eva Mendes and their two daughters, for example, Gosling provides media outlets with a wide range of opportunities to speculate and write about his relationship status and family life. Likewise, by not saying much in his films, the audience is forced to rely on visual and audio cues to interpret narrative. Adewunmi praises his 'old-fashioned movie star's aesthetic, in which he purposefully holds out on much of his personal life, and lets his deliberately unconventional choices do the majority of talking for him'.[8] Silence is an essential device for Gosling in both his private and public personas. By defining Gosling in her title as a *Star After His Time*, Adewunmi notes the inherently complicated nature of his position within the star system. Yet like both Villeneuve and Refn, Gosling remains a relative outsider to contemporary Hollywood not just because of his Canadian nationality, but also through his determination not to take on big-budget, commercially driven roles. Paul McDonald remarks that 'stars are a form of investment, employed in film productions as a probable guard against loss'.[9] However, in the following section, it becomes clear that Gosling's star persona does not necessarily align with financial success, despite critical acclaim and the efforts of ingenious marketing techniques which might appeal to a commercial audience.

Critical Responses

Pappademas's 'weirdos and sociopaths' summary of Gosling's character choices aptly fit the three films starring the actor that I have analysed so far. The silent hero figures of K, Driver and Julian are all positioned outside the

---

[6] Ted Kotcheff, dir. (1982, Orion Pictures), DVD.
[7] 'Ryan Gosling Is a Star after His Time' (2007). *Buzzfeed News*. https://www.buzzfeednews.com/article/bimadewunmi/ryan-gosling-is-a-star-after-his-time.
[8] Ibid.
[9] McDonald, *The Star System*, 10.

boundaries of civilized society and barely know how to interact within its confines. In terms of critical responses from film critics to Gosling's recent performances, reactions vary from regarding them as either 'intense' or 'robotic', creating an interesting parallel to debates about expressionist styles of acting. The frequent references to these robotic or mechanical aspects of Gosling's performances, for instance, match Styan's interpretation of expressionist styles of acting which he regards as a 'deliberate departure from the realism of Stanislavsky' and notes that 'in avoiding the detail of human behaviour, a player might appear to be overacting, and adopting the broad mechanical movements of a puppet'.[10] In this section I will also introduce the 2018 film *First Man*.[11] While its settings do not reflect the same heightened realities of the previous films I've discussed and the film has a more grounded biographical context, it features another central performance that illustrates the essential outsider persona of the silent hero. As Neil Armstrong, Gosling portrays a man who is far more comfortable on the lonely surface of the moon than he is on Earth. Through analysing these critical debates in this section and looking at how Gosling's films are marketed to appeal to a wider audience, the continuing allure of the anti-social, laconic hero is highlighted.

In *Nicolas Winding Refn and the Violence of Art*, Justin Vicari points to Gosling's 'robotic' performance in *Drive*. He notes how the film has the seemingly archetypal Hollywood romance set-up between Driver and Irene and observes how 'feelings of love immediately go to feelings of needing to protect the loved object from violation; in this, the numbed hero often gives the aura of being traumatized, violated'.[12] This idea is summed up in the stylized, 'hyper-romantic'[13] elevator scene, where dramatic artificial lighting and extradiegetic sound envelop Driver as he protectively kisses Irene in slow motion (Figure 57).

Reality is distorted to the extent that it is not even clear if this 'reality' is real or a figment of Driver's imagination. Once the scene returns to real time, however, and Driver proceeds to violently stamp on an assailant's skull, reality quickly catches up as he stares blankly at a horrified Irene. The blood that adorns his scorpion jacket is a symbol that he can never truly change his violent nature. Refn notes that 'he kisses her goodbye because now he knows what he has to do … to turn himself into a superhero'.[14] Violence and sacrifice are essential characteristics of heroism in Refn's central characters. Driver

---

[10] Styan, *Modern Drama*, 5.
[11] Damien Chazelle, dir. (2018, Universal Pictures), DVD.
[12] Vicari, *Nicolas Winding Refn*, 180.
[13] Ibid., 186.
[14] Drive, Special Features (2012), DVD, Sony.

FIGURE 57 *Time stops as Driver turns and kisses Irene, whether in reality or in Driver's imagination. Sacrifice is a key characteristic of the silent hero, and it features heavily across Refn's filmography.*

is, as Vicari mentions, 'numbed' to this act of violence; as a silent hero, he is the only one able to perform this service efficiently and unemotionally, as he operates outside the boundaries of society. This is represented symbolically when Irene leaves the elevator and a blank-faced Driver remains inside with the brutalized body, unable to escape from the repercussions of his primal instincts.

Links between Gosling's portrayal of heroism and a disturbed emotional state are taken further by Vicari when he considers if Driver is not a human hero, but a 'cyborg'[15] in his mechanical movements and seeming invincibility after being stabbed with a blade. In the diner scene, for example, Gosling is framed on the left, calmly and methodically eating food. He looks up, and the camera cuts to a wider shot of the diner as he observes a former business partner and returns to his food, not moving from his seat, with the back of the menacing scorpion jacket in clear view. The partner decides to pick a seat closer to Gosling, knocking on the table surface briefly before talking as if to check if Gosling is functioning properly. He asks rhetorically about Driver's association with Shannon, receives no answer, then remarks that they met last year. Still, no answer. The partner tilts his head slightly as if to encourage a physical response, but no movement is provided by Gosling in recognition. The partner proceeds to give descriptions of a botched job and offers Driver another opportunity of work. The camera then focuses on Gosling, who finally raises his head in close-up and calmly suggests that the partner shuts his

---

[15] Vicari, *Nicolas Winding Refn*, 189.

FIGURE 58 *Gosling keeps his face still and composed as he stares at the departing co-worker. By keeping the camera focused on Gosling's facial expression in favour of swift cuts between the two figures, intimidation is created through Gosling's tense focus and silence.*

mouth before he kicks his teeth in and shuts it for him. The camera continues to linger on Gosling's stony glare as the partner leaves (Figure 58).

As contemporary actor Felix Granger notes, Gosling 'creates a blank slate for the viewer to put their interpretations of their own emotions on him' and that by revealing 'very little, you can allow lots of people to have different reactions'.[16] If Gosling had provided the audience with an animated monologue during this scene, then the blank slate would have been removed, and Driver's mysterious persona diminished. In the space of a few words, Gosling has asserted menace through his cold, robotic tone of phrase and still facial features.

Ideas of this 'robotic' nature of Gosling's Driver are frequently cultivated by actions he does not do and that he chooses to withhold, actions which might encourage more human, immediately relatable responses in an audience. This deliberate distancing strategy forces them to actively engage in the narrative and discover what is taking place, as well as work out how to respond emotionally. When a doctor removes a bullet from Driver's arm following the motel shootout, Driver, with the blood on his face accompanied by copious amounts of blood on his shirt, watches on passively, exhibiting little more emotional distress than the Terminator when it has bullets removed from its back by Sarah Connor in *Terminator 2: Judgement Day*.[17] Driver's lack of visible pain suggests he is something more than human. A similar sense

---

[16] Epton, Interview with Felix Granger, 12 April 2021.
[17] James Cameron, dir. (1991, Tri-Star Pictures), DVD.

of Driver's apparent robotic nature is implied when he admits his involvement in Standard's death to Irene. As Driver mentions to Irene that he still has the stolen money from the pawn shop and offers it to Irene, she replies with a slap, whose impact is heard in crisp, loud volume despite Driver's head barely moving an inch. While the audience might expect Driver to react with a verbal outburst, or even a shocked facial expression, he exhibits neither as he simply pauses and stares down at the ground, reconfiguring himself with a few awkward spoken sentences before they retire to the elevator. Both scenes display Driver's apparent lack of any human emotion and come across as almost comical in their lack of expository sentiment and passion. Minimal dialogue and economical body movement add to the sense of numbed passivity with which Driver receives Irene's loud, physical slap.

Robotic tendencies in *Drive* have frequently been related to Refn's portrayal of violence. For example, the film critic Jim Schembri describes Driver as a 'robotic, monosyllabic stuntman' and derides the film's narrative development as: 'People get shot, blood spurts everywhere, he [Driver] slowly loses control.'[18] Laconicism and pace are apparently at fault, implying that if Gosling had been loud-mouthed as opposed to monosyllabic, then his character's violent actions would somehow be more acceptable or understandable, or that the violence would have been more appropriate if Gosling had conveyed his emotions through verbal, violent outbursts. Yet other critics such as Peter Bradshaw and Philip French praise the intensity of Gosling's performance, linking his minimalist style to that of Steve McQueen, suggesting that Gosling's 'permafrost-cool'[19] and 'slight grimaces'[20] provide the audience with a constantly engaging persona. Like Lang and Leone before him, Refn is obsessed with the *pathology* of violence and the effect it has on audience response. He described art as an 'act of violence',[21] noting the way he himself seeks to provoke reactions from audiences.

The performances and direction of Refn's 'robotic' main star have been deliberately left open for audience interpretation and debate, and this is a debate about acting technique and visual aesthetics that goes right back to the early days of Expressionist drama. In his analysis of Expressionism on the

---

[18] 'Drive' (2011). *The Age*. https://www.theage.com.au/entertainment/movies/drive-20111026-1mjau.html.
[19] 'Drive – Review' (2011). *The Guardian*. https://www.theguardian.com/film/2011/sep/22/drive-ryan-gosling-film-review.
[20] 'Drive – Review' (2011). *The Guardian*. https://www.theguardian.com/film/2011/sep/25/drive-ryan-gosling-film-review.
[21] Jack Giroux, 'Interview: Nicolas Winding Refn on Violent Men, Valhalla and Pretty Woman' (2010). *Film School Rejects*. https://filmschoolrejects.com/interview-nicolas-winding-refn-on-violent-men-valhalla-and-pretty-woman-f96c21a797f7.

stage, for example, Kurtz notes: 'What first came to light, in the harsh glare of the spotlights, was a little slice of intense unreality',[22] going on to describe how actors were integrated into this space through the use of stylized gestures and exact motions. Directors like Fritz Lang were criticized at the time for 'false theatricals' and the 'too stylized' nature of character and plot.[23] Fred Hildenbrandt went so far as to describe *Metropolis* as an 'artificial, coldly calculating bit of business with magnificent photography'.[24] In *Only God Forgives* (a far more critically polarizing film than *Drive*), criticism is often intriguingly focused on Refn himself for the stylized nature of the filmmaking, which reinforces the character of Julian as a symbolic rather than a realistic figure. Damon Wise notes how, unlike his performance in *Drive*, Gosling is merely 'making a guest appearance in a Refn movie',[25] emphasizing how, in typical expressionist fashion, Refn's visual environments take centre stage over realistic character development. Even when *Only God Forgives* received praise, it is interesting to note the ongoing robotic language used to describe Gosling's performance, with Kevin Lincoln remarking how 'Gosling, in his silence and broken face, performs the part of the son as archetype and *prototype* to perfection'.[26] Gosling is described as a machine still in the process of creation, and the audience is encouraged to cultivate meaning from this frequently inscrutable, imperfect enigma, summarized by Lincoln as 'completely untouchable and bizarre, both masculine and weirdly beautiful' (Figure 59).[27]

It is perhaps apt that Gosling subsequently plays a literal robot in *Blade Runner 2049*. Although far more critically praised than *Only God Forgives*, the critics' focus was still often directed towards the film's visual aesthetic or comparisons made to its iconic original. Jade Bastién, however, argues that here we see Gosling begin to move away from the robotic, tough guy persona that he developed in *Drive*, and highlights 'the striking contradiction in his face and body during the more action-orientated scenes'[28] suggesting a far more vulnerable character that does not wholly align with traditional notions of the silent hero. Actor Felix Granger notes how Gosling's 'emotional intensity

---

[22] Kurtz, *Expressionism and Film*, 43.
[23] Ihering, 'Der Metropolis, Ufa-Palast am Zoo'.
[24] Hildenbrandt, 'Metropolis', *Berliner Tageblatt*, 11 January 1927.
[25] 'Only God Forgives Review' (2012). *Empire*. https://www.empireonline.com/movies/reviews/god-forgives-review/.
[26] 'What Is Cool? Ryan Gosling, Jake Johnson, and the Not-Dead Movie Star' (2013), Pacific Standard. https://psmag.com/social-justice/what-is-cool-ryan-gosling-jake-johnson-and-the-not-dead-movie-star-64155. Emphasis added.
[27] Ibid.
[28] 'The Vulnerability of Ryan Gosling in Blade Runner 2049' (2017). *Vulture*. https://www.vulture.com/2017/10/ryan-goslings-vulnerable-performance-in-blade-runner-2049.html.

FIGURE 59 *A battered Julian sits in the darkness as fractured light shines over his bruised body in a grotesque yet compelling image of suffering and angst.*

comes through that roboticness', pondering 'What's scarier than seeing a robot who suddenly emotes?'[29] Guns are frequently used by K, but rarely with conviction or self-confidence – at least not until the film's final act, when K has realized he is not the prophesied child and fights to protect the man he once thought was his father. However, passivity remains a key element in Gosling's performance as K, just as it does in his portrayals of both Driver and Julian. Behind the violent, authoritative exteriors of all Gosling's 21st-century silent heroes lie distinctly vulnerable and passive individuals. His characters emphasize the double-bind of the silent hero – they are ultimately trapped in their own stories.

This passivity reaches a peak in Gosling's performance in *First Man*. As Kermode asserts, 'It is the quintessential Ryan Gosling role. The character who doesn't say very much, but implies loads', agreeing that 'it's his impassiveness that does it'.[30] The audience are frequently met with the use of the word 'intense' in critical reviews of this particular film when writers talk about Gosling's performance, carrying far more positive connotations than the 'robotic', mechanical descriptions of Gosling's performance in *Drive*. John Nugent highlights the actor's perfectly fitting 'stiff Buster Keaton-esque

---

[29] Epton, Interview with Felix Granger, 12 April 2021.
[30] Epton, Interview with Mark Kermode, 10 February 2021.

features' for this particularly 'internal' role.[31] By drawing comparisons with 'Great Stone Face', it is clear how much emotion and critical audience response Gosling is able to cultivate through his minimal movements and expressions. 'Stiff' is not used in a derogatory sense. These subtle and still facial expressions allow Gosling to effectively externalize the internal griefs of his character by allowing the audience to pour their own imaginations into the performance. As with many expressionist characters, internal emotions are manifested through controlled action, gesture and facial expression rather than expository dialogue. Geoffrey MacNab describes Gosling's portrayal of Neil Armstrong as being 'played with quiet intensity',[32] suggesting that Gosling's silence evokes far more response in an audience than any amount of grandstanding or monologuing. Gosling utters the famous moon speech ambivalently, with little pomp or grandeur assigned to this moment, and the US flag is not in sight. The man takes precedence over the event. Again, the audience are intrigued by what they do not know and must work hard to fill in the gaps – as is made clear by MacNab's statement that the film's 'only slight frustration is the stoic-to-a-fault central character'. The audience are left to ponder 'America's most reluctant hero',[33] whose essential loneliness and isolation are highlighted, thanks to Gosling's minimalist performance.

It is significant that marketing techniques were employed in these films to appeal to the tastes of commercial audiences, as well as to disguise the arthouse nature of their experimental narratives. In *Drive*, for example, posters constantly featured Gosling and a car, either inside the vehicle or outside it, with his iconic scorpion jacket in clear view. While subsequent DVDs featured similar covers, the 4K Blu-ray edition cover released in 2022 reinforced just how iconic the jacket had become, with a three-dimensional, shining gold scorpion adorning a white background half obscured in shadow, highlighting Driver's morally questionable methods of protection. Acknowledging the film's minimal dialogue, Kermode describes Driver's jacket as 'the loudest thing in the movie'.[34] Driving – and thus the idea of high-octane, *Fast and Furious*-style action – is implied in the promotional posters for the film, even though, despite *Drive*'s title, driving is not the central focus of the film. The film's laconic tagline 'Get in. Get out. Get away' also implies an action-driven heist movie, when only one brief, failed theft takes place. The tagline rather serves as an eloquent summary of the classical silent hero's journey. The film's alternative tagline,

---

[31] 'First Man Review' (2018). *Empire*. https://www.empireonline.com/movies/reviews/first-man-review/.
[32] 'First Man Review: Damien Chazelle's gripping Neil Armstrong Biopic Is an Inspiration' (2018). *The Independent*. https://www.youtube.com/watch?v=Vxxifb6Wclw.
[33] Ibid.
[34] Epton, Interview with Mark Kermode, 10 February 2021.

'There are no clean getaways', mirrors the precise wording of the tagline for *No Country For Old Men*,[35] alluding to the dark, violent undertones of the neo-Western. Michigan citizen Sarah Denning sued *Drive*'s trailer for having 'very little driving' as well as 'antisemitic' undertones and, tellingly, marketing itself as 'a Fast and Furious style action piece'.[36] She ultimately won the grand total of the single ticket refund that she had demanded. During an interview, Refn responded disingenuously that Denning was simply 'accusing him of being a lot more clever than I am',[37] but also stated that he would love to talk to her about ideas in his film that he had not recognized or intended. *Arrival*'s posters function in a similar fashion, highlighting the ominous alien ship and containing the tagline 'Why Are They Here?', suggesting an alien invasion tale in the vein of commercial hits like *Independence Day*,[38] when this science fiction element is ultimately secondary to the personal journey of Louise herself.

Like *Drive*, the experimental narrative of *Only God Forgives* is hidden behind the masquerade of an action-driven set-up, in this case through the guise of a boxing movie. In the promotional poster, Ryan Gosling is shown with raised fists, playing on the tough-guy image he had already established in *Drive*, and the actual, Oedipus-laden narrative is masked behind this commercial, *Rocky*-like facade. The promotional poster for *Blade Runner 2049* likewise sets up an apparent conflict between K and Deckard by using contrasting colours of orange and blue, yet the actual clash does not take place until over halfway through the movie and, like *Drive*, takes up little screen time in the film's wider plot. *First Man* subverts the action-filled narrative of space films like *Apollo-13*[39] by employing the tropes of earlier 'quiet' science fiction films like *Silent Running*,[40] choosing instead to market the film by evoking a sense of nostalgia. In terms of box office, the marketing techniques of these films, which have so often sat at odds with directors' stated artistic, expressionist aims, have not been a clear-cut success. *Drive* was a smash-hit for Refn, catapulting him into the stratosphere of Hollywood, while *Only God Forgives* was both a financial and critical failure. *Blade Runner 2049* suffered a similar financial fate to its 1982 original, despite rave reviews and a significant budget, suggesting that it too will gain a later cult status.

---

[35] Joel Coen and Ethan Coen, dirs. (2007, Miramax Films), DVD.
[36] Ben Child, 'Woman Sues to Stop "Drive" Getting Away with a "Misleading Trailer"' (2011). *The Guardian*. https://www.theguardian.com/film/2011/oct/10/woman-sues-drive-trailer.
[37] 'Drive, Director Nicolas Winding Refn' (2011). *YouTube*. https://www.youtube.com/watch?v=5Vv0E_-Fi5g&t=1747s.
[38] Roland Emmerich, dir. (1996, 20th Century Fox), DVD.
[39] Ron Howard, dir. (1995, Universal Pictures), DVD.
[40] Douglas Trumbull, dir. (1972, Universal Pictures), DVD.

While the practice of auteur studies has become increasingly unpopular in the realm of film analysis, it is nonetheless important to look at each individual director's personal approach to film not just in relation to their opinions on silence and the silent hero, but also recognizing their positions as outsiders who often work within the Hollywood system. Refn, for example, refers to Leone, another outsider I have discussed, as setting his films 'in a heightened reality, in an artificial world', and yet notes that Leone was 'concerned with heroes in the real world who have struggles because they're not meant to be here'.[41] Refn points to the necessary outsider nature of the silent hero who is barred from the very society in which he operates.

When he considers Refn's admission that he does not regard himself as a director,[42] Justin Vicari observes that 'such borderlessness, in particular, has a special meaning in the world of film, whose best practitioners have often been freely moving citizens of the world'.[43] This borderlessness is key to the expressionist traits outlined by Kurtz in his earlier analysis of Expressionism as a desire to 'get away from the time-bound, away from the moment' in its drive towards emotional 'creation'.[44] Having lived and worked in several countries, Refn has been exposed to an eclectic mix of cultural influences. His own career so far has been comprised of successive financial failures and successes: his debut *Pusher*[45] was a huge success, although the financial fallout from his third film *Fear X*[46] nearly led to bankruptcy. Refn was then forced to film two sequels to *Pusher* in order to make ends meet, and he subsequently refused to make another film in his home country of Denmark.

Following the success of *Bronson*[47] – where Refn stretched his auteur muscles, only agreeing to direct the film on the condition that he could rewrite it – *Drive* represented his first venture into the Hollywood system. Working on the film's screenplay with Hossein Amini, Refn remarked that the first draft of his co-writer's initial script for Universal Studios was 'much more in the vein of a $60 million *Fast-and-Furious* movie'.[48] An intriguing link is made between budget and commercial film, as if to suggest that increased financial backing implies a more action-driven production. Hugh Jackman, known best for his

---

[41] Robert Koehler, 'Nicolas Winding Refn and the Search for a Real Hero' (2011). *CinemaScope*. https://cinema-scope.com/cinema-scope-magazine/interview-nicolas-winding-refn-and-the-search-for-a-real-hero/.
[42] Giroux, 'Interview' (2010). https://filmschoolrejects.com/interview-nicolas-winding-refn-on-violent-men-valhalla-and-pretty-woman-f96c21a797f7/.
[43] Vicari, *Nicolas Winding Refn*, 12.
[44] Kurtz, *Expressionism and Film*, 11.
[45] Refn, dir. (1996, RCV), DVD.
[46] Refn, dir. (2003, Lionsgate), DVD.
[47] Refn, dir. (2008, Vertigo Films), DVD.
[48] Koehler, 'Nicolas Winding Refn'.

various appearances as superhero Wolverine, was the initial actor in mind for the role of Driver when film production was in its early, action-driven plot stages.

Once Gosling, who had contacted Refn personally, got on board, he described the character of Driver as a man who is 'lost in the mythology of Hollywood and he's become an amalgamation of all the characters he admires'.[49] The actor also notably summarized *Drive* as depicting 'a guy who wants to be a superhero'.[50] Hollywood conventions and audience expectations are challenged by a character who has become disengaged with reality. With Gosling working alongside Refn and Amini, the script's dialogue was significantly cut from the original draft. Referring to the source novel, Refn notes how 'all of his [Driver's] prior life in the novel was deliberately eliminated for the movie. I think this increases his sense of being a fairy-tale creature'.[51] Like both Western and film noir heroes, mystery is an essential characteristic of the silent hero. Refn's own professed dyslexia also plays an interesting role in terms of Sontag's ideas of the increasing contamination of language: by struggling with language, Refn is compelled to strip dialogue down to its most economic state.[52] By the time Refn had negotiated with studios, the film's final budget stood at $15 million, far below any *Fast and Furious* budget yet still more than all Refn's previous films combined. As in the case of *Caligari*, where Wiene had a restricted budget and was forced to create many of the now-iconic sets himself, by having fewer materials at his disposal, Refn was able to craft a far more economic and powerfully emotional film.

Villeneuve has experienced a similar mix of failures and successes during his career. His first two feature films, *August 32nd on Earth*[53] and *Maelstrom*[54] both received unimpressive critical reviews, leading the director to take a nine-year break from feature films. His return to the cinema with *Polytechnique*,[55] a retelling of the 1989 Montréal Massacre, garnered both controversy and rave reviews, paving the way financially for Villeneuve's future works.

As with *Drive*, issues of directorial control played an important role in the production of Villeneuve's *Arrival*. Villeneuve noted, 'I will deform scenes, I will cut dialogues, I will make it my own, I will be a bit of a barbaric arsehole

---

[49] Luke Goodsell, 'Ryan Gosling on Drive: This is My Superhero Movie' (2011). *Rotten Tomatoes*. https://editorial.rottentomatoes.com/article/ryan-gosling-on-drive-this-is-my-superhero-movie/.
[50] Ibid.
[51] Koehler, 'Nicolas Winding Refn'.
[52] Sontag, 'The Aesthetics of Silence', 13.
[53] Villeneuve, dir. (1998, Epicentre Films), DVD.
[54] Villeneuve, dir. (2000, Alliance Atlantis), DVD.
[55] Villeneuve, dir. (2009, Alliance Films Remstar), DVD.

with the material, because I need to invade the screenplay.'[56] *The French Canadian* director's need to remove speech from the script also suggests a similar interest to Refn in terms of his use of silence and laconic dialogue. Villeneuve's interest in the expressive possibilities available without speech is particularly evident when he notes that 'For me, cinema is not about dialogue, it's about choreography that ends between sounds and images'.[57] Verbal, expository narration is at odds with the emotional drive of Villeneuve's filmmaking. Speaking about his own responses to the source material of *Arrival* (Ted Chiang's *Stories of Your Life and Others*) Villeneuve expressed his hopes that *Arrival* 'will convey the emotions that I felt when I was reading the short story, and I fought to protect those emotions to the process'.[58] The director is not only interested in silence, but the critical emotional responses that it can cultivate in an audience. The fact that Villeneuve himself fought personally to make sure that these emotions translated to the screen emphasizes his enthusiastic investment in the cinematic experience. Audience critical response is paramount. Upon hearing that his most recent work *Dune*[59] was planned to be streamed at the same time as its cinematic release, for instance, Villeneuve released a scathing public criticism of Warner Bros' decision, stating that 'there is absolutely no love for cinema, nor for the audience'[60] in such a move.

'Literally Me': Ryan Gosling and Silent Hero Masculinities

It's a sweltering day in downtown LA. Traffic lines the road as far as the eye can see. Tensions are running high. You're just trying to get home from work, but then your air conditioning breaks. You're frustrated and you leave your stationary car to walk. Yet by the end of the day you've managed, among other activities, to accost fellow citizens with a bat, shoot someone in the leg, shoot up a phone booth, shoot a guy, then get yourself shot. These things happen.

---

[56] FilmisNow, 'Arrival: On-Set Visit with Denis Villeneuve "Director"' (2016). *YouTube*. https://www.youtube.com/watch?v=qzKLJ4GeFto&t=0s.
[57] Mark Mangini, 'Soundworks Collection – the Sound of *Blade Runner 2049*' (2018). *YouTube*. https://www.youtube.com/watch?v=Vxxifb6WcIw.
[58] FilmIsNow, 'Arrival'.
[59] Villeneuve, dir. (2021, Warner Bros. Pictures), DVD.
[60] Villeneuve, 'Dune Director Denis Villeneuve Blasts HBO Max Deal' (2020). *Variety*. https://variety.com/2020/film/news/dune-denis-villeneuve-blasts-warner-bros-1234851270/.

The narrative journey of Michael Douglas's William 'D-Fens' Foster in *Falling Down*[61] represents an archetypal image of masculinity in crisis on screen, films in which the central character abandons his meaningless profession in society to fight 'the man' and try to get his due, usually ending up either critically injured or dead. Perhaps the most iconic iteration of this archetype can be found in *Taxi Driver*'s[62] disturbed Vietnam veteran Travis Bickle (Robert De Niro), whose awkward attempts to fit into society with a regular job and a steady girlfriend prove unsuccessful, leading him to befriend then attempt to assassinate a presidential candidate, achieving a warped 'salvation' through shooting a pimp and saving a young girl in the process. Again, the role of the child in the hero's act of 'heroism', however twisted, is key.

In contemporary pop culture, however, films such as these (other examples of 'man vs society' include the protagonists in *American Psycho*,[63] *Fight Club*[64] and *American Beauty*[65]) have often fallen under the banner of Literally Me films, feeding into a particularly interesting debate about the nature of intense audience response. Whilst these films do not represent a particularly 'silent' take on masculinity and the role of men in society generally – all the above examples contain very verbal central characters who frequently resort to loud emotional outbursts and expository dialogue – there are still evident links to the emotional journeys of many of the silent heroes that I have discussed. In a recent article, journalist Faris Firoozye stipulates that, despite these characters' psychosis, they 'consistently gain a form of supreme consciousness, usually completing a journey from a life of complete existential emptiness ... into a transformation of true self-affirmation and self-acceptance'.[66] Direct links to many of the silent heroes I have discussed are made, with the 'supreme consciousness' that Firoozye refers to suggesting both omniscience and omnipotence which allows heroes to dispatch their enemies with expert skill and with a sincere belief that they are putting the world to rights. Again, the outsider status of the protagonist and their process of 'transformation' is key in the hero's journey as they begin in existential crisis and progress to a state of greater identity and sense of purpose, even if it is ultimately a misguided one.

The films that frequently appear in this recent Literally Me social media trend are nothing new in terms of their portrayals of dissatisfied loners and the dark depictions of the societies they position themselves against (Christian

---

[61] Joel Schumacher, dir. (1993, Warner Bros.), DVD.
[62] Martin Scorsese, dir. (1976, Columbia Pictures), DVD.
[63] Mary Harron, dir. (2000, Lionsgate Films), DVD.
[64] David Fincher, dir. (1999, 20th Century Fox), DVD.
[65] Sam Mendes, dir. (1999, DreamWorks Pictures), DVD.
[66] '"Literally Me" Characters: A Take on Modern Pop Culture' (2023). *The Oxford Blue*. https://www.theoxfordblue.co.uk/literally-me-characters/.

Bale's commercially driven Patrick Bateman in American Psycho, for example, represents a brutal critique of Reagan's economic policies), nor is the tendency for these depictions to be misinterpreted and glamourized by segments of the audience. In its extreme interpretation, powerful audience identification with these films has led to such damaged and dangerous manifestations as the Incel movement, in which young men glorify the perceived qualities of the martyred loner. At the very least, these films stir up huge debate about the intentions of the filmmakers and the kind of response they were hoping to encourage in an audience. Given Refn's adamant refusal to list his artistic intentions (beyond his general stated urge towards expression) and the laconic nature of his male protagonists, it is particularly interesting to note how the phenomenon of Literally Me found its origins in *Drive*.[67] *Drive* provides an acerbic commentary on Hollywood mythology through the violent interactions of its laconic, emotionally repressed leading man – for example, the audience see Driver reacting unemotionally during a stunt scene when an assistant asks him to sign a contract granting the company liability if he is injured or killed. Instead of following traditional Tinsel Town romances, Driver doesn't get the girl and the audience do not even know if he will survive at the end of the film. It is this dissatisfied loner archetype that appeals to an audience who can admire his actions from afar but are unable to perform these actions themselves. As Firoozye asserts, 'The allegory is clear: it is the alienation from a cold, modern society that drives association to these "literally me" characters.'[68] The trend has likewise identified *Blade Runner 2049* in its category of disillusioned male figures, establishing Gosling as a go-to actor for portraying emotionally repressed men of few words who fight against the barriers and confines of human society. However, it is the element of sacrifice within the narrative progression of these male protagonists that lies at the heart of much of their popular appeal. Firoozye notes the essential sacrificial trait in Literally Me characters when he mentions how K 'decides to [re]affirm his humanity by sacrificing himself for a noble cause when he saves Deckard and reunites him with his replicant child, hence giving his own short life some fulfilment and meaning. Despite being manufactured as a machine, he chooses to live and die as a human'.[69] Sacrifice is essential to create a meaningful, affective story arc in the silent hero figure, a trait which intersects with Literally Me narratives of the grieved martyr.

It is fruitful to consider the precise points at which characters such as Driver and K achieve their greatest points of audience relatability. Driver's

---

[67] 'Literally Me Guys'. *Know Your Meme.* https://knowyourmeme.com/memes/literally-me-guys.
[68] ' "Literally Me" Characters'.
[69] Ibid.

FIGURE 60 *Driver's outburst carries shock due to his previously passive behaviour. He has never once even said a bad word against Shannon, but Irene potentially being in danger flips an emotional switch.*

key moment of externalized and verbalized anger occurs when he questions Shannon about how the assailant in the elevator scene knew where he lived, made all the more emotionally affective because of his usual taciturn nature. When Shannon initially mentions that he contacted Bernie for help, Driver remains superficially unconcerned, adopting the same cool expression that the audience has viewed throughout the movie. As soon as Shannon admits that he mentioned 'the girl' to Bernie, however, Driver explodes both in terms of volume and body language (Figure 60).

He lunges and grabs Shannon by the neck, with Driver's next furious rhetorical phrase 'What the fuck did you just say?' barely audible behind his rage, intercut with images of Driver's tense expressions inside his car (a vehicle inside which he had previously been shown to be calm and collected). With a distressed Shannon still in his grasp, he asks another rhetorical question: 'You fucking told him about Irene?' Shannon tries to placate him with a few weak pleas to 'calm down', but Driver ignores him, repeating his previous phrase in louder, maniacal fashion. The instant Driver realizes that Irene, his one hope at entering human society, is in danger, he snaps. Driver continues his rant, threatening to kill Shannon, repeating the rhetorical phrase one more time as his voice becomes slightly calmer. Shannon tries to placate him with weak extended assurances that he'll sort out the situation, but Driver lets Shannon go as he gives him a final rhetorical question about 'why [he] has to fuck everything up'. Bleak depictions of masculinity are cultivated here through redundant repetitions alongside an overuse of terse insults.

FIGURE 61 *As with Figure 60, it is K's sudden, loud outburst that comes across as so shocking alongside his physical movement because he has not displayed this behaviour before. His contorted facial features are a far cry from the mute passivity he has previously displayed.*

Likewise in *Blade Runner 2049*, it is K's sudden rise in volume and verbal exclamation upon mistakenly interpreting Ana's Stelline's comment to mean that the horse memory is his own that causes such intense audience response. In a similar fashion to the bleating cries of the baby on the beach in *Under the Skin*, the audience are distressed not only because of the sheer volume and pathos of the noises, but also because they are hearing it in relation to the relative silences that have gone before. As the audience feels for the baby that is alone and unprotected on the shore, they feel for a man whose greatest cry of protest against the brutal emotionless life he is required to function in is articulated by a single, pained word: 'Goddammit' (Figure 61). Body language again also plays an important role; K's face, previously still and passive, becomes contorted with anger as he exclaims, with his pent-up rage articulated through the futile action of kicking over a bin.

The emotional breaking point of Julian in *Only God Forgives*, however, is particularly terrifying both in the context of the scene and the sheer high pitch of his voice which accompanies his violent actions. After Mai (Yayaying Rhatha Phongam) questions why Julian lets his mother treat him so badly, Julian pushes her against a nearby wall, noting threateningly that, if she doesn't appreciate the dress he bought for her, she should 'take it off'. The first time Julian utters this phrase, he says it in the usual quiet tones that the audience has become accustomed to. When Mai refuses to undress, however, he screams 'take it off' a second time (Figure 62).

These are not the angry shouts of Driver or even the short, intense exclamation of K, but a high-pitched, crazed noise of insanity. Mai then dutifully

FIGURE 62 *Sound plays a particularly pivotal role in evoking shock in the audience through Julian's loss of control. This is a character who has been particularly laconic and reticent in terms of dialogue. The first time he reprimands Mai in standard volume, the audience is relatively unperturbed. The second time, however, he screams the words so loudly and unexpectedly that the sudden rise of volume and pitch encourages a jump scare.*

complies as Julian returns to silence. His primal utterance – issuing from Mai's reference to Julian's unhealthy relationship with his mother – cultivates far more emotional audience response precisely because of his minimal resort to dialogue previously.

Although Armstrong never provides any key moments of vocalized emotion in *First Man* (the only emotive outburst the audience are witness to is when he retires to a room during Karen's funeral, where he covers his face with his hands as he cries uncontrollably, with no words of discernible human language necessary), the scene where he discovers the deaths of his colleagues during a pre-launch test over the phone presents an interesting display of *repressed* emotion. When an assistant informs him that Deke Slayton (Armstrong's chief) is on the phone, Armstrong responds with a passive 'oh' as he walks to the phone in a distancing tracking shot; the audience is not permitted to read any emotion on his face. Initially thinking that he is being called to be relieved of attending the conference, he begins the conversation amicably. When Slayton responds that there were problems with the plugs-out test, Armstrong nonchalantly remarks that tests are there to find these problems, not yet understanding the gravity of the situation. Slayton explains the fire and that all the astronauts were killed, with Armstrong's face now in close-up, still and inscrutable as he receives the news. Armstrong drops the niceties and leaves a pregnant pause, as does Slayton, before the voice explains that there may have been a wiring issue. Armstrong's face remains blank and unemotive as he listens to the details, providing the audience with an affective space to try and decipher his emotional state. When the voice stops speaking to ask if Armstrong understands, Armstrong leaves another pause before uttering a simple laconic 'yeah', finishing the conversation with a blunt 'ok'. On the surface, nothing in Armstrong's demeanour has altered. The audience linger on Armstrong's face as he looks down to one side, then to the other as they hear a clink of glass. The camera cuts to Neil's bloodied hand and the partially shattered wine glass within it (Figure 63). Armstrong silently wipes off the blood with a handkerchief. Instead of an open outpouring of grief between two men at the death of their comrades, the broken glass stands in as an affective signifier of Armstrong's unspoken anguish.

In relation to the pop culture phenomenon from which Literally Me originated, it is also interesting to briefly consider the meme-related context that the trend derived from, as well as the amusing memes that have cultivated a public aura around Gosling himself. One of these involved the 'Ryan Gosling Won't Eat His Cereal' vines, a series of short seven-second clips in which sequences of poorly rendered footage of Gosling's still facial expressions play while the creator introduces the said spoonful of cereal and moves it slowly

FIGURE 63 *In stark contrast to Figure 62, Armstrong evokes concern in the audience through his complete lack of reaction and apparent lack of pain from shattering part of the glass in his hand. It is what Gosling doesn't do in this moment that provokes a strong emotional audience response.*

towards Gosling's mouth. Gosling's on-screen characters then amusingly appear to either passively reject the offer or actively slap the spoon away. Beyond their comedic content, the vines provide an interesting commentary about the intense nature of the taciturn characters that Gosling has tended to play in his later career, but they also represent a warm affection towards the actor and his acting techniques. Gosling even paid a tribute to the creator upon his passing. Another bizarre yet amusing meme creation was the 'Hey Girl' meme that derived from a fan blog in 2008, which involved various captions pasted onto an image of the actor's face with Gosling making complimentary statements, as if to a prospective girlfriend. One of these examples includes an image of Gosling's laughing expression with the attached text: 'Hey Girl, Feel My Sweater' at the top, accompanied with the cheesy rejoinder: 'Know What It's Made Of? Boyfriend Material' at the bottom of the image. Gosling himself claimed to have no idea of the huge popularity of these memes when he was being interviewed to promote *The Nice Guys*[70] and the meme reached a new level of meta when, during Gosling's MTV interview for *Blue Valentine*, interviewers presented Gosling with a series of these captions for him to read, prompting huge attention from the internet. Gosling's public persona has garnered huge appeal on the web from both male and female audience members who have invested emotionally, albeit sometimes in sinister fashion, sometimes humorously, in the characters he portrays on screen.

Acting Techniques

Gosling has been reluctant to describe the precise inspirations and processes of his acting style. However, he is known to have worked with Sandra Seacat, an acting coach versed in Method (she was a protégé of the technique's founder Lee Strasberg) and in her own original acting practice of dream work developed from the theories of Carl Gustav Jung. With this technique she encourages actors to use characters from dreams in their real-life performance and to channel the powers of the unconscious. During an interview at Cannes, when Gosling was questioned on how he creates internalized characters, he casually deflected the question towards Refn, who provided an equally noncommittal response.[71] When the interviewer again tried to quiz Gosling on his stylized form of acting, Gosling continued to avoid answering the question

---

[70] Shane Black, dir. (2016, Warner Bros. Pictures), DVD.
[71] 'Drive – Interview with the Cast at Cannes 2011'. *YouTube*. https://www.youtube.com/watch?v=Y0AGBO7w7dA.

FIGURE 64 *Alongside the emotive tones of Katyna Ranieri, the audience is also drawn to the unique distanced framing of Driver staring in his car, with filmmakers having previously framed him in more claustrophobic shots within the vehicle itself. This rare editing choice heightens the already palpable emotive atmosphere as Driver silently broods on the death of his father figure and the acts he is about to carry out in retaliation.*

directly, and the interviewer pointedly reminded Gosling of this fact, yet he once again refused to give a direct response. Gosling deliberately cultivates mystery by refusing to explain his techniques.

At first glance, the potential Method acting influences in Gosling's style seem directly at odds with the expressionist, symbolic silent hero figures he so often conveys. Gosling himself has certainly shown stereotypical Method tendencies, such as gaining 60 pounds for the role of Jack Salmon in *The Lovely Bones*[72] (the process, which involved eating colossal amounts of Häagen-Dazs ice cream, apparently inspired *Elvis* actor Austin Butler in his preparation for the eponymous role) and living with on-screen partner Michelle Williams for *Blue Valentine*. Yet the actor's controlled, precise movements in his performances, particularly in terms of his 'stone face' expressions, point to a distinctly physical, expressionist and movement-orientated acting technique. As Styan elaborates, Expressionist acting involved 'avoiding the detail of human behaviour', in which the performer's 'mechanical movements' would often take centre stage.[73] He acknowledges that this style of acting was 'suitable for certain kinds of comedy',[74] which align with Keaton in films such as *One Week*,[75] when the actor, dressed in worker's garb – the realism

---

[72] Peter Jackson, dir. (2009, Paramount Pictures), DVD.
[73] Styan, *Modern Drama*, 5.
[74] Ibid.
[75] Buster Keaton and Edward F. Cline, dirs. (1920, Metro Pictures), *YouTube*.

FIGURE 65 *The stylized aesthetic is on full display as Driver's masked figure walks up to the window in menacing slow motion. He is apparently not even seen by any of the people inside the pizzeria, reinforcing the idea of Driver as a ghostly, omnipotent instrument of vengeance.*

of which is deliberately undercut by the clothing's exaggerated Expressionist style – employs a deadpan expression as wedding guests hurl shoes at him instead of confetti. Yet so too can these still facial expressions and slow stylized movements be employed during more serious drama such as *Drive*, when Driver, after finding the body of father-figure Shannon in the garage (at which point Riz Ortollani's emotional 'Oh My Love' begins to play), stares blankly at the criminals laughing inside Nino's pizzeria from within his car (Figure 64).

The audience watch Driver walk to the back of the car to retrieve the latex face mask he wore during a previous stunt scene (in which the mask received its own song, Cliff Martinez's 'Rubber Head'), although they do not witness him putting on the item, making the image of him walking up to the pizzeria door in slow motion with the mask already on decidedly unsettling and deliberately dehumanizing (Figure 65).

The mask further emphasizes the impersonal, terrifying idea of what Styan refers to as the 'grotesque and unreal', quoting Yvan Goll's assessment that the prop is 'unchangeable, inescapable ... it is Fate'.[76] Adopting the role of a superhero, an unnatural force of nature, Driver continues to wear the mask as he crashes into Nino's car, and Ortollani's extradiegetic song reaches its dramatic crescendo in tandem with the loud motor of Driver's speeding vehicle. An injured and petrified Nino views his masked figure from a distance on the beach, before Driver proceeds to drown him without mercy. Again, Driver disappears into the role of an ironic Hollywood superhero as he anonymously

---

[76] Styan, *Modern Drama*, 5.

dispatches the bad guy with ease. The mask that Gosling dons is also a literal representation of his character's inscrutable and symbolic nature. He remains unable to change the violent path he is set upon and can never achieve the tranquility and human connection he desires with Irene and Benicio.

Despite Gosling's refusal to elaborate on any precise stylistic influences, his work with directors in pre-production suggests a strong interest in and intense focus on his craft. There are well-documented instances where he was directly involved in contributing to filmic narratives during pre-production that help audiences to analyse Gosling's performance both in front of and behind the camera. In the key area of dialogue delivery, for instance, Gosling played a major role in shaping the language of *Blade Runner 2049*. He noted how the repeated baseline test, which encapsulates both the robotic and dreamlike qualities of much expressionist dialogue, 'held the key to understanding K'[77] and acting coach Natsuko Ohama was employed to realize his vision. Ohama used a technique called 'Dropping In', where language is repeated and considered in every context until it is exhausted of its effect. Much like Sontag's theories of speech, words are exhausted of any meaning through their constant repetition. Gosling praised the technique's 'trance-inducing effect that can be very powerful and unsettling'.[78] The actor's interests in the dehumanizing effects of language also align with his own fascination with the power of silence. Referring to *Drive*, Gosling pondered that 'a lot of action movies these days, they're more action and they have a little less character'.[79] He highlights that, like speech, the overload of hollow action movies that are focused on explosions and quick edits have removed any possibility of narrative intrigue. In a separate interview about *Drive*, Gosling significantly observes:

> I don't think you need all this talking in movies. Sometimes it's easier to get the point across if you're not saying something. Sometimes when you're talking, it gets in the way of it, and it was a real relief to just take that out of this and let people just watch it and make their own assessments of what they think the characters are going through.[80]

Gosling's statement highlights the power of saying less, but also the importance he puts on cultivating audience response. By 'not saying

---

[77] Lapointe, *The Art and Soul*, 117.
[78] Ibid.
[79] Screenslam, 'Drive: Ryan Gosling is Character Driven – Screenslam' (2011). *YouTube*. https://www.youtube.com/watch?v=A1uolzUc60Q.
[80] The Celeb Factory, 'Ryan Gosling on the Dialogue in Drive' (2011). *YouTube*. https://www.youtube.com/watch?v=1GrF4bO9sUA.

something' the audience is forced to focus their attention on a character's movement and how they react to their surroundings. Body language can act as a more effective, universal form of communication through its expressive gestures. Referring to the script he helped condense alongside Refn (the source novel on which *Drive* is based contains far more dialogue than is uttered in the final film), Gosling notes how audience understanding of characters' emotional states is far more insightful and meaningful when they utilize 'their own assessments' as opposed to following more explicit narrative signposts such as dialogue.

    The concept of *Drive* as a film was also largely a result of Gosling's personal involvement. Apart from his dyslexia and colour-blindness, Refn was also (and remains) unable to drive, requiring Gosling to drive him around the streets of LA to get used to the city and find potential shooting locations. Gosling noted at Cannes how, when he was driving Refn home, REO Speedwagon's 'I Can't Fight This Feeling Anymore' began playing on the radio 'and I turned it up because we weren't talking. He [Refn] started singing at the top of his lungs'[81] ultimately giving Refn the central idea of *Drive*. Both silence and sound played a key role in the film's inception. Although Refn ultimately chose most of the locations, Gosling personally picked the environment of the LA river and its concrete banks, where the driving scene with Driver, Irene and Benicio takes place to the soundtrack of ambient music. Gosling describes the area as 'this one spot where out of nowhere there was this patch of shrubs and trees, and you couldn't go any further. There was no reason for it to be there. It was kind of magical'.[82] This dreamlike expressionist notion of setting, with the unlikely juxtaposition of nature within a very unnatural, urban landscape, grabbed the actor's attention. Gosling even built his own car for the production, with Refn describing how 'he built his own heart'[83] in the process, again evoking the links with the almost mechanical, robotic quality that so many critics have drawn attention to in Gosling's acting style as well as reinforcing the passionate, emotional commitment Gosling brings to his film choices.

---

[81] Edward Davis, 'Nicolas Winding Refn Says RAO Speedwagon Helped Him & Ryan Gosling Seal the "Drive" Deal' (2011). *IndieWire*. https://www.indiewire.com/2011/05/nicolas-winding-refn-says-reo-speedwagon-helped-him-ryan-gosling-seal-the-drive-deal-118596/.
[82] Locations Hub, 'The 12 Film Locations of Drive in Los Angeles' (2012). *Locations Hub*. https://www.locationshub.com/blog/2013/10/26/the-12-film-locations-of-drive-in-los-angeles.
[83] CELEBS.com, 'Ryan Gosling behind the Scenes on "Drive"' (2011). *YouTube*. https://www.youtube.com/watch?v=BwAPER0lm48&t=3s.

Gesture

So far, my discussion of Gosling's physical performance has often centred on his facial expressions. While this feature is an important means by which the audience can form their own emotional responses, Gosling's hands play a similar – if not more important – role in conveying meaning in scenes where no dialogue is spoken. Both Villeneuve and Refn (as well as *First Man* director Damien Chazelle) frequently frame the actor's hands in close-up instead of focusing on his whole figure, and Refn's theories on hands and their relationship to masculinity will be analysed in this section. Kim Newman notes of German Expressionist silent films that, in terms of acting, 'it's all in the hands',[84] emphasizing the integral importance of gesture in films without spoken dialogue. Conrad Veidt, for example, in another starring role after *Caligari*, played a man controlled by transplanted hands in *The Hands of Orlac*.[85] Another link can be seen between the 21st-century films I discuss here as well; hands, like the face, are constantly framed as vessels to cultivate mood and narrative development. Nathaniel Dorksy stresses their sanctified nature in *Devotional Cinema*, exalting that 'the total genius of your hand is more profound than anything you could have calculated with your intellect. One's hand is a *devotional object*'.[86] Dorsky highlights the intense emotionality involved in this specific body part when he mentions the 'profound' affect that it produces, directly opposing the rational element of 'intellect' in its usage. As with the figure of the actor itself, hands, and particularly hands in close-up, become key affective vessels into which the audience is compelled to pour their emotions. Highlighting the use of editing techniques in the opening shot of his own film, Hawkins ponders how 'The hand too is deterritorialised, as through framing it is cut off from its owner. It is an anonymous hand, an orphan hand'.[87] As seen with the opening shot of Luv's hand in *Blade Runner 2049*, affect is cultivated by introducing character through this imagery of synecdoche; the hand we first see stands for the whole body, representing the character's identity in miniature. Gesture, and the economy of gesture, are key techniques to convey meaning to an audience.

Discussing the performances of Krauss and Veidt in *Caligari*, Lotte Eisner describes how 'through a reduction of gesture they attain movements which are almost linear and which – despite a few curves that slip in – remain brusque,

---

[84] Epton, Interview with Kim Newman, 9 March 2021.
[85] Robert Wiene, dir. (1924, Pan-Film), DVD.
[86] Dorksy, *Devotional Cinema*, 38. Emphasis added.
[87] Hawkins, 'The Concept', 84.

like the broken angles of the sets'.[88] Gosling's controlled performances in the films I have discussed likewise could be described as 'brusque', suggesting an economy of dialogue as well as of movement. Sontag asserts, 'A person who becomes silent becomes opaque for the other; somebody's silence opens up an array of possibilities for interpreting that silence, for imputing speech into it.'[89] Movement and gesture therefore become central routes to deciphering narrative in films which lack expository dialogue. Through analysing hand shots in these films, tactility's central role in both eliciting emotional critical responses from the audience and shaping the masculinity of the silent hero is emphasized.

In *Blade Runner 2049*, hands are frequently used to introduce characters and to symbolize their marginalization in society – an important trait in expressionist silent heroes. In the opening scene, the audience are provided with a close-up, interior view of K's spinner, where three screens are on display, with the one on the right listing K's name and status alongside a picture of his face. The next shot shows the audience the back of Gosling's lowered, sleeping head. The camera then provides the audience with a wide shot of the bleak, plastic landscape as the spinner continues to fly forward. It is only in the next shot that we finally witness Gosling's face for the first time. Yet his expression is deliberately blurred and in the background of the picture, with his right hand shown in extreme close-up and sharpened focus. A beeping sound then wakes K up. However, his figure remains blurred, with the hand still in clear view. The filmmakers provide the audience with an exercise in visual abstraction. By showing the image of K on screen and the outside environment before showing the face of the actual man sitting in the spinner, his mysterious, outsider persona is cultivated through audience anticipation. The audience might expect to see Gosling's face as the first image within the spinner, yet this image is withheld to symbolize K's fragmented, oppressed position within the world in which he works. Through focusing on the hand instead of the face (the natural 'money shot' in the star system), the filmmakers force the audience to seek meaning through unconventional corporeal signifiers (Figure 66).

Representations of visual isolation are also employed in the character of Sapper Morton. Before the audience are introduced to his full physical figure, they witness his body reflected against water in shadow. Suddenly, in close-up, a left hand arises from the liquid holding a group of maggots. These insects are inspected with the other hand, as a finger pokes the creatures before the left hand tosses them back into the water. It is only after this tactile interaction, designed to create a queasy unease, that the camera zooms out

---

[88] Eisner, *The Haunted Screen*, 25.
[89] Sontag, 'The Aesthetics of Silence', 16.

FIGURE 66 *The hand of a sleeping K is shot in the foreground in sharp focus, contrasted with his blurred figure in the background.*

to a wide shot of Sapper's figure within his workspace. Although he is framed from the back in the next shot, with his facial expression obscured behind his suit, the previous image of his hands symbolizes Sapper's relative autonomy in comparison to K. While K's hand sat mechanically on the controls of his spinner, only moving slightly when alerted by the noise of an alarm to continue his prescribed mission, the audience witness both of Sapper's hands, free to touch, keep and dispose of the organisms in his palms as he wishes. These brief images act as a non-verbal prelude to the dialogue that subsequently takes place, where Sapper taunts K and declares that K has never seen a miracle. Subtle gestures are employed in both scenes as visual signifiers. By focusing on this single body part, the filmmakers create a physical synecdoche, with hands representing the mindsets of their respective characters.

Hands play a pivotal role in K's personal development. Catherine Payne and Alexandra Pitsis note how 'an implicit narrative about the role of the senses, particularly tactility, in the development of human consciousness' takes place throughout the film.[90] This development can be seen emerging moments after K has killed Sapper and notices a yellow flower under a tree. While the filmmakers had the option of showing K pick up the flower in a wide shot, the audience are instead provided with a close-up of K's hand, a devotional object, picking up the flower. K is then shown in medium shot holding the flower between two fingers and smelling it, then looking around before the camera cuts to K's hands holding a plastic bag containing the flower inside his spinner. Again, instead of the filmmakers simply transitioning from the shot of K picking up the flower to this shot inside the spinner, the fact that K is

---

[90] Payne and Pitsis, 'On Nature and the Tactility of the Senses in Blade Runner 2049', 3.

FIGURE 67 *Instead of immediately proceeding to the dilapidated casino, K's curious hand stops to feel creatures he has presumably never seen or felt before.*

shown holding, staring at and smelling the flower emphasizes the character's narrative journey through the focus on the senses.

K constantly uses his hands to touch, explore and attempt to understand his surrounding environments. When walking through the apocalyptic environment of Las Vegas, for example, a bee sits briefly on K's hand. The audience witness this hand and bee in close-up before the camera cuts to K's still expression. K continues walking slowly through the dystopian environment. Villeneuve noted that in this scene he 'wanted a frontier between reality and dreams to be blurred' and kept instructing Gosling to 'walk slower, walk slower'.[91] This heightened reality emphasizes the already hypnotic atmosphere of Gosling's slow, concentrated movements. In another close-up, his hand reaches slowly underneath a beehive, becoming covered with insects that seemingly do not attack him (Figure 67).

The only sounds we hear in this moment are those of the bees buzzing as K remains silent. Villeneuve also remarked how he wanted the insects to be 'a sound that is like gold, and an overwhelming presence'.[92] The soundscape that takes place mirrors the bright orange, near-gold texture of the dystopian LA, with the noise of the bees directing attention to the sparse, surreal surrounding environment of beehives rather than K himself. Like expressionist figures before him, K's state of mind is articulated through sets and sound.

Upon entering the derelict casino, K's moments of discovery remain rooted in touch. When he spots a roulette table, an item he has presumably never

---

[91] *The New York Times*, 'A Scene from Blade Runner 2049 – Anatomy of a Scene' (2017). *YouTube*. https://www.youtube.com/watch?v=S75OKnM_BKU.
[92] Ibid.

FIGURE 68 *K is constantly fascinated by objects he appears not to have encountered. Beyond touch, sound also comes across as a significant point of intrigue. He plays the exact same note on this piano as he does in Sapper's house, as if curious to learn about differences in pitch.*

FIGURE 69 *K's hand is surrounded by the characteristic shadows of film noir, but instead of a world-weary monologue of a bedraggled private detective, the audience only hear the single broken piano note K plays which provokes him to discover and silently inspect the box beneath it.*

seen before, the audience is provided with a close-up of his hand, which delves into the object, picks up the ball and lightly throws it around the wheel. While K's action could have been presented in a medium shot, this choice to focus on the hand this closely represents an explicitly tactile technique in conveying K's approach to the world around him. Moving on, he walks over to the piano and plays a single note with his gloved hand, instantly creating a sonic link with the action he performed at Sapper's house when he spots a piano key that is suspiciously stuck down (Figures 68 and 69).

In that previous instance, a distinctly corporeal moment takes place when K retrieves a small box from within Sapper's piano, and the song 'Memory' begins to play; the audience is instantly alerted to the fact that this object holds significant meaning for K that he does not express in words. Instead, the camera provides a close-up of K's gloved hands. They hold the box to one side, turn it with delicate precision, then slowly lift the lid to reveal a small baby's sock. The camera continues to linger on the hands as they carefully examine the sock, briefly cutting back to K's inscrutable facial expression before returning to the item. K then retrieves a photo. Again, the camera lingers on his hands as he views the image. A single note on the piano provides an emotive connection between two distinct scenes where hands are shown constantly discovering through feeling, 'feeling' understood both in the sense of touch as well as the emotive reaction it creates in the character, and thereby the audience.

Tactility is essential in creating emotions of hope and sorrow within the character of K and in eliciting critical audience response – the audience is forced to travel on K's journey of discovery alongside him. When K enters the darkened orphanage, he is met with the glances of a group of sitting children, who stand up and touch him as K reacts passively; even in the isolated environment of the trash mesa, he remains an outsider, yet also something to be regarded with awe and fascination. When K is eventually granted access to the orphanage records, the camera pans up on his dominating figure before switching around to his back, surrounded by the pitch black of the orphanage as the camera slowly pans down to his hand in close-up, which moves away from his blaster towards a cigarette plate. His hand turns the plate around, revealing part of the item to be shaped in the image of a horse's head. The hand then rests on the table, tightening into a fist. K proceeds to search for the wooden toy horse that he 'remembers' hiding here. The subtle affective signifier of the horse motif, as with the steaming pan in Sapper's house, plays an integral role in elevating the scene's emotional atmosphere.

K reaches slowly into literal darkness as both he and the audience wait in anticipation to see if the horse is real, and if K is truly the prophesied replicant child. After finding a wrapped object in the furnace, the audience witness K slowly and meticulously unfold the material to reveal the horse. Instead of cutting straight to K's shocked expression, the camera lingers for several seconds as K feels the object, as if to check that the item in his hand is truly real and conforms to his touch-memory. The camera then frames K's fingers in extreme close-up as the date on the feet of the horse is focused on, then finally cuts to his disturbed face. His destiny to be the 'chosen one' has seemingly been confirmed upon finding this mythical object (Figure 70).

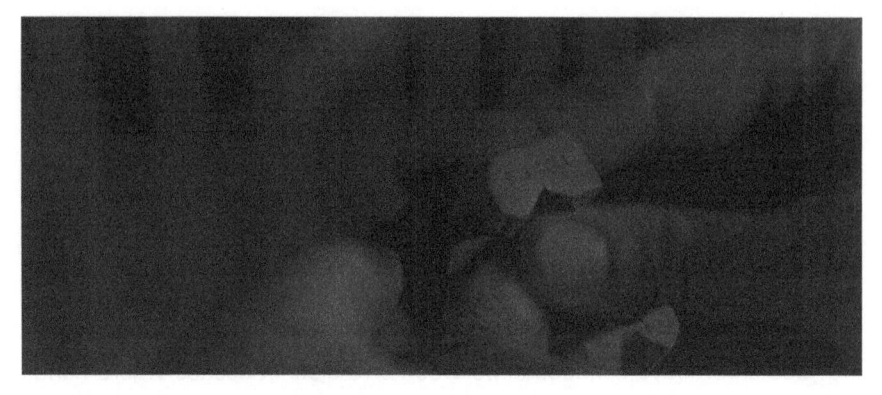

FIGURE 70 *K's fingers feeling the object of his dreams. Rather than simply filming Gosling's whole figure as he touches the object, the filmmakers focus directly on the horse and K's fingers, emphasizing the integral role of tactility in this silent hero's journey of discovery.*

FIGURE 71 *K feels snow for the final time as he stares at his open palm. Snow becomes a physical means for K to explore reality through tactility and to develop his own sense of humanity.*

However, when the audience reaches the final scene in the film and the quest is at an end, K returns Deckard to his daughter, along with the treasured horse. Only Gosling's lower body is in view as K reluctantly reaches into his pocket to return the object to the man he once hoped was his father, emphasizing K's ultimate outsider role despite the nobility of his sacrifice. Once Deckard has gone to meet his daughter, K sits on the steps, checks the wounds which he knows will end his life, and raises a palm to feel the snow on his hand as he did previously after believing himself to be the replicant child (Figure 71).

While the gesture is brief, it takes on a whole new significance when the audience witnesses Ana, the true replicant child, touching artificial snow inside her cell. Even though K is not the chosen one, he nonetheless has felt the real snow Ana has never truly touched. In a poignant echo of Roy Batty's final monologue in *Blade Runner* (also acknowledged here as a form of sonic memory through Hans Zimmer and Benjamin Wallfisch's 'Tears in the Rain' rendition of Vangelis's original track), the audience is shown K silently feeling things that Ana has never felt, just as Batty saw things Deckard had never seen. K's gestural hands have become the ultimate arbiters of self-discovery and expression, devotional objects of grand import.

Hands play a similarly integral characterizing role in the films of Refn. During an interview about *Only God Forgives*, he asserted: 'The idea of a male fist is obviously a sexual extension. It's a combination of sex and violence in the male's hand. But when you open it, it's about submission. And I thought that movement was a movie.'[93] Close-ups of the hand are littered throughout Refn's second collaboration with Gosling, urging the audience to derive meaning from these expressive body parts of a character who barely speaks at all. In a very revealing statement, Gosling has noted that 'the audience is the driver in a sense, and that my character is more like an avatar, a vehicle in which to experience the world and the characters in it',[94] suggesting the importance he places on silence, symbolism and audience response. Through the simple gesture of a contracting hand, Refn claims that masculinity and violence can be voiced. Vicari concurs with Refn's phallic viewpoint, noting how 'the hand substitutes for the penis again and again in the film, and Julian's nightmare is also his most fervent wish: to have it cut off'.[95] Considering these arguments, it is also interesting to observe how this portrayal of masculinity in *Only God Forgives* plays into the idea of the silent hero, particularly in comparison to *Drive*, where Refn presents the audience with what appears to be a far more macho iteration of this silent figure.

The claustrophobic halls that Julian walks through are constantly saturated in a dark, ominous red that pervades the environment and reflects Julian's tortured psyche. Refn, in a very similar fashion to Villeneuve's directions of Gosling during *Blade Runner 2049*'s Las Vegas scene, noted how he and Gosling 'very much talked about the sleepwalk. The man was caught

---

[93] Film at Lincoln Center, 'Nicolas Winding Refn on the Power of Silence' (2013). *YouTube*. https://www.youtube.com/watch?v=6sLr5_1eo7U&t=7s.
[94] Nigel M. Smith, 'Ryan Gosling on Not Understanding All of "Only God Forgives" and How He's Highly Influenced by Violence' (2013). *IndieWire*. https://www.indiewire.com/2013/07/ryan-gosling-on-not-understanding-all-of-only-god-forgives-and-how-hes-highly-influenced-by-violence-36594/.
[95] Vicari, *Nicolas Winding Refn*, 196.

between two worlds and had no will other than to confront his mother'.[96] Like *Caligari*'s Cesare, Julian is a passive walking symbol with little basic directive. When Julian enters a room that is filled with contrasting blue light to wash his hands, the audience might expect a comparative respite from this visual oppression of red. When the camera provides the audience with a close-up of Julian's hands in the sink, however, blood appears to pour out of them in a dream-like sequence. Although the audience are not explicitly told that Julian has killed his father, that he has taken another life with his hands, the recognizable symbolism of imagined, flowing blood already confirms this thought; as Macbeth was unable to wash away his violent actions with all of Neptune's ocean, so too is Julian unable to wipe out the act which his hands have performed. From Refn's phallic point of view, these open, submissive hands represent Julian's stifled masculinity, unable to kill the man who killed his brother. His hands provide an externalized symbol of the guilt Julian still harbours and is unable to reconcile. Instead of seeing heroic hands that beat up bad guys and protect the girl, the filmmakers use hands to tell a far darker and more complicated narrative of vulnerability and torment.

In *Drive*, however, the audience's first exposure to Driver's use of violence takes place in scenes of comparatively controlled action and authority. Driver sits in a motel room following the botched heist. Looking down at the phone belonging to Blanche, he says nothing, but a slow turn of his head towards the door and the camera panning in on his face immediately alerts the audience to impending danger. Slow motion shots ensue as brutal violence takes place, with Gosling preparing to initiate his defence. Once he is prepared, the scene returns to real time as Driver grabs the assailant's gun, punches him repeatedly then employs a curtain rack to impale him. Driver then swiftly grabs the gun and uses it to kill the second attacker. He checks outside the window, then looks back again, with another close-up emphasizing his still, now-bloody facial expression. In both expressionist close-ups, Driver has remained calm and composed despite the chaos and violence he has delivered. His hands have efficiently and economically ended the lives of his enemies, and no symbolic remorse is evident in his act. Instead, Driver's closed fists and violent actions represent a silent hero that is in his element when he is killing, not saying a word or receiving a single wound as he dispatches his enemies (Figure 72).

Ultimately, as in *Blade Runner 2049*, both *Drive* and *Only God Forgives* involve filmmakers using gesture to offer up their silent heroes as symbols of sacrifice. After a battered Julian has saved Chang's daughter and has been

---

[96] JoBlo Movie Trailers, 'Nicolas Winding Refn NY Interview – Only God Forgives' (2013). *YouTube.* https://www.youtube.com/watch?v=R3n-TG4V4-U.

FIGURE 72 *Driver coolly surveys the motel after his murders to check for any more potential targets. Blood is splattered on the wall and his face, but none of the blood is his own. As such, the red liquid resembles a form of war paint, a bloody mark of acknowledgement for the deaths that Driver has successfully delivered.*

freed from his mother, he sits on a sofa and is approached by Chang. Neither exchange a word, and the camera suddenly cuts to an image of Julian's open, sacrificial palms moving slowly onto the screen. The ground below him is no longer the darkly lit room Julian was sitting in, but a forest. Chang is then shot in this dreamlike sequence as jarring music begins to play. The cuts between Julian and Chang's facial expressions do not reflect the tension of the standoff between Bernie and Driver in *Drive*; Julian stands still as Chang approaches, clenching his fists in anticipation of Chang's judgement. The camera cuts back and forth between the darkened image of a sword held in Chang's hand – which has been shown repeatedly throughout the film – and the scene in the forest where Chang raises his sword. Julian is shot in close-up with his head bowed and eyes closed, and the action of the blade cutting Julian's hands is not shown, as the camera instead cuts to a bizarre karaoke scene with Chang.

In the penultimate scene of *Drive*, when the camera slowly pans up from the bottom of the car to reveal Driver's still, potentially dead body, the unnatural golden light that sears through the car's window implies a symbolic death, as if Driver has passed into the next life (Figure 73). Yet Driver's single blink, and the camera's panning back to a close-up of his hand as he starts his mythical vehicle signify his apparent resurrection. While Julian sacrifices his hands to pay for the deaths he has enacted, the final images of Driver's hands calmly commanding the steering wheel of his car as he drives into the darkness present a wildly different perception of masculinity. Driver fulfils the

FIGURE 73 *Driver sits still in his car after being stabbed, making the audience question if he is alive. Once the golden light is particularly strong, a single blink confirms he is living.*

role of the classical silent hero by retaining his violent nature and his distance from society, whereas Julian purges his violent past with the physical removal of Refn's symbols of sex and violence entirely.

Gesture, as a means of encouraging an audience's critical response through economic use of movement, is highlighted particularly effectively during the dramatic crescendo of *First Man*, as Gosling's Neil Armstrong stands on the moon. After watching his colleague move into the distance, the camera cuts to flashbacks of Armstrong on Earth with his daughter Karen, with one of these images showing him holding Karen in his arms. The camera then cuts back to Armstrong by a crater. With his outer visor now removed, revealing his sad facial expression, the camera cuts to an image of his closed hand, which significantly opens to reveal Karen's bracelet in his palm, which he lets slide into the abyss (Figure 74).

The audience have only witnessed Armstrong holding the object a few times throughout the movie, never speaking to another person about it. By only filming the object of the bracelet sparingly, its symbolic inclusion and sacrifice in the crater scene makes its loss – and Armstrong's emotional acceptance of the loss of Karen – all the more poignant and heartfelt. In a similar fashion to K and the horse, these affective signifiers are invested with an emotional significance beyond their mere physical form. Armstrong's moment of sacrifice takes place inside his space suit, a metaphorical armour in which he can finally express his personal pain away from the Earth – he is literally far from the boundaries of human civilization. The other silent male heroes I have discussed go through a similar process of physical and emotional pain before they can carry out their ultimate sacrificial act. K is savagely attacked by Luv, Julian by Chang and Driver by Bernie. Through Gosling's various bloody,

FIGURE 74 *Only the open hand of Neil Armstrong and the bracelet he has let go of are shown, emphasizing the intimate relationship between a father and daughter whose loss has now been accepted through this release.*

broken faces and emotive hands, a frequently violent yet distinctly vulnerable depiction of the silent hero is enacted.

Throughout all these films, gesture, in the form of both heightened facial expression and controlled movements, is highlighted by filmmakers through the use of stylized editing techniques. The emotive power of the Kuleshov effect, for example – a montage technique developed in early 20th-century film – is at play in the supermarket scene in *Drive*, in which Driver 'meets' Irene and Benicio. No verbal interaction takes place, but we witness Driver in a series of sequential shots, his blank face staring into the distance as he walks down an aisle, only to turn a corner and stop and stare. The following image of Driver's focus of attention is of Irene and Benicio shopping. Yet the camera then cuts to Driver in tracking shot, now focusing on his back as he walks then stops to eavesdrop on their conversation. Rather than showing intimacy between the characters, the filmmaker's use of the effect does the opposite, emphasizing disconnect and Driver's own antisocial tendencies. It is also important that it is Driver's face we see first in this example of the Kuleshov effect. John Preston Isenhour refers to a filmic experiment by scholar J. M. Foley where, 'given a close-up of an actor with a neutral expression and a shot of a pretty girl, the meaning of a sequence depends on whether one sees the shot of the girl or the shot of the man first'.[97] If the audience had

---

[97] Isenhour, 'The Effects of Context and Order in Film Editing', 72.

FIGURE 75 *Freed from prison, Standard toasts his wife Irene during a house party.*

FIGURE 76 *In the second part of this Kuleshov effect, the image of Irene clearly indicates that it is her that Standard is toasting.*

witnessed the shot of Irene and Benicio first in this instance, then the switch to Gosling eavesdropping may have come across as decidedly more sinister. However, in the film's order of images, the first shot of Gosling's blank, still facial expression provides the audience with the opportunity to form their own subjective interpretation of his psychological state.

The Kuleshov effect is also employed during Standard's party, where Driver is working in a darkened room and Irene is in her nearby flat, characteristically framed in front of a symbolic, orange-coloured wall. Although Irene appears to be staring at Standard during his speech, the camera zooms in on her facial expression after he finishes talking and cuts back to Gosling in his room staring despondently at his work desk (Figures 75, 76 and 77).

FIGURE 77 *In this next image, however, the Kuleshov effect is subverted, suggesting that, while Irene is looking at Standard, she is actually thinking about Driver in a separate location.*

The camera cuts to Irene, then to Gosling, who stands up, dons the scorpion jacket, and leaves his apartment. This stylized editing technique implies a relationship across different locations, breaking any sense of reality as the man Irene is implied to be thinking about is not the husband in front of her eyes, but the man several rooms away. The Kuleshov effect emphasizes the powerful effect of still, intense facial expressions through aesthetic filmic techniques.

Filmmakers in *Only God Forgives* also employ the Kuleshov technique to powerful effect. Gosling's Julian says even fewer words than Driver, and the audience are thereby forced to use his long, traumatized stares as a primary source of narrative exposition. Tied to a chair while he watches Mai, Gosling is framed in medium shot as he sits still, then the camera pans in on his blank facial expression. The next shot the audience see is of a darkened door, followed by an image of Julian walking through claustrophobic, saturated red halls towards this entrance. Both images are separated from the room we see Julian in during the first image, suggesting that the character is in a hallucinatory dream state. Julian places a hand on the door, and the audience witness a close-up panning shot of Julian's arm, which is swiftly cut off by Chang, who appears outside the door in a subsequent image before the camera returns to a close-up of Julian's disturbed expression. Through this stylized filming technique, Gosling's facial expression is scrutinized to decipher his confused emotional state. Editing is employed in this example to disorientate the audience, and the chronological ordering (or lack of order) of each image is essential to creating these feelings of narrative unease. Gosling's face is necessarily shown first so the audience can understand that the subsequent images are what this man is witnessing in his mind. Likewise, the image of his disturbed expression at the end of the sequence is essential to convey the fact that he has witnessed Chang and the metaphorical removal of his own arm.

4

Sound and Music

Speaking about his inspirations for 'A Real Hero', the song that made *Drive* iconic, co-writer David Grellier cited the character Max Rockatansky from the *Mad Max* series of films, describing how he 'wanted to give a homage to that lonely hero that we see in movies like *Mad Max*. People who make their own choice and try to save lives'.[1] Loneliness is a central trait of the silent hero, and the lyrics of 'A Real Hero' fit perfectly with Driver's sacrificial journey. Electric Youth frontman Austin Garrick notes that the line about a man saving 'One-hundred fifty-five people on board' is a direct reference to the actions of US pilot Sully Sullenberger, who saved all these citizens on his plane by initiating a water landing during a flight in 2009. However, the subsequent lyrics stating that these people are 'All safe and rescued/From the slowly sinking ship' neatly fit with the saved characters of Irene and Benicio. In *Drive*, the song first plays during Driver's trip through LA with the family, and the joyous nature of the journey is mirrored in the pathetic fallacy of heightened, intense sunlight, a far cry from the darkness in which the city has previously been shot. When the song is heard for the second and final time during the film's climax, it is after the audience has endured the silence of painful anticipation as the camera stays fixed on Driver's face, knowing he has finally secured Irene and Benicio's safety, but unsure whether Driver is dead. The audience hears the song begin slowly as the face remains still. However, as the volume slowly increases and the trance-like techno pulses start to build, the face finally blinks and the volume increases further into triumphant synth beats. Like his Western predecessor Shane, we see a revived Driver

---

[1] Mikey O'Connell, ''Drive Song Inspired by Captain Sully Sullenberger and Mad Max' (2011). *The Hollywood Reporter*. https://www.hollywoodreporter.com/movies/movie-news/drive-soundtrack-captain-sully-254349/.

disappear into the distance. The images of light that the audience witness alongside their first hearing of the song are revisited with its second inclusion, creating a heavenly visage for the hero through its associations with healing and heroism.

Chion's theories of sound will play a key role in this chapter, particularly in the area of what he terms synchresis, 'the forging of an immediate and necessary relationship between something one sees and something one hears'.[2] While Chion outlines the notion of synchresis primarily in terms of a sound that appears to emanate 'naturally' from that contained in the image, I want to expand the notion of synchresis to engage those music-to-image relations usually conceived more simplistically in terms of 'association'. By extending the notion of synchresis to address music-to-image relations (something that is suggested but not fully realized in Chion) the audience are better able to explore the intimate and vital role music plays in constructing our narrative understanding. For example, in *Drive*, the first use of 'A Real Hero' links with the chivalric image of Driver as he chaperones the innocent Irene and Benicio across LA in his car. Once we begin to hear this song again near the film's conclusion, as Driver's body slumps motionlessly inside the car, it provides the audience with a form of sonic memory and the hope that this song will now resurrect Driver as a reward for his heroic act. If the song was not repeated in this scene, then the emotional link between Driver's acts of heroism in the two scenes would not be fully established. This song, which is about heroism and sacrifice, becomes synonymous with the figure of Driver.

The Heroic Leitmotif

Music not only directs audience critical response in scenes containing nonverbal communication, but it can also evoke a character's whole narrative journey and emotional development, particularly through the device of the leitmotif, which allows audiences, through synchresis, to connect the music to recurrent narrative themes. In *Film Music: A History*, James Wierzbicki describes how, in the simple notion of this term, leitmotifs 'signal the mere presence of whatever character, object, action or emotion with which they are associated'. In their more complex form, however, 'they indicate serious changes in affect or situation'.[3] The audience witness this complex musical development in *Drive* when Irene talks to a monosyllabic Driver in her home and asks about his profession, a scene previously referred to in

---

[2] Chion, *Audio-Vision*, 5.
[3] Wierzbicki, *Film Music*, 60.

the introduction. When Driver responds with the simple phrase 'I drive', Cliff Martinez's song of the same name begins to play as the two characters stare at each other. Chion's concept of added value is clear in the first instance of the song's usage: Martinez's heavenly sounds articulate the connection that is beginning to surface between the two laconic characters who, at no stage in the film, ever feel the need to utter that overused, three-word phrase. Martinez described this music as the film's 'love theme', which was also the thing that had 'the most hymnal quality, the most overtly religious theme'.[4] Martinez also noted his use of wind chimes in the love theme as one of his 'main ambient textures' and that this was one of the instruments 'that was manipulated the most'.[5] This musical manipulation continues with the slow, ambient sounds of Martinez's 'He Had a Good Time'. The song, like 'I Drive', plays shortly after Irene has made this same short statement. In both cases, music is used to fill the space that is left by pauses in speech. Music can play an important role in constructing narrative – in this case the growing relationship between Irene and Driver has been forged and solidified in the audience's imagination through Martinez's ambient score.

The next time the audience hears these hymnal sounds is in the elevator scene, where Martinez's 'Wrong Floor' begins playing, again, as in the previous examples, after a character (in this case, Driver's assailant, named in the credits only as Tan Suit) has spoken these exact words. The love theme reaches its climax in this particular scene, as the two figures embrace before Driver prepares to violently protect the woman he now knows he will never be able to stay with. Without the confirmation provided by Martinez's now-familiar refrain, the love between Irene and Driver would not be fully realized in the audience's imagination. With the inclusion of 'Wrong Floor', the emotional connection between these two figures is cemented. When the audience hears these same ambient chimes for the final time, however, they appear over two-thirds of the way through Martinez's six-and-a-half-minute song 'On the Beach'. Unlike previous examples, no character ever utters this phrase, and Irene is not pictured alongside Driver as the song begins to play. Instead, it plays shortly after Bernie has assured Driver of Irene's safety, an assurance that he evidently does not believe. As Driver reaches the final stages of his heroic development, no words are necessary. When he is stabbed by Bernie and he stabs Bernie in turn, he knows without a doubt that Irene's safety is secured. Although she is no longer physically next to Driver in these final images of the film, Martinez's familiar heavenly chimes play and the audience's

---

[4] Lakeshore Records, 'Cliff Martinez – Driver Composer Interview HD' (2011). *YouTube.* https://www.youtube.com/watch?v=sTwpfUbkxcQ.
[5] Ibid.

knowledge of her safety that results from Driver's heroic act releases the two from their previous sound-image relationship. The leitmotif has reached its final stage, with Driver separated from Irene but safe in the knowledge that he has performed a noble act, having finally evolved into the real hero of the film's last song.

Just as Martinez makes his love theme one of *Drive*'s central leitmotifs, composer Benjamin Wallfisch cites his *Blade Runner 2049* 'puzzle theme'[6] in the film's opening composition '2049' as an important means to signal K's narrative development. He notes how 'whenever there's another piece of the puzzle that propels K's discoveries and sense of personal crisis, we hear those chords as a reminder that there's a sense of fate to the maze he is in'. Like Martinez's chimes, Wallfisch also describes how this acoustic piano 'was heavily processed using granular synthesis as a kind of granular analogue to the idea of something natural being transformed, almost like a replicant'.[7] Musical manipulation is an essential element required to articulate the feelings of a character who is withdrawn. Wallfisch also describes the importance of the four notes that play during *Blade Runner 2049*'s opening shots, remarking how he refers to this simple tune as either the 'horse theme' or the 'soul theme'.[8] The physical object that K becomes so entranced by receives its own musical cue and articulates an obsession which K refuses to voice in words. As Wallfisch observes, 'The melody takes on different guises, expands and contracts as the story unfolds and we hear it mainly when K makes a significant discovery' and Wallfisch praises 'the idea of complexity built on immense simplicity'.[9] Echoing Sontag, less defiantly asserts itself as more. Only four piano notes are used in the opening titles to convey this sense of mystery and confusion; a more complex composition might bombard the audience with too much sensory material to process as they witness the opening text onscreen (itself a nod to the expository intertitles used in expressionist film, albeit far more intricate). By starting simply, Wallfisch can then manipulate these four notes far more effectively to elicit critical audience responses.

Accepting Chion's idea of the empathetic effect, which he describes as music that 'can directly express its participation in the feeling of a scene by taking on the scene's rhythm, tone, and phrasing',[10] audience critical response

---

[6] Adam Chitwood, '*Blade Runner 2049* Composer Benjamin Wallfisch on the Unique Score, Experimenting, & Vangelis' (2017). *Collider*. https://collider.com/blade-runner-2049-benjamin-wallfisch-interview/.
[7] Ibid.
[8] Ibid.
[9] Ibid.
[10] Chion, *Audio-Vision*, 8.

to K's journey becomes more active. In the first use of the four notes, K's subservience is emphasized. The notes play during a bleak wide shot, where the camera pans over a dystopian California. K's spinner appears in the middle of the shot, yet the vehicle's size pales in comparison to the gargantuan, lifeless structures beneath it, and the spinner disappears into the distance only seconds after it has appeared. Nothing is discovered at this point and K is rendered as little more than an ant within the totalitarian structure of the world in which he works. These sharp, cacophonic notes participate in the scene to create an empathetic effect by mirroring K's marginalized, oppressed position as well as commenting on the plastic environment that surrounds him.

Wallfisch's four notes resurface when Joshi asks K to provide her with a memory from when he was a child. A reluctant K begins to relate a story about a horse and a flashback scene appears as the music begins to play. The notes sound much gentler and less synthesized as K tells the tale. Confusion and intrigue are cultivated here on several levels through the disruption of chronology with the use of flashback imagery, K's voiceover and the slow, hypnotic sounds of the piano, all evoking a heightened, dream-like atmosphere. Even though K is unsure about the nature of this memory, believing himself to be a replicant at this stage in the plot, the lack of sharpness in tone nonetheless suggests the relaxing and comforting sense of humanity and stability that these images are designed to instil in him. At this stage, the music signals K's passivity through his acceptance of the memory's artificial nature.

As the notes occur again in 'Furnace', however, they are far more abrasive and intense, underlaid with an apocalyptic drone. K slowly moves towards the furnace that he both fears and hopes will contain the horse of his memory. When he finds the horse and notices the inscription on its feet, the percussive piano sounds reach an emotional crescendo. Bassist Nico Abondolo was told to play his double-bass 'uncomfortably high', and co-composer Hans Zimmer noted in relation to musical composition that, 'If it doesn't hurt, it can't be right.'[11] Distortion and jarringly high sounds are necessary in *Blade Runner 2049* to fully articulate K's internal turmoil. Abondolo's cello and violins were incorporated in 'a pivotal, unbelievable point of *Blade Runner 2049*'.[12] Although this specific scene is not revealed in the article, the quote likely refers to this key moment of discovery where, through empathetic effect, the heightened music is precisely designed to mirror K's facial expression and emotional state (Figure 78).

When the leitmotif reappears in 'Someone Lived This', where Ana reveals that the memory of the horse is real, the four notes serve to return the audience to the uneasiness and emotional pain of these earlier scenes, as

---

[11] Lobenfeld, '*Blade Runner 2049*'.
[12] Ibid.

FIGURE 78 *K's expression of hope and fear is accompanied by apocalyptic synth drones alongside Wallfisch's haunting 'soul theme', articulating emotions that K will not describe in words.*

K lets out his only verbal outburst in the movie – the single, angst-ridden exclamation of 'Goddammit'.

Once K has been told that he is not the prophesied child, however, the four notes that resurface in 'That's Why We Believe' are gentle, quiet and distinctly mournful. Alongside K, the audience learns he is not the person he craved to be. Following this moment of discovery, the four notes subsequently disappear from the score and are only used again briefly during the film's end credits song 'Blade Runner'. In this final ten-minute compilation, the four notes are included alongside previously used songs such as 'Mesa' and 'Sea Wall', the latter song playing during K's final heroic act as he saves Deckard. The audience are invited to relive K's emotional journey through a compilation of repeated sounds. Images alone are no longer required to evoke the pain and heroism of K's lonely sacrifice.

In *First Man*, a leitmotif is used in powerful empathetic effect to elegize Armstrong's daughter Karen (Lucy Stafford), who dies when his journeys into space have barely begun. In the leitmotif's first iteration, which composer Justin Hurwitz appropriately titled 'Karen' and composed with gentle harp notes, the titular character is lying in bed at home, with Armstrong's hand stroking through her hair. The camera pans to Armstrong's concerned facial expression, but quickly cuts back to his hand in extreme close-up, which continues to tentatively feel Karen's hair strands. The camera holds this poignant image as Hurwitz's song continues to play and the camera slowly pans down to Karen's sleeping face. Yet in the next brutal cut, as Hurwitz's song stops, the audience see the tragic facial expression of Armstrong's wife Janet (Claire Foy) outside, followed by that of their son Ricky (Gavin Warren), before a small coffin is seen being lowered into the ground. The audience have been disorientated both by the change in location, from internal to external, as well as the loss of Hurwitz's music. When the camera cuts to Armstrong, the audience witness both his still, controlled facial expression and, significantly, another extreme close-up of his hands holding Karen's bracelet, a shot referred to later in the film's climactic scene when Armstrong holds the bracelet in space. With Karen gone, the song likewise disappears, underlining a sense of pain alongside shots of the silent, grieving family members.

Despite Karen's death, her constant presence in Armstrong's thoughts is signalled throughout the film with the repetition of this gentle tune. When Janet encourages Armstrong to join the Apollo 11 project, it is her character that speaks the title of the song, 'It'll Be an Adventure'. Yet the melody which plays, with the exception of its louder, bombastic conclusion, mirrors the notation of 'Karen', suggesting that the 'adventure' for Neil is not centred around his wife, or even about the adventure of going to the moon, but the opportunity to try and come to terms with his personal grief about his lost daughter. The concept of Chion's anempathetic effect can also start to be seen, where 'music can ... exhibit conspicuous indifference to the situation, by progression in a steady, undaunted, and ineluctable manner, like a written text or a *machine* that's running'.[13] What is being said by Janet and what is being thought by a laconic, emotionally insulated Armstrong are shown to be at odds through the dissonance between speech and music. A similar example can be noted again during Hurwitz's 'Baby Mark'. As this song plays and Neil stares blankly at his second son in a cot, the audience might expect a different song to signify this new arrival, perhaps something heart-warming and joyous, yet the music that plays is the same heart-breaking leitmotif of 'Karen'. Despite the expected happy presence of Armstrong's third child, Hurwitz's music undercuts the images on screen to suggest that no child can replace his first and only daughter. Chion also notes how the anempathetic mode 'has the effect not of freezing emotion but intensifying it, by inscribing it onto a cosmic background'.[14] By highlighting this discordance between what is said and seen and what is heard, Armstrong's blank facial expression is rendered more emotive and pathetic, and the audience's critical response is intensified.

When Armstrong has left the boundaries of Earth and is searching for the Agena Target Vehicle, 'Squawk Box' (a further iteration of the 'Karen' leitmotif) starts to play and the camera focuses on a wide shot of space. The earth is framed on the left and Armstrong's ship on the right, with only the darkness of space in between. Armstrong's basic directives, docking his ship with the

---

[13] Chion, *Audio-Vision*, 8. Emphasis added.
[14] Ibid.

Agena and returning home, are laid out in a clear image. Yet the song continues as the camera cuts to Armstrong's son Ricky pulling up the American flag back on Earth. In a brief visual and aural metaphor, the audience are shown that both country and family are secondary factors to Armstrong's solitary ruminations on Karen as he floats in space. The camera subsequently cuts back and forth between Armstrong's family and the mission in space. Even when the leitmotif starts to intercut and combine with the booming sounds of the ship as Armstrong is framed in extreme, shaky-cam close-ups when he tries to stabilize the vehicle, the soft harp sounds remain until the ship has stopped in a safe position. The gentle sounds that the audience have come to associate with Karen act as a form of musical protection, as if Armstrong's daughter is guiding him to safety from the heavens.

By the time the Karen motif reaches its emotional crescendo in Hurwitz's 'Crater', the harp sounds have evolved into an otherworldly theremin, an instrument which Ryan Gosling discovered was a favourite of the real Armstrong, and which Adam Epstein describes as the film's 'unlikeliest star',[15] almost becoming a character in itself. The camera shows the distraught Armstrong in complete silence, echoed by the surrounding cosmic silence of space, as he regards his beloved daughter's bracelet in his hand. It is only after he releases this object into the darkness of the abyss that 'Crater' begins to play, signifying Armstrong's release from grief and torment in extradiegetic form. The motif makes its final appearance in the film's last scene, where Hurwitz's 'Quarantine' articulates the silent relief of the reunited family and where, as in *Blade Runner 2049*, reconciliation is conveyed visually with the simple gesture of hands pressed against glass (Figures 79 and 80).

Emotive Sound

All the films I have discussed so far employ sound – specifically extradiegetic sound – as an integral device to cultivate audience response. Since one of the primary forms of diegetic sound – speech – is largely absent in these silent hero films, the audience are provided with an opportunity to pour their imagination and critical responses into a less expository medium. This effect is clear in *Drive*, for example, when Driver goes to a nightclub to confront Cook about threatening Benicio, seemingly unarmed. The diegetic music emanating from the club is heard in the background as Driver strides down a corridor

---

[15] '"First Man" Stars One of the World's Weirdest Musical Instruments' (2018). *Quartz.* https://qz.com/quartzy/1422234/the-other-star-of-first-man-is-one-of-the-worlds-weirdest-musical-instruments/.

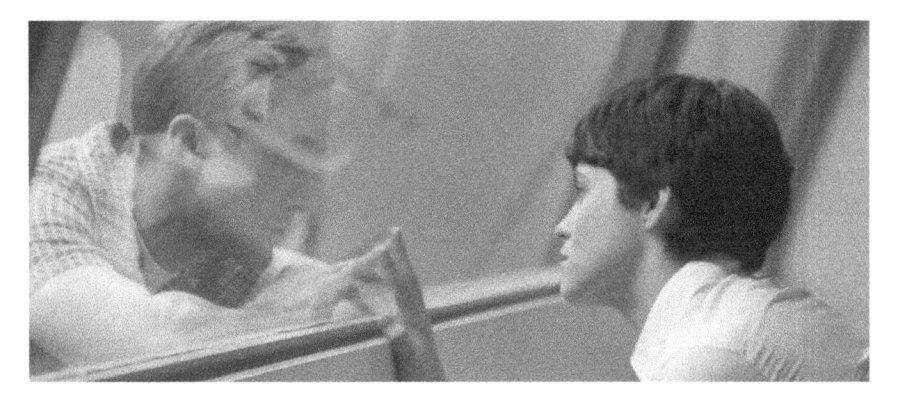

FIGURE 79 *Instead of extensive dialogue or even pithy phrases, the Armstrongs' reconciliation is rendered through small but significant hand gestures.*

FIGURE 80 *Meeting his daughter for the first time, Deckard likewise chooses not to engage in any futile uses of speech, instead beginning his reconnection by offering a single, open hand.*

and bluntly asks a worker about Cook's whereabouts. The distracted worker directs him towards his location before returning to her phone. Everything the audience witness so far in terms of sound is diegetic. The music that opens the scene positions the audience in the realm of a nightclub, a position which is confirmed by the tacky imagery of tinsel adorning the wall by the worker, the dull brick wall on the right and the blunt expository dialogue. As Driver turns, the camera briefly frames him in tracking shot and then films him from a distance, as if wary, as he walks down the final corridor to Cook's location. With his iconic scorpion jacket in full view, Driver reaches into his pocket to retrieve a hammer. The next cut only shows him below the neck as he wields the weapon, at which point the nightclub music stops and a loud 'braaam' noise floods the audience's aural perception. Distinctly booming, synthetic and designed to 'impart a sense of apocalyptic momentousness'[16] to the film, these sounds as used here are unlike anything the audience have heard before and are clearly positioned outside the world of the film, symbolically representing the menace of a weapon whose wielder's face does not even need to be shown to evoke threat. From the moment this extradiegetic sound is heard, the audience know violence is about to take place, even though the noise clearly does not emanate from the hammer itself.

As Driver enters Cook's domain, the intimidating braam noise disappears as Driver proceeds to methodically slam down the hammer three times on Cook's exposed hands. The braam noise plays again as Cook is kicked to the floor, replaced by a low synth as Driver threatens him with the hammer. When Cook refuses to give him a satisfactory answer, Driver raises his hammer arm, with the camera switching to a medium shot as the surrounding women passively look on. The subsequent extreme close-up of Gosling combined with the barely audible extradiegetic synth rumbles creates a disturbing image of masculine menace. With a speech-blocking toothpick placed firmly in his mouth and framed by the popping reds of the curtains, the image of Driver dominating the entire image with his unseen weapon and expression of derisive anger could be lifted straight out of a comic book (Figure 81). No loud dramatic sound is required here to articulate the fact that Driver is not a man to be trifled with.

The following phone conversation between Driver and Nino also plays out with a particularly coded masculinity. Nino does not even bother to acknowledge Driver with a 'hello', getting straight to the point by tersely asking: 'You got something that fuckin' belongs to me?' The camera switches to an extreme low angle shot of Driver as the audience also listen to the palpable diegetic sounds of his gloved hand squeezing the hammer in violent anticipation. Driver follows up with a taciturn 'seems that way' as the low synth sounds continue in the background. After switching to Nino's bemused reaction in the pizzeria, the camera cuts back to a tense Driver, evidenced by the subtle shakes of his hammer hand and his increased breaths along with a slightly higher voice pitch; imagery and sound work in tandem to evoke the nervous tension behind Driver's surface cool. When Nino mocks the fact that Driver isn't working with anyone and hasn't discussed his plan with anyone else, the camera slowly zooms in on Nino's face as if to suggest that he has won the argument, but Driver's silence followed by the sound of the phone

---

[16] 'Braaams for Beginners: How a Horn Sound Ate Hollywood' (2015). *Hollywood Reporter*. https://www.hollywoodreporter.com/movies/movie-news/braaams-beginners-how-a-horn-793220/.

FIGURE 81 *Tension and unease are created in the audience here through recognizable signifiers; Driver never performs his acts of violence without his faithful scorpion jacket, and the signature toothpick in his mouth signals danger for his hapless victim. The heightened reality of the scene is accentuated by the extreme close-up alongside the theatrical element added by the blood-red curtains which frame Driver's furious, violent figure.*

cutting off lets the audience know that Driver has gained the upper hand. By refusing to acknowledge Nino's taunts with a single word, he retains control in the masculine power play, intimidating Nino to the extent that he sends a hitman after Driver as the tense synths continue to rumble quietly in the soundscape. Nothing has been resolved and the ominous synth sounds telegraph that more violence is about to take place.

Sound design is also a central means of conveying stylized violence in *Drive*'s subsequent elevator scene. Award-winning sound editor Mark Berger notes how, in terms of audio design, 'the criterion isn't authenticity. It's *perceived* authenticity'.[17] Sound is used in the scene to evoke the *idea* of violence, just as music and imagery were used in earlier expressionist film to evoke a sense of dread and foreboding in the audience's imagination without ever actually showing the violent acts themselves, such as the murders in *Cailgari*. *Drive*'s supervising sound editor Lon Bender acknowledges how he 'removed the elevator noise in the moments before the action begins', mirroring the sound techniques used in Martin Scorsese's 1980 film *Raging Bull* . From the start of the scene, stylized sound design is central to evoking an atmosphere of tension, with silence anticipating the arrival of sound. The extradiegetic sounds employed to resemble noises of diegetic violence during the skull-crushing moment are not those of real kicking or punching, but are

---

[17] 'The Sounds of Violence' (2012). *Slate*. https://slate.com/culture/2012/02/drive-the-sound-editing-in-the-elevator-stomping-scene.html. Emphasis in original.

FIGURE 82 *Aside from a very brief cut to the corpse of Driver's brutalized assailant, disgust is evoked in the elevator scene primarily through sound. While Driver's crazed maniacal expression evokes a certain amount of unease within the audience, it is the sounds they hear and gory images they are forced to imagine that create the greatest emotional and visceral impact.*

'the slowed-down noise of cracking nuts', 'the sloshing of a viscous liquid' and even a track of 'Ryan Gosling breathing and snorting and firing spittle'.[18] A wide variety of strange, distorted sounds are utilized to convey the horror of Driver's gory actions (Figure 82).

The origins of the sounds of violence that take place on screen are decidedly unnatural and stylized and it is significant that all naturalistic sounds of the physical environment – elevator noises – are removed completely.

First Man composer Justin Hurwitz uses a similarly stylized approach to sound, particularly in the moon landing scene. The camera swiftly pans to the door of the ship as it opens, and the audience hear the rushing of air, followed by a wide shot of the moon's surface. In the following images of the men undoing their seatbelts, the audience might expect to hear the diegetic sound of the object unclicking, but Hurwitz lets the audience experience silence as the men prepare to walk on the moon's surface. Only Armstrong's breathing can be heard as we finally hear diegetic noise. His breaths are heard while the camera frames a point-of view shot, with the audience experiencing Armstrong's journey alongside him in a similar fashion to that of Louise in *Arrival*. After providing obligatory responses to his superiors, including his 'One small step' lines, he experiences the wonder of the moon in silence, with a swift panning shot of the surface as Hurwitz's 'Moon Walk' begins to

---

[18] Ibid.

FIGURE 83 *Armstrong allows his mournful face to be seen as he releases Karen's bracelet into the abyss. Affective response is all the more powerful in this scene because of Armstrong's repressed emotions on Earth, only exhibiting his grief in a short moment far away from his home.*

play. No expressions of amazement or shock are spoken by Armstrong, with image and extradiegetic sound replacing expository dialogue (Figure 83).

Emotional audience response is also cultivated through the stylized split cut technique of the J-cut, where audio from the following scene starts playing during the preceding scene, as in the example of the baseline test discussed in Chapter 2. Image and sound are not synched. In the films I have discussed, J-cuts are employed to intensify audience critical responses through disorientation, with off-screen sounds, described by Chion as those which 'meander at the surface'[19] contrasted by onscreen sound when sound and image subsequently synch. In *First Man*, for example, these effects provoke a foreboding pathos regarding the death of Karen. After Armstrong has completed his perilous flight in the X-15 vehicle, he walks silently through a desert landscape, where only the quiet sounds of wind can be heard. However, the noise of a machine suddenly starts to be heard that is clearly not connected to the image on screen. The audience is compelled to wonder where this alien sound is originating from. In the space of a couple of seconds, the camera cuts to an extreme close-up of a hand in a darkened room and images of unrecognizable faces. The sound's source is still unclear. In the next image, however, the audience finally discover its origin as they witness a radiotherapy

---

[19] Chion, *Audio-Vision*, 68.

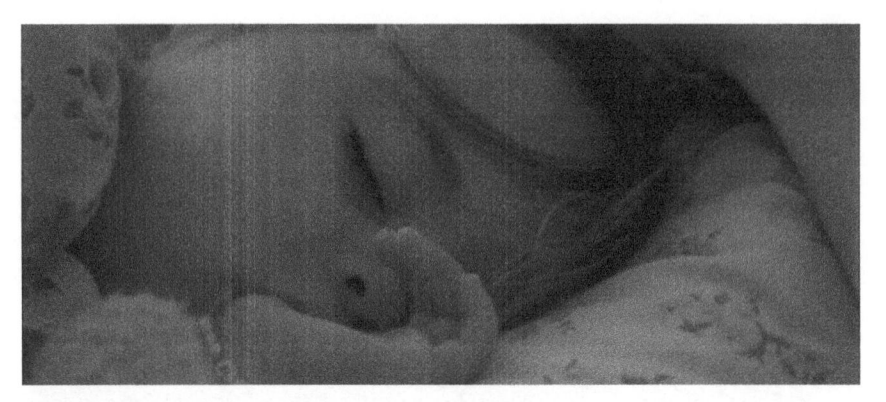

FIGURE 84 *During this J-cut, Karen Armstrong sleeps in bed while her father feels her hair, and unknown squeaking sounds start to be heard.*

FIGURE 85 *After cutting to the facial expressions of Janet and Mark Armstrong in an external environment, the source of the squeaking is revealed to be a casket-lowering device.*

machine towering above a still Karen. Image and sound are now connected, thereby transitioning the noise into an onscreen diegetic sound. Through this audial transition, the audience experience confusion followed by sadness as image and sound become coherent. In a similar use of the J-cut, the noise of Hurwitz's 'Karen' that plays over the image of her sleeping face becomes intertwined with the sound of a turning wheel. As before, the audience have no idea where this sound emanates from, and the camera cuts to an outside environment with Janet and her son Ricky's sad facial expressions, before an image reveals the source of the sound to be a casket-lowering device as Karen's coffin descends into the ground (Figures 84 and 85). This swift movement from off-screen to onscreen sound creates a powerful emotional response, where the audience are forced to both anticipate and contemplate a child's death.

In *Blade Runner 2049*, J-cuts are used to represent K's oppressed role as a replicant and to emphasize the brutality of the world in which he is forced to work. In the forensic department of the LAPD, K zooms in on an image of the remains he found under Sapper's tree. A close-up of the number that K discovers is displayed, indicating that the woman who gave birth was a replicant. As this image is on screen, we hear his boss Joshi declaring that such a discovery is not possible. The audience might expect the camera to cut back to an image of her saying these words, but the next cut shows that the conversation between herself and K is actually taking place in a separate LAPD room. Rather than provide shots of K and Joshi walking from the laboratory to this separate room, the filmmakers instead cut directly to this next interaction, initially shot from outside the building with their figures blurred by rain, which has the effect of revealing the bleak functionality of their daily routine and the harsh nature of their relationship. In similarly brutal fashion, after a worker is killed by Luv in order to steal the remains, the audience do not hear any extensive eulogy for the worker from the department. Instead, while the camera shows the body still lying on the floor, the audience hear the off-screen sound of Joshi's voice laconically mentioning his death, before it cuts to her continuing speech, now in clear diegetic form as the audience see her talking to K in his apartment. Joshi's dialogue, already economic and frequently terse towards her junior officer, is highlighted even more intensely through the use of swift cuts and disorientating sounds.

K's alienation is particularly clear when he goes to a retirement home to speak to Gaff (Edward James Olmos) about Deckard. The filmmakers provide the audience with a wide shot of the environment as K utters the statement that Gaff worked with Deckard, yet K himself is not seen. The sound remains diegetic in the sense that it matches the chronology and action of the narrative on screen – K's utterance takes place in the environment of the retirement home, and the audience are fully aware of the identity of the voice that is asking questions, even though K himself is deliberately left out of shot. The camera switches to Gaff as he provides a verbal response, implying his comparative freedom despite his own solitary position in the retirement home. The camera pans out as Gaff speaks, but the audience barely see the back of K's listening figure before the camera cuts to another wide shot of the retirement home, with K and Gaff shot from a distance. When the camera finally focuses on K's speaking face, it is only briefly, and the scene finishes by focusing on Gaff and his origami sheep, a taunting visual metaphor of K's passivity and compliance.

Imagery works alongside sound in a form of negation, making the audience consider K's marginalization through what is heard but not shown.

In contrast to the often-disorientating effects of J-cuts and off-screen sounds, both in terms of character development and audience response, these techniques are often used to symbolize the progress of self-discovery in *Arrival*. After Louise's first experience on the alien ship, she listens to the noise of the aliens in the tent on the computer. However, rather than instantly framing Louise in this shot, the camera initially focuses on a wide shot of people working in the tent, where the alien noise is heard, before eventually panning to Louise listening to this sound on her computer. Using these sound and image techniques, the filmmakers subtly imply that this noise is extradiegetic and occurring in Louise's mind as she learns the alien's language, even though the eventual reveal of Louise listening to the noise on her headphones reveals the source to be diegetic. This scene acts as a precursor to the film's increasing use of sound to cultivate audience critical response to character development and to narrative orientation.

Louise's gradual emotional development is symbolized using the sound of a bird noise. In a J-cut, Colonel Webber is on the ground looking at a live screen of Louise and Ian in the ship and instructs them to start their session. However, the tweets of the bird caged on the ship are already heard in this scene. The camera then cuts to Louise, and the bird noise is heard, but the bird is still not shown. It is only when Louise gets frustrated by her inability to communicate due to her suit that she looks at the bird and the source of the sound is finally revealed. Similarly, when Louise is stressed after experiencing images of Hannah and sits down despondently, Ian questions whether she is dreaming in the alien's language. Louise provides no direct answer, but the bird tweets are now heard in extradiegetic and anempathetic sound, extracted from their physical location on the alien ship and symbolizing her increased immersion in the atemporal state of the aliens. By using sound that conflicts with the imagery and speech taking place on screen, Louise's personal, solitary role as a silent hero is prioritized.

Conclusion: 'To Be Born Is to Have a Soul, I Guess'

In the climactic scene of Miloš Forman's 1975 film *One Flew Over the Cuckoo's Nest*,[1] Chief Bromden (Will Sampson), a mute character only revealed to be able to talk halfway through the film with his laconic phrases 'Thank you' and 'Mmm, juicy fruit', launches into his longest passage of speech in the film, telling the lobotomized Randle McMurphy (Jack Nicholson) that he feels 'as big as a damn mountain'. Once he realizes McMurphy's condition, however, Bromden returns to silence and out of mercy kills his comrade, only issuing a few grunts as he lifts the water fountain and triumphantly hurls it through the glass window to make his escape. Although the loud, joyous cheers of Taber (Christopher Lloyd) are heard alongside the rising, mighty score, the final image is of a silent Bromden running into the wilderness accompanied only by the sound of a soulful theremin and shaker.

My work has focused on such ideas of a silent hero in their 21st-century iterations, heroes whose narrative journeys are frequently existential and fragmented as they seek to find their place in the world. Characters such as K and The Woman, for example, try to seek meaning and sanctuary in societies that refuse to integrate and accept them, and both ultimately sacrifice their lives in the process. Highlighting two key facets of the silent hero, they both exist on the outskirts of the dystopian societies in which they operate and they both make the sacrifice in order to save a human life, despite remaining excluded from the human connection they ardently desire (Figure 86).

---

[1] Miloš Forman, dir. (United Artists, 1975), DVD.

FIGURE 86 *K is shot in silhouette after being told he is not the child, with most of his figure unclear due to the dark wall next to him. Strips of light seep into the room in a similar fashion to* Double Indemnity, *but none of these strips adorn K's figure, suggesting that his conscience is free from wrongdoing and guilt now that he is aware of his unimportance.*

These notions of heroism are frequently tied up with the elements of angst, cynicism and moral ambiguity of earlier iterations of the silent hero in film noir and the Western. Driver, while heroic in saving Irene and Benicio from harm, must commit acts of bloody violence and aggression, acts which make any chance of joining human society impossible. These acts of violence separate the hero from the society that he or she yearns to join, yet also suggest an omnipotent, supernatural level of skill. They are able to injure and kill those that pose a threat to the object of their sacrifice (generally an innocent, often a child, as seen in *Drive*, *Blade Runner 2049*, *Valhalla Rising* and *Only God Forgives*). One-Eye, the only entirely mute character in this study, exudes power both through the frequently bloody actions he carries out and through his verbal reticence, forcing the other characters – and thus the audience – to interpret meaning from corporeal signifiers and the elemental landscape he is positioned within.

This potentially productive nature of silence is articulated particularly powerfully by Shilina-Conte as she espouses how such silence offers the chance for 'a renewed positive examination of elective mutism' in film 'which might appear to be a negative and powerless (dis)order that inspires creative inspiration in cinema'.[2] Shilina-Conte argues that while some silences may have represented a negative articulation of existence in many post-Second

---

[2] Shilina-Conte, 'Silence as Elective Mutism'.

World War films, they can nonetheless be seen to have come to symbolize 'a mode of protest and resistance', particularly in those films made by minorities and outsiders. Rather than being viewed largely in terms of negation and reduction, the experimental uses of silence as seen in these 21st-century films present fruitful 'new ways of conceptualizing and thinking about life'.[3]

Since these silences cultivate more thoughtful and conflicted analyses of emotional character arcs, the silent heroes in many of these 21st-century films also offer an intriguing move away from traditional notions of 'strong silent type' masculinity. Instead of the tough, supposedly casual cool of Rick Blaine or The Man, audiences are faced with a fragile exterior of toughness that could fall apart at any moment. Many of Ryan Gosling's later silent hero roles present audiences with far more vulnerable and angst-ridden psychological depictions of men in emotional turmoil. While Gosling adopts familiar visual signifiers like the toothpick and the scorpion jacket in reference to previous laconic silent hero icons – Eastwood's 'cool' The Man with No Name, Alaine Dion's loner hitman in *Le Samouraï*[4] – he invests his heroes with far more traumatized vulnerability and disillusionment. Although his characters still retain the classic silent hero dilemma of being trapped in a role, the concepts of what it means to be a man (and, in other films I have discussed, what it means to be a woman) often become entangled with the idea of what it means to be human, summed up perfectly in the lyrics of College's song that contributed to *Drive*'s mythology – 'And a Real Hero, Real Human Being'.

Audience response plays an essential role in deciphering these vulnerabilities, with affect theory placing direct emphasis on bodily experiences, in which sensory and motor systems of the body are fundamentally integrated with cognitive processes. The audience must actively engage both visual and aural faculties in order to fully appreciate the nuances of the sounds and images presented to them on film, an experience that threatens to become distinctly passive in many contemporary films that are overloaded with noise and expository dialogue. Expressionism becomes a useful tool with which to consider the world when the search for meaning and what it means to be 'real' becomes increasingly relevant in the 21st century. The romantic idea of stripping back the layers (including language) to discover a primal notion of self becomes a central part of the current AI debate. Fundamental questions about the nature of human consciousness are raised – significantly the discussions around feelings and emotional experience as something distinct from the concept of the intellect. The complex ethical

---

[3] Ibid.
[4] Jean-Pierre Melville, dir. (1967, S. N. Prodis), DVD.

and moral issues that arise from these discussions feed into the inherently psychological, introverted iterations of contemporary silent heroes.

Just as German Expressionist films reflected the tumultuous nature of their political and social landscape, so too are my 21st-century films reflective of the era in which they are produced. *Arrival*, for example, provides a particularly bleak but prescient picture of the chaos that can ensue when nations refuse to work together and instead strive for individual gain, while disillusioned figures such as K and Driver hold up a mirror to the feelings of alienation individuals can experience in a world of seemingly unending conflict and division (a relatability which can lead to potentially dangerous misinterpretations of heroism, as analysed in the 'Literally Me' section). Many of the films present audiences with a depressing outlook on the position of women, outsiders and 'innocents' in society. Lots of these films also reflect Sontag's ideas of the redundancy of language, both in the positive ways it can encourage the audience to focus on image and sound as alternative narrative and emotional signposts, but also in the ways that characters are trapped by the systems of language. These are particularly recurrent themes in both *Blade Runner 2049* and *Drive*, where emotionally inarticulate characters are constantly failed by language; there is frequent inability to engage in rational debate and conversation and violence often becomes a surrogate for the spoken word.

As for Gosling himself, his current projects suggest an interesting trajectory in their continued adherences to and potential divergences from a silent hero archetype. In *The Grey Man*,[5] with the exception of a worryingly verbal opening scene, Gosling largely adheres to taciturn expectations with his mysterious, morally questionable Six. In keeping with silent hero traditions, a fundamental element of mystery is maintained, despite the film's divergence from expressionist aesthetics due to its action-driven, linear narrative. As a result, it does not retain the soul-searching emotionality that is on full display in Gosling's previous role in *Blade Runner 2049*. His role as the central Ken doll in *Barbie*[6] is also particularly apt considering Gosling's robotic character in *Blade Runner 2049*. As a doll designed specifically as a partner for Barbie (an interesting comparison with his role as a man obsessed with a sex doll in *Lars and the Real Girl*),[7] Ken spends much of the film craving her attention and becomes despondent when she does not greet him with a simple hello. He acts as a mirror, albeit a more comedic one, to Ana de Armas' holographic Joi. In the supposed utopia of Barbieland, Ken serves as Barbie's go-to boyfriend. Boi, if you will.

---

[5] Anthony Russo and Joe Russo, dirs. (2022, Netflix), Netflix.
[6] Greta Girwig, dir. (2023, Warner Bros. Pictures), DVD.
[7] Craig Gillespie, dir. (2007, MGM Distribution Co,), DVD.

It is difficult at this point not to recall Joi's description about becoming a 'real girl' once K removes her from the main system, thereby meaning she will be 'killed' if her emanator is destroyed. 'Real' for Joi then becomes intrinsically linked with the concept of mortality. To die is to be human, as Roy Batty poignantly acknowledged in the original *Blade Runner*: 'All these memories will be lost in time, like tears in rain. Time to die.' This idea of 'real' lies at the heart of the discussion about the role expressionism has in the search for meaning. With its stylized aesthetic, minimal dialogue and use of visual and aural signifiers to cultivate narrative, expressionism allows the audience to actively experience a connection with the characters on screen. The audience do not need to see or hear the same sights and sounds as Batty has seen and heard, but they have been given the ability to form a range of varied emotional interpretations from their own brilliant, inherently subjective imaginations.

Filmography

American Beauty (DreamWorks Pictures, 1999)
American Psycho (Lionsgate Films, 2000)
Apollo 13 (Universal Pictures, 1995)
Arrival (Paramount Pictures, 2016)
August 32nd on Earth (Epicentre Films, 1998)
Barbie (Warner Bros. Pictures, 2023)
The Believer (Fireworks Pictures, 2000)
The Big Trail (Fox Film Corporation, 1930)
Blade Runner (Warner Bros., 1982)
Blade Runner 2049 (Warner Bros. Pictures, 2017)
Blue Valentine (Derek Cianfrance, 2010)
Bronson (Vertigo Films, 2008)
The Cabinet of Dr. Caligari (Decla-Film, 1920)
Casablanca (Warner Bros., 1942)
Double Indemnity (Paramount Pictures, 1944)
Drive (FilmDistrict, 2011)
Enemy (Entertainment One, 2013)
Falling Down (Warner Bros., 1993)
Fight Club (20th Century Fox, 1999)
First Man (Universal Pictures, 2018)
A Fistful of Dollars (Unidis, 1964)
The Good, the Bad and the Ugly (United Artists, 1966)
The Hands of Orlac (Pan-Film, 1924)
Half-Nelson (THINKFilm, 2006)
Incendies (micro_scope, 2010)
L.A. Confidential (Warner Bros., 1997)
Lonely Are the Brave (Joel Productions, 1962)
The Lovely Bones (Paramount Pictures, 2009)
Mad Max (Roadshow Film Distributors, 1979)
Maelstrom (Alliance Atlantis, 2000)
The Maltese Falcon (Warner Bros., 1941)
Metropolis (Parufarnet, 1927)
The Neon Demon (Wild Bunch et al., 2016)
No Country for Old Men
Nosferatu (Film Arts Guild, 1922)
The Notebook (New Line Cinema, 2004)
One Flew Over the Cuckoo's Nest (United Artists, 1975)
One Week (Metro Pictures, 1920)

Only God Forgives (RADiUS-TWC, 2013)
Pickup on South Street (20th Century Studios, 1953)
The Place beyond the Pines (Focus Features, 2012)
Polytechnique (Alliance Films Remstar, 2009)
Pusher (RCV Film Distribution, 1996)
Raging Bull (United Artists, 1980)
Rambo: First Blood (Orion Pictures, 1982)
Le Samourai (1967, S. N. Prodis)
Shane (Paramount Pictures, 1953)
Stagecoach (United Artists, 1939)
Sunset Boulevard (Paramount Pictures, 1950)
Terminator 2: Judgement Day (Tri-Star Pictures, 1991)
The Third Man (British Lion Film Corporation, 1949)
True Grit (Paramount Pictures, 1969)
Under the Skin (BFI et al., 2014)
Valhalla Rising (Scanbox Entertainment, 2009)

Bibliography

Abramovitch, Seth. 'Braaams for Beginners: How a Horn Sound Ate Hollywood'. 2015. *Hollywood Reporter*. https://www.hollywoodreporter.com/movies/movie-news/braaams-beginners-how-a-horn-793220/ (Accessed 30 May 2021).

Adewunmi, Bim. 'Ryan Gosling Is a Star after His Time'. 2007. *Buzzfeed News*. https://www.buzzfeednews.com/article/bimadewunmi/ryan-gosling-is-a-star-after-his-time (Accessed 28 May 2021).

Adler, Reneta. '"The Good, the Bad and the Ugly" Begins Run: Brutal Italian Western Stars Clint Eastwood'. 1968. *The New York Times*. https://www.nytimes.com/1968/01/25/archives/the-screen-zane-grey-meets-the-marquis-de-sade-the-good-the-bad-and.html (Accessed 10 May 2021).

Altman, Rick. *Silent Film Sound*. New York: Columbia University Press, 2004.

Angel, Maria, and Anna Gibbs. 'Media, Affect and the Face: Biomediation and the Political Scene', *Southern Review: Communication, Politics and Culture*, 38.2 (2005): 24–39.

Ball, Zoe. 'Nicolas Winding Refn Interviewed by Zoe Ball'. 2013. *YouTube*. https://www.youtube.com/watch?v=taNev9I5Xzs (Accessed 23 April 2021).

Bastién, Jade. 'The Vulnerability of Ryan Gosling in Blade Runner 2049'. 2017. *Vulture*. https://www.vulture.com/2017/10/ryan-goslings-vulnerable-performance-in-blade-runner-2049.html (Accessed 17 April 2021).

Berg, Charles. *An Investigation of the Motives for and Realisation of Music to Accompany the American Silent Film, 1896–1927*. New York: Arno Press, 1976.

Berlin, Isiah. *The Roots of Romanticism*. London: Chatto & Windus, 1999.

Books and Boots. 'Edvard Munch: Love and Angst @ the British Museum'. *Wordpress*. https://astrofella.wordpress.com/2019/07/22/edvard-munch-love-and-angst-british-museum/#:~:text=I%20would%20not%20cast%20off,art%20of%20one%27s%20innermost%20heart (Accessed 20 May 2022).

Bradshaw, Peter. 'Drive – Review'. 2011. *The Guardian*. https://www.theguardian.com/film/2011/sep/22/drive-ryan-gosling-film-review (Accessed 20 May 2021).

Britannica. 'Edvard Munch: Norwegian Artist'. *Britannica*. https://www.britannica.com/biography/Edvard-Munch (Accessed 10 May 2022).

Brooks, Xan. '"My Father and I Disagree on the Purpose of Cinema": Anders and Nicolas Winding Refn on Film-making'. 2021. *The Guardian*. https://www.theguardian.com/film/2021/feb/11/my-father-and-i-disagree-on-the-purpose-of-cinema-anders-and-nicolas-winding-refn-on-film-making (Accessed 13 March 2021).

Buckland, Warren, ed. *Puzzle Films: Complex Storytelling in Contemporary Cinema*. Chichester: Blackwell, 2009.

Burns, William. 'From the Shadows: Nosferatu and the German Expressionism Aesthetic', *Mis-En-Scéne: The Journal of Film & Visual Narration*, 1 (2016): 1–12.

TheCelebFactory. 'Ryan Gosling on the Dialogue in Drive'. 2011. *YouTube*. https://www.youtube.com/watch?v=1GrF4bO9sUA (Accessed 14 June 2021).

CELEBS.com. 'Ryan Gosling behind the Scenes on "Drive"'. 2011. *YouTube*. https://www.youtube.com/watch?v=BwAPER0lm48&t=3s (Accessed 14 June 2021).

The Chic League, 'The Neon Demon Analysis: High Fashion & Neuroaesthetics in Film'. 2021. *YouTube*. https://www.youtube.com/watch?v=95FICC4M1_w&t=253s (Accessed 13 February 2023).

Child, Ben. 'Woman Sues to Stop Drive Getting Away with a "Misleading Trailer"'. 2011. *The Guardian*. https://www.theguardian.com/film/2011/oct/10/woman-sues-drive-trailer (Accessed 7 May 2021).

Chilvers, Ian. *The Oxford Dictionary of Art & Artists*, 4th edn. Oxford: Oxford University Press, 2009.

Chion, Michel. *Audio-Vision: Sound on Screen*, ed. Claudia Gorbman, 2nd edn. New York: Columbia University Press, 2019.

Chion, Michel. *The Voice in Cinema*, ed. Claudia Gorbman. New York: Columbia University Press, 1999.

Chitwood, Adam. '"Blade Runner 2049" Composer Benjamin Wallfisch on the Unique Score, Experimenting, & Vangelis'. 2017. *Collider*. https://collider.com/blade-runner-2049-benjamin-wallfisch-interview/ (Accessed 28 May 2021).

D'Artenay, Alyssa. 'The Influence of Film Music on Emotion', Monterey Bay: California State University, 2019. https://digitalcommons.csumb.edu/cgi/viewcontent.cgi?article=1570&context=caps_thes_all (Accessed 16 February 2023).

Darwin, Charles. *The Expressions of Emotions in Man and Animals*. Oxford: Oxford University Press, [1872] 1998.

Davis, Edward. 'Nicolas Winding Refn Says RAO Speedwagon Helped Him & Ryan Gosling Seal the "Drive" Deal'. 2011. *IndieWire*. https://www.indiewire.com/2011/05/nicolas-winding-refn-says-reo-speedwagon-helped-him-ryan-gosling-seal-the-drive-deal-118596/ (Accessed 4 May 2021).

Desowitz, Bill. '"Blade Runner 2049": The Most Difficult Craft Challenges for Director Denis Villeneuve'. 2017. *Indiewire*. https://www.indiewire.com/2017/11/blade-runner-2049-roger-deakins-denis-villeneuve-1201900768/ (Accessed 23 January 2021).

Dick, Bernard. 'Columbia's Dark Ladies and the Femmes fatales of Film Noir', *Literature/Film Quarterly*, 23 (1995): 155–62.

Dorsky, Nathaniel. *Devotional Cinema*. 2nd edn. Berkeley: Tuumba Press, 2005.

'DP/30: The Oral History of Hollywood. Drive, Director Nicolas Winding Refn'. 2011. *YouTube*. https://www.youtube.com/watch?v=5Vv0E_-Fi5g (Accessed 4 March 2021).

BIBLIOGRAPHY

'Drive – Interview with the Cast at Cannes 2011'. 2015. *YouTube*. https://www.youtube.com/watch?v=Y0AGBO7w7dA (Accessed 25 January 2021).

Dudek, Duane. 'Under the Skin,' with Scarlett Johansson, Confounding, Captivating'. 2014. *Milwaukee Journal Sentinel*. https://archive.jsonline.com/entertainment/movies/under-the-skin-with-scarlett-johansson-confounding-captivating-b99269582z1-259400161.html/ (Accessed 1 March 2023).

Ebert, Roger. 'Urban Renewal on a Very Large Scale'. 2010. *Roger Ebert*. https://www.rogerebert.com/reviews/great-movie-metropolis-2010-restoration-1927 (Accessed 6 April 2021).

Eisner, Lotte. *The Haunted Screen: Expressionism in the German Cinema and the Influence of Max Reinhardt*. Trans. by Roger Greaves. New York: University of California Press, [1952] 1974.

Engber, Daniel. 'The Sounds of Violence'. 2012. *Slate*. https://slate.com/culture/2012/02/drive-the-sound-editing-in-the-elevator-stomping-scene.html (Accessed 30 April 2021).

Entwistle, Brady. 'One Blade Runner 2049 Scene Was Almost Too Expensive, Details Cinematographer'. 2023. *Screen Rant*. https://screenrant.com/blade-runner-2049-scene-too-expensive-cinematographer-response/ (Accessed 11 March 2023).

Epstein, Adam. '"First Man" Stars One of the World's Weirdest Musical Instruments'. 2018. *Quartz*. https://qz.com/quartzy/1422234/the-other-star-of-first-man-is-one-of-the-worlds-weirdest-musical-instruments/ (Accessed 28 May 2021).

Epton, Nancy. Interview with Felix Granger, 12 April 2021.

Epton, Nancy. Interview with Kim Newman, 9 March 2021.

Epton, Nancy. Interview with Mark Kermode, 10 February 2021.

Fernandez, Chantal. "'The Neon Demon' Costumes Are as High-Fashion as the Modelling World It Portrays'. 2016. *Fashionista*. https://fashionista.com/2016/06/neon-demon-costumes (Accessed 3 March 2023).

Film at Lincoln Center. 'Nicolas Winding Refn on the Power of Silence'. 2013. *YouTube*. https://www.youtube.com/watch?v=6sLr5_1eo7U&t=7s (Accessed 12 May 2021).

FilmisNow Movie Bloopers & Extras 'Arrival: On-Set Visit with Denis Villeneuve "Director"'. 2016. *YouTube*. https://www.youtube.com/watch?v=qzKLJ4GeFto&t=0s (Accessed 15 June 2021).

Firoozye, Faris. '"Literally Me" Characters: A Take on Modern Pop Culture'. 2023. *The Oxford Blue*. https://www.theoxfordblue.co.uk/literally-me-characters/ (Accessed 15 March 2023).

Fleuckiger, Barbara. 'Colour Analysis for the Digital Restoration of Das Cabinet des Dr. Caligari'. 2015. *Moving Image*, 15 (2015): 22–43.

French, Philip. 'Drive – Review'. 2011. *The Guardian*. https://www.theguardian.com/film/2011/sep/25/drive-ryan-gosling-film-review (Accessed 20 May 2021).

Giroux, Jack. 'Interview: Nicolas Winding Refn on Violent Men, Valhalla and Pretty Woman'. 2010. *Film School Rejects*. https://filmschoolrejects.com/interview-nicolas-winding-refn-on-violent-men-valhalla-and-pretty-woman-f96c21a797f7/ (Accessed 24 April 2021).

Gombrich, E. H. *The Story of Art*. London: Phaidon, 1950.

BIBLIOGRAPHY

Goodsell, Luke. 'Ryan Gosling on Drive: This Is My Superhero Movie'. 2011. *Rotten Tomatoes*. https://editorial.rottentomatoes.com/article/ryan-gosling-on-drive-this-is-my-superhero-movie/ (Accessed 24 April 2021).

Graham-Dixon, Andrew. *The Art of Scandinavia*. 2016. BBC 4.

Hall, Mordaunt. 'Movie Review Metropolis (1927) a Technical Marvel'. *New York Times*. 7 March 1927.

Hall, Mordaunt. 'Goldwyn Urges Caution'. *New York Times*. 5 August 1928.

Hawkins, Matthew. 'The Concept of Affective Tonality and the Role of the Senses in Producing a Cinematic Narrative'. PhD diss., University of East London, 2016. https://repository.uel.ac.uk/download/983013beab892a8bb051711b30ec7454168963a6ea84eca32bb4cdc5dac6dc4f/7445538/__DLSTAFF1_USERS_D22_nazmin_DESKTOP_ROAR_Matthew%20Hawkins_Ammended%20Thesis.pdf (Accessed 20 February 2023).

Herber-Percy, Colin. 'The Flesh is Weak. Empathy and Becoming Human in Jonathan Glazer's "Under the Skin"', *Philosophy of Film without Theory*, 3, no. 2 (2020): 347–64. https://doi.org/10.58519/aesthinv.v3i2.11943 (Accessed 15 February 2023).

Hildenbrandt, Fred (1927), 'Metropolis' *Berliner Tageblatt*. 11 January.

Hirsch, Foster. *The Dark Side of the Screen: Film Noir*. Boston: Da Capo Press, 1981.

Hirsch, Foster. *Detours and Lost Highways: A Map of Neo-Noir*. New York: Limelight, 1999.

Hodges, Brian. 'Tears of a Machine: The Humanity of Luv in "Blade Runner 2049"'. 2017. *Roger Ebert*. https://www.rogerebert.com/features/tears-of-a-machine-the-humanity-of-luv-in-blade-runner-2049 (Accessed 20 March 2023).

Ihering, Herbert (1927), 'Der Metropolis, Ufa-Palast am Zoo'. *Berliner Borsen-Courier*. 11 January.

IMDb, 'Trivia'. *IMDb*. https://www.imdb.com/title/tt0013442/trivia (Accessed 8 May 2021).

Isenhour, John Preston. 'The Effects of Context and Order in Film Editing'. *AV Communication Review*, 23 (1975): 69–80.

JoBlo Movie Trailers. 'Nicolas Winding Refn NY Interview – Only God Forgives'. 2013. *YouTube*. https://www.youtube.com/watch?v=R3n-TG4V4-U (Accessed 23 April 2021).

Johnson, Brian D. 'How a Pair of Canadians Infused Their DNA into Blade Runner 2049'. 2017. *Macleans*. https://macleans.ca/culture/movies/how-a-pair-of-canadians-infused-their-dna-into-blade-runner-2049/ (Accessed 6 March 2023).

Know Your Meme, 'Literally Me Guys', *Know Your Meme*. https://knowyourmeme.com/memes/literally-me-guys (Accessed 16 March 2023).

Koehler, Robert, 'Nicolas Winding Refn and the Search for a Real Hero'. *CinemaScope*. https://cinema-scope.com/cinema-scope-magazine/interview-nicolas-winding-refn-and-the-search-for-a-real-hero/ (Accessed 13 April 2021).

Kurtz, Rudolph. *Expressionism and Film*. New Barnet: John Libbey, 1926.

Lakeshore Records. 'Cliff Martinez – Driver Composer Interview HD'. 2011. *YouTube*. https://www.youtube.com/watch?v=sTwpfUbkxcQ (Accessed June 24 2021).

Langer, Susan K. *Feeling and Form*. New York: Scribner's, 1953.

BIBLIOGRAPHY

Lapointe, Tanya. *The Art and Soul of Blade Runner 2049*. Los Angeles: Alcon Entertainment, 2017.

Lincoln, Kevin. 'What Is Cool? Ryan Gosling, Jake Johnson, and the Not-Dead Movie Star'. 2013. *Pacific Standard*. https://psmag.com/social-justice/what-is-cool-ryan-gosling-jake-johnson-and-the-not-dead-movie-star-64155 (Accessed 17 April 2021).

Lobenfeld, Claire. '*Blade Runner 2049*: How Hans Zimmer and Benjamin Wallfisch Followed Up the Most Influential Sci-Fi Score of all Time'. 2017. *FactMag*. https://www.factmag.com/2017/10/20/hans-zimmer-wallfisch-blade-runner-2049-interview/ (Accessed 28 May 2021).

LoBrutto, Vincent. *Becoming Film Literate: The Art and Craft of Motion Pictures*. Connecticut: Praeger, 2005.

Locations Hub. 'The 12 Film Locations of Drive in Los Angeles'. 2012. *Locations Hub*. https://www.locationshub.com/blog/2013/10/26/the-12-film-locations-of-drive-in-los-angeles (Accessed 20 March 2021).

MacNab, Geoffrey. 'First Man Review: Damien Chazelle's Gripping Neil Armstrong Biopic Is an Inspiration'. 2018. *The Independent*. https://www.independent.co.uk/arts-entertainment/films/reviews/first-man-film-review-ryan-gosling-neil-armstrong-claire-foy-release-date-trailer-a8578796.html (Accessed 15 November 2020).

Mangini, Mark. 'Soundworks Collection – the Sound of Blade Runner 2049'. 2018. *YouTube*. https://www.youtube.com/watch?v=Vxxifb6Wclw (Accessed 24 May 2021).

McDonald, Paul. *The Star System: Hollywood's Production of Popular Identities*. New York: Colombia University Press, 2000.

Minden, Michael, and Holger Bachmann, eds. *Fritz Lang's Metropolis: Cinematic Visions of Technology and Fear*. New York: Camden House, 2002.

Monique, 'Hollywood's Obsession with Toxic Masculinity, as Seen in "Blade Runner 2049" ', *Just Add Colour*. https://www.colorwebmag.com/2017/10/16/hollywoods-obsession-toxic-masculinity-seen-blade-runner-2049/ (Accessed 10 March 2023).

Muncy, Julie. 'Blade Runner 2049 Director Opens up about the Film's Treatment of Women'. 2017. *Gizmodo*. https://gizmodo.com/blade-runner-2049-director-opens-up-about-the-films-tre-1820747134 (Accessed 10 March 2023).

Munden, Kenneth J. 'A Contribution to the Psychological Understanding of the Cowboy and His Myth'. *American Imago*, 15 (1958): 103–48.

Museum of Cinema. 'Valhalla Rising Interview with Nicolas Winding Refn'. 2009. *YouTube*. https://www.youtube.com/watch?v=HH06a3Y4lgw&t=211s (Accessed 14 May 2021).

The New York Times. A Scene from Blade Runner 2049 – Anatomy of a Scene'. 2017. *YouTube*. https://www.youtube.com/watch?v=S75OKnM_BKU (Accessed 20 May 2021).

Nugent, John. 'First Man Review'. 2018. *Empire*. https://www.empireonline.com/movies/reviews/first-man-review/ (Accessed 22 May 2021).

O'Connell, Mikey. "Drive' Song Inspired by Captain Sully Sullenberger and Mad Max'. 2011. *The Hollywood Reporter*. https://www.hollywoodreporter.com/movies/movie-news/drive-soundtrack-captain-sully-254349/ (Accessed 30 April 2021).

Oddy, Chris. 'Behind the Scenes of Under the Skin'. 2014. *Dazed Digital*. https://www.dazeddigital.com/artsandculture/article/19225/1/behind-the-scenes-of-under-the-skin (Accessed 17 February 2023).

Ordana, Michael. 'How Do You Follow up a Sci-Fi Classic Without Cloning It? If It's "Blade Runner", You Rewrite Its DNA'. 2018. *LA Times*. https://www.latimes.com/entertainment/envelope/la-en-mn-denis-villeneuve-20170104-story.html (Accessed 24 May 2021).

Osenlund, Kurt R. 'Interview: Jonathan Glazer Talks Under the Skin'. 2014. *Slant*. https://www.slantmagazine.com/film/interview-jonathan-glazer/ (Accessed 5 March 2023).

Pappademas, Alex. 'The Loner'. 2007. *GQ*. https://www.gq.com/story/ryan-gosling?currentPage=3 (Accessed 24 May 2021).

Pavek, Hannah. 'Taciturn Masculinities: Radical Quiet and Sounding Linguistic Difference in Valeska Grisebach's *Western*'. 2020. Edinburgh University Press. https://www.euppublishing.com/doi/full/10.3366/film.2020.0128?role=tab (Accessed 6 March 2023).

Payne, Catherine, and Alexandra Pitsis. 'On Nature and the Tactility of the Senses in Blade Runner 2049'. *Journal of Asia-Pacific Pop Culture*, 3 (2018): 55–74.

Phillips, Jacob. 'Did Not Christ Appear to You? Commentary by Jacob Phillips'. *VCS*. https://thevcs.org/psalters-darkest-hour/did-not-christ-appear-you (Accessed 15 March 2023).

Porfirio, Robert. 'Interview with Billy Wilder', in *Film Noir Reader Three*. Porfirio, Alain Silver and James Ursini (eds). New York: Limelight, 101–19, 2002.

Radio Times. 'Blade Runner 2049 Will Be Almost Entirely Free of Green Screen Effects'. 2017. *Radio Times*. https://www.radiotimes.com/tv/sci-fi/blade-runner-2049-will-be-almost-entirely-free-of-green-screen-effects/ (Accessed 24 April 2021).

Rayhan, Abdullah, 'The Scream is One of the World's Most Famous Paintings. But What Does it mean?' *bdnews24*. https://bdnews24.com/arts/obydgcu7g2 (Accessed 20 March 2022).

Rikhardsdottir, Sif. *Emotion in Old Norse Literature: Translations, Voices, Contexts*, Woodbridge: Brewer, 2017.

Refn, Nicolas. Special Features, *Drive* DVD, 2012, Sony.

Robson, Leo. 'Scarlett Johansson in Under the Skin: 'prick her and she doesn't bleed'. 2014. *The Guardian*. https://www.theguardian.com/film/2014/mar/15/scarlett-johansson-under-skin-extraterrestrial (Accessed 17 March 2023).

Schembri, Jim. 'Drive'. 2011. *The Age*. https://www.theage.com.au/entertainment/movies/drive-20111026-1mjau.html (Accessed 4 April 2021).

Schneider, Steven Jay. *1001 Movies You Must See Before You Die*. 2nd edn. London: Hachette, 2018.

Schrader, Paul (1996), 'Notes on Film Noir', in *Film Noir Reader*, Alain Silver, James Ursini (eds). New York: Limelight, 53–63, 1996.

ScreenSlam. 'Drive: Ryan Gosling Is Character Driven – ScreenSlam'. 2011. *YouTube*. https://www.youtube.com/watch?v=A1uolzUc60Q (Accessed 14 June 2021).

Shanahan, Timothy. 'Do You Long for Having Your Heart Interlinked?', in *Blade Runner and Philosophy: This Breaks the World*, Robin Bruce and Trip McCrossin (eds). Chicago: Open Court, 3–10, 2019.

Sherlock, Ben. 'Drive & 9 Other Ultraviolent Neo-Noirs'. 2021. *ScreenRant*. https://screenrant.com/drive-similar-bloody-violent-neo-noir-movies/ (Accessed 20 May 2022).

Shilina-Conte, Tanya. 'Silence as Elective Mutism in Minor Cinema' 2021. Edinburgh University Press. https://www.euppublishing.com/doi/10.3366/film.2021.0165 (Accessed 1 March 2023).

Silberman, Marc. 'Soundless Speech, Wordless Writing: Language and German Silent Cinema'. 2010. *Imaginations*. http://imaginations.glendon.yorku.ca/?p=181 (Accessed 3 April 2021).

Silman, Anna. 'The Complete Illustrated History of Ryan Gosling, From Child Star to Heartthrob to Movie Director. 2014. *Vulture*. https://www.vulture.com/2014/05/illustrated-comprehensive-history-bio-biography-ryan-gosling.html (Accessed 5 March).

Sinnerbrink, Robert. 'Stimmung: Exploring the Aesthetics of Mood', *Screen*, 53 (2012): 148–63.

Smith, Nigel M. 'Ryan Gosling On Not Understanding All of "Only God Forgives" and How He's "Highly Influenced by Violence"'. 2013. *IndieWire*. https://www.indiewire.com/2013/07/ryan-gosling-on-not-understanding-all-of-only-god-forgives-and-how-hes-highly-influenced-by-violence-36594/ (Accessed 28 May 2021).

Sontag, Susan. 'The Aesthetics of Silence', in *Styles of Radical Will*, ed. David Rieff. London: Penguin Classics, 3–34, [1969] 2009.

Stang, Ragna. *Edvard Munch: The Man and the Artist*. London: Gordon Fraser, 1979.

Styan, J. L. *Modern Drama in Theory and Practice 3: Expressionism and Epic Theatre*. Cambridge: Cambridge University Press, 1981.

Tate, 'German Expressionism'. *Tate*. https://www.tate.org.uk/art/art-terms/g/german-expressionism (Accessed 20 September 2020).

Tomkins, Silvan. *Affect, Imagery, Consciousness*. 4 vols. New York: Springer. 1962–92.

Touet, Emmanuel. *Birth of the Motion Picture*, trans. by Susan Emmanuel. New York: Harry N. Abrams, 1995.

Thomson, David. *'Have You Seen ...?' A Personal Introduction to 1,000 Films*. New York: Alfred A. Knopf, 2008.

Thomson, David. 'Thomson On Films: "Drive", a Cool, New Noir That Degenerates Into a Bloodbath'. 2011. *The New Republic*. https://newrepublic.com/article/95110/drive-ryan-gosling-refn-noir (Accessed 2 April 2021).

Vincent van Gogh: The Letters, 'To Theo van Gogh. Arles, Monday, 3 September 1888'. https://www.vangoghletters.org/vg/letters/let673/letter.html (Accessed 13 April 2021).

Vincent van Gogh: The Letters, 'To Theo van Gogh. Arles, Saturday, 18 August 1888'. https://www.vangoghletters.org/vg/letters/let663/letter.html#translation (Accessed 13 April 2021).

Vicari, Justin. *Nicolas Winding Refn and the Violence of Art: A Critical Study of the Films*. Jefferson: McFarland, 2014.

Vice. 'Inside the Making of 'Blade Runner 2049 – Created with Blade Runner 2049'. 2017. *YouTube*. https://www.youtube.com/watch?v=T0kobbjpdUg (Accessed 16 May 2021).

Villeneuve, Dennis. "Dune' Director Denis Villeneuve Blasts HBO Max Deal'. 2020. *Variety*.https://variety.com/2020/film/news/dune-denis-villeneuve-blasts-warner-bros-1234851270/ (Accessed 25 March 2021).
Weta Workshop. 'Weta Workshop – Blade Runner 2049 Miniatures'. 2017. *YouTube*.https://www.youtube.com/watch?v=sLxxbfsj8IM&t=195s (Accessed 28 April 2021).
Wierzbicki, James. *Film Music: A History*. New York: Routledge, 2009.
Wikipedia, Metropolis, 'Release and Reception', *Wikipedia*. https://en.wikipedia.org/wiki/Metropolis_(1927_film) (Accessed 14 May 2021).
Will, Barbara. 'The Nervous Origins of the American Western', *American Literature*, 70 (1998): 293–316.
Winkler, Martin M. 'Classical Mythology and the Western Film', *Comparative Literature Studies*, 22 (1985): 516–40.
Wise, Damon. 'Only God Forgives Review'. 2012. *Empire*. https://www.empireonline.com/movies/reviews/god-forgives-review/ (Accessed 21 May 2021).
Wright, Will. *Sixguns and Society: A Structural Study of the Western*. Los Angeles: University of California Press, 1975.

Index

Note: Figures are indicated by page number followed by "f". Endnotes are indicated by the page number followed by "n" and the endnote number e.g., 20 n.1 refers to endnote 1 on page 20.

Abbey, E. 48
absence of sound 19, 25–6
Adewunmi, B. 111
Adler, R. 52
aestheticism 14
aesthetics 65
The Aesthetics of Silence (Sontag) 3
alienation, feelings of 30, 168
Altman, R. 26
American Beauty (film) 123
American Psycho (film) 123, 124
Angel, M. 18
animated figures 26
Apollo-13 (film) 119
Are You Afraid of the Dark? (television series) 110
Armstrong, N. 112, 118, 144, *145*, 154–157, *161*, *162*
Arrival (film) 6, 56, 80, 84–7, 119, 121, 122, 160, 164, 169
artificial CGI method 94
The Art of Scandinavia (television series) 13
asceticism 3
audience response 19, 21, 27, 31, 33, 34, 49, 57, 94, 115, 123, 126–8, 152, 156, 164, 167
Audio-Vision: Sound on Screen (Chion) 2, 16, 22, 26, 27
August 32nd on Earth (film) 121
autonomous mood, concept of 20

Barbie (film) 168
The Believer (film) 110

Benach, E. 98
Berg, C. 26
Berlin, I. 10, 11
The Big Trail (film) 50, 51
Blade Runner 2049 (film) 3, *5*, 11, 13, 16, 21, 30, 55, 59, 61, 73, 82, 126, 141, 163
 dystopian world of 99
 promotional poster of 119
Blue Valentine (film) 129, 130
Bradshaw, P. 115
The Brave Cowboy (Abbey) 48
Brinkema, E. 20
Bronson (film) 120
Buckland, W. 65
Burns, J. 48, 49
Burns, W. 33

The Cabinet of Dr. Caligari (film) 27–9, *32*, 35, 36, 40, 42, 49, 61–3, 71
 expression of *31*
Casablanca (film) 42–4, 51
chaos, themes of 7
Chaplin, C. 26
Chion, M. 2, 3, 16, 22, 27, 55, 150–2, 155, 161
Citroen, P. 35
Coleman, B. 50
The Concept of Affective Tonality and the Role of the Senses in Producing a Cinematic Narrative (Hawkins) 20
Critique of Silence (Brinkema) 20
Curtiz, M. 42

INDEX

Danish Nordisk Films industry 15
D'Artenay, A. 20, 23, 49
Darwin, C. 18
Da Vinci, L. 12
Deakins, R. 79
Deleuze, G. 19, 20
Devotional Cinema (Dorksy) 134
dialogue, sparse use of 6
Dick, B. 41
Did Not Christ Appear to You (Phillips) 9
disillusionment 7, 11, 30, 38, 39, 50, 61, 109, 167
Dollars Trilogy (film) 52, 53
Dorksy, N. 134
Double Indemnity (film) 39, 41, 42
Dracula (film) 32
Drive (film) 1–3, 16, *17*, 21, 34, 70, *71*, 73, 142, 143, 149
   mythology 167
   supermarket scene in 145
   violence in 169
Dune (film) 122

Eisner, L. 6, 28, 29, 134
emotional audience 6, 27
emotional experience 29, 167
Emotion in Old Norse Literature: Translations, Voices, Contexts (Rikhardsdottir) 9
emotions 7, 11
emotive responses 85
Enemy (film) 82
expressionism 7, 8, 10, 13, 15, 19, 30, 34, 37, 56, 75, 115, 120, 167, 169
Expressionism and Film (Kurtz) 6
Expressionist films 6, 11, 16
   central elements of 28
   in 21st-century 61
The Expressions of Emotions in Man and Animals (Darwin) 18

facial expressions 8, 9, 16, 18, 19, 30
Falling Down (film) 123
fascination, sense of 43
Fast and Furious ix, 63, 66–7, 118, 120, 121
Fear X (film) 120

Fight Club (film) 123
filmmakers 4, 15, 40, 45, 48, 53, 54, 58, 60, 61, 89, 100, 124, 136, 140, 142, 147, 163
Film Music: A History (Wierzbicki) 150
film-music system 26
film noir 15, 19, 38–46, 61
Firoozye, F. 123, 124
First Man (film) 112, 117, 119, 127, 144, 154, 160, 161
First World War 10, 13, 30, 39, 51
A Fistful of Dollars (film) 47
Foley, J. M. 145
Forman, M. 165
Frederson, J. 35
French, P. 115

Gassner, D. 73
German Expressionist films 11
   aesthetic and thematic influences 41
   archetypal madman in 31
   background in 30
   Blade Runner 2049 61
   The Cabinet of Dr. Caligari 27, 61
   musical elements of 28
   screenings 28
   silent films 26
   themes and styles 39
   visual and metaphorical darkness 38
Germany 7, 12–15
gestures 16, 19, 30, 31, 36, 38, 47, 53, 55, 56, 61, 83, 95, 113, 118, 133
ghosts 27
Gibbs, A. 18
Glazer, J. 4, 91
Goldwyn, S. 26, 27
Gombrich, E. H. 12
The Good, the Bad and the Ugly (film) 50, 52
Goosebumps (film) 110
Gorky, M. 25–7
Gosling, R. 19, 20, 30, 54, 57, 66, 83, 98, 109–14, 121
   acting style 133
   facial expression 147
   on-screen characters 129
   physical performance 134
   'robotic' performance 112

INDEX

Graham-Dixon, A. 13
Granger, F. 19, 114, 116
Great German Art 14
Grellier, D. 149
The Grey Man (film) 168
Grosz, G. 34, 35
The Guardian (newspaper) 92

The Hands of Orlac (film) 134
The Haunted Screen: Expressionism in the German Cinema and the Influence of Max Reinhardt (Eisner) 6
Hawkins, M. 20, 28, 29, 42, 78, 134
Herber-Percy, C. 91
Hildenbrandt, F. 116
Hoermanseder, M. 98
Hollywood 9, 15, 120
human language 4
Hurwitz, J. 154, 160

imagery 4, 6, 33, 34, 55, 56, 58, *69*, 88, 90, 134, 153, 158, 159, 164
impressionism 14
Incendies (film) 6, 87, 88
The Influence of Film Music on Emotion (d'Artenay) 20

Jackman, H. 120
Janowitz, H. 30
Johnson, B. D. 75

Karas, A. 44
Kermode, M. 13, 16, 19, 42, 54, 117
Korda, A. 44
Krauss, W. 30, 134
Kuleshov effect 17
Kurtz, R. 6, 7, 9, 28, 34, 116

L.A. Confidential (film) 41
laconicism 44, 48, 56, 58, 115
landscape 9, 27, 35, 49, 52, 54, 62, 63, 88, *90*, *92*, 133, 135
Langer, S. K. 22
Lang, F. 34–7, 42, 52, 75, 115, 116
Lars and the Real Girl (film) 168
The Last Laugh (film) 27

Leone, S. 47, 49–50, 52, 53, 75, 92, 115, 120
leitmotifs 153, 154, 156
Le Samourai (film) 167
lighting effects 7, 8, 33, 40, 73, 79, 80, 94, 99
Lincoln, K. 116
Literally Me 123, 124, 128
LoBrutto, V. 30
Lonely Are the Brave (film) 48, 107
Los Angeles 1, 42, 66, *69*, 73–6, 81
The Lovely Bones (film) 130

MacNab, G. 118
Mad Max (film) 149
Maelstrom (film) 121
male silent heroes 5
The Maltese Falcon (film) 41
Martinez, C. 8, 151
Mayer, C. 27, 30
McDonald, P. 111
McQueen, S. 115
Metropolis (film) 34–7, *39*, 42, *56*, 62, 73, 74–6, 80, 85, 94, 116
Mikkelsen, M. 62, 64, 66
Modern Drama in Theory and Practice 3: Expressionism and Epic Theatre (Styan) 7
Mouawad, W. 88
movement 15–19, 25, 30, 31, 33, 64, 71, 113, 130, 133, 135, 141, 145, 162–3
Munch, E. 11–13
Munden, K. J. 72
Murch, W. 3, 27
Murnau, F. W. 30, 34
music 21–3, 98, 150–3, 155, 156
mystery, sense of 1, 61, 83, 91, 121, 152

Nancy, J.-L. 21
narrative ambiguity 4
narrative confusion 4
Nazi film industry 14
The Neon Demon (film) 6, 96, 98
Newman, K. 16, 19, 21, 41, 51, 53, 134
New York Times 52

Nicolas Winding Refn and the Violence of Art (Vicari) 112
Night Café (paint) 11
No Country For Old Men (film) 119
noiseless screen 3, 4
Nordau, M. 14
Norse mythology 9, 10
Nosferatu (film) 30, 31, 42, 75
    Count's screen time 34
    shadows in *33*
The Notebook (film) 110
Nugent, J. 117

Oddy, C. 94
Ohama, N. 132
One Flew Over the Cuckoo's Nest (film) 165
One Week (film) 130
Only God Forgives (film) 3, *6*, 16, 57, 61, 71, 81, 126, 141, 147
    aesthetic feature in 34
    colour usage in 34
    critics of 116
    experimental narrative of 119
The Oxford Dictionary of Art & Artists (Van Gogh) 11

Pappademas, A. 111
Pavek, H. 20, 21, 54
Payne, C. 136
Phillips, J. 9
Pickup on South Street (film) 41
Pitsis, A. 136
The Place Beyond the Pines (film) 111
Pollock, C. 35
Polytechnique (film) 121
Pusher (film) 120
Puzzle Films: Complex Storytelling in Contemporary Cinema (Buckland) 65

'radical quiet,' concept of 20–1
Raging Bull (film) 159
Rambo: First Blood (film) 111
reality 7, 12–14, 112
Reed, C. 44
Refn, N. W. viii, 3, 7–10, 16, 19, 35, 56, 62, 63, 65, 66, 71, 72, 80–3, 96–8, 109, 110–13, 115, 116, 119, 120, 122, 124, 129, 133, 134, 141, 142, 144
    The Neon Demon 96
    Only God Forgives 81
    Valhalla Rising 66
Reimann, W. 27
responses 7, 58
Rikhardsdottir, S. 9
'robotic' acting style 20
Robson, L. 92
The Roots of Romanticism (Berlin) 10

Sallis, J. 1
Salmon, J. 130
Schembri, J. 115
Schmidt-Rottluff, K. 9, 10
Schreck, M. 31, 32
Scorsese, M. 159
The Scream (paint) 13
Second World War 39, 41, 42, 49–50, 52
shadows 28, 29, 33, 34, 40, 42, *45*, 64, 71, 73, 75, 118, 135, *138*
Shane (film) 48, 66, 67, 69, 70
Shilina-Conte, T. 16, 19, 20, 62, 63, 90, 166
Shrader, P. 41
Silberman, M. 27
silence 15–19, 56, 57, 82, 102, 159, 166, 167
silent heroes 1, 2
    as affective vessel 19–21
    masculinities 122–9
    in 21st-century film 3, 15
Silent Running (film) 119
Sinatra, F. 105
Sinnerbrink, R. 20, 29
Sontag, S. 3, 19, 56–8, 60, 71, 73, 83, 121, 132, 135, 152, 168
sound 57, 127, 150
    emotional development 156–64
    musical 21–3
Spaghetti Western 52, 53
Stagecoach (film) 50, 51
Stimmung: Exploring the Aesthetics of Mood (Sinnerbrink) 29

Stoker, B. 32
The Story of Art (Gombrich) 12
storytelling, unconventional mode of 99
Styan, J. L. 7, 32, 56, 61, 73, 81, 87, 112, 130, 131
Summer Wind (song) 105, *106*
Sunset Boulevard (film) 41
symbolism 14

tactility 139
Tate Gallery 7
Taxi Driver (film) 123
Terminator 2: Judgement Day (film) 114
terror, feelings of 31
The Third Man (film) 44, 73
Tomkins, S. 18
True Grit (film) 50
truth 14
21st-century expressionist films *see* Expressionist films

Under the Skin (film) 6, 21, 91, 93, 96, 126
   noises of 96–7
   opening scenes of 4
   untrained actors in 94

Valhalla Rising (film) 9, 62, 64, 66, 166
Van Gogh, V. 11–13
Veidt, C. 30
Verhaeghe, V. 75
Vicari, J. 1, 81, 83, 112, 113, 120
Villeneuve, D. viii, 3, 7, 8, 16, 19, 55, 56, 62, 73–5, 80–4, 87, 100, 111, 121, 122, 134, 137, 141
violence 62, 83, 115, 159
visual isolation 135
visual symbolism 34

Wallfisch, B. 152, 153
Wayne, J. 49, 50
the Western 15, 46–54
Wiene, R. 28–30, 34, 121
Wierzbicki, J. 26, 150
Wilder, B. 15, 39, 41, 42, 75
Williams, M. 130
Winkler, M. M. 54
Wise, D. 116
The Woman 92–6, 165
Wright, W. 70, 87

Young Hercules (television series) 110

Zimmer, H. 153